T0228015

IET SECURITY SERIES 14

Privacy by Design for the Internet of Things

Other volumes in this series:

Privacy by Design for the Internet of Things

Building accountability and security

Edited by
Andrew Crabtree, Hamed Haddadi and
Richard Mortier

The Institution of Engineering and Technology

Published by The Institution of Engineering and Technology, London, United Kingdom

The Institution of Engineering and Technology is registered as a Charity in England & Wales (no. 211014) and Scotland (no. SC038698).

© The Institution of Engineering and Technology 2021

First published 2021

The Institution of Engineering and Technology
Michael Faraday House
Six Hills Way, Stevenage
Herts, SG1 2AY, United Kingdom

www.theiet.org

British Library Cataloguing in Publication Data
A catalogue record for this product is available from the British Library

ISBN 978-1-83953-139-2 (hardback)
ISBN 978-1-83953-140-8 (PDF)

Typeset in India by Exeter Premedia Services Private Limited
Printed in the UK by CPI Group (UK) Ltd, Croydon

Contents

List of figures

List of tables

About the editors

Andrew Crabtree is a professor in the School of Computer Science at the University of Nottingham, UK. A sociologist by background, he started working with computer scientists and software engineers when he did his PhD with John Hughes at Lancaster University, UK. He has championed the use of ethnography in systems design and has been working on shaping computing around the social world for the last 25 years. He has written three textbooks on ethnography for design. In 2014, he became the first ethnographer to be awarded a senior EPSRC Fellowship to respond to the privacy and accountability challenge created by the IoT and the technological transformation of the home into a key site of personal data production.

Hamed Haddadi is a reader in human-centred systems at the Dyson School of Design Engineering at The Faculty of Engineering, Imperial College London. He leads the Systems and Algorithms Laboratory, is a Security Science Fellow of the Institute for Security Science and Technology, and an Academic Fellow of the Data Science Institute. He is also a Visiting Professor at Brave Software where he works on developing privacy-preserving analytics protocols. He is interested in User-Centred Systems, IoT, Applied Machine Learning, and Data Security & Privacy. He enjoys designing and building systems that enable better use of our digital footprint, while respecting users' privacy. He has spent time working and collaborating with Brave Software, Intel Research, Microsoft Research, AT&T Research, Telefonica, NEC, and Sony Europe. When not in the lab, he prefers to be on a ski slope or in a kayak.

Richard Mortier is Professor of Computing & Human-Data Interaction in the Department of Computer Science & Technology (a.k.a. the Computer Laboratory), Cambridge University, UK, and Fellow and President of Christ's College, Cambridge. Past research has included distributed system performance monitoring and debugging, incentives in Internet routing protocols, and real-time media platform design and implementation. Current work includes platforms for privacy preserving personal data processing, IoT security, smart cities, and machine learning for knowledge management platforms. Alongside his academic career, roles have included platform architect, founder, and CTO while consulting and working for startups and corporates in both the US and the UK.

Chapter 1

Privacy by design for the Internet of Things

Andy Crabtree[1], Hamed Haddadi[2], and Richard Mortier[3]

This book brings together a collection of interdisciplinary works that are in various ways concerned to address the societal challenge to privacy and security occasioned by the Internet of Things (IoT). The chapters in this book cover legal, social science, systems and design research perspectives. Taken together, they seek to enable the broader community to understand the multi-faceted contexts in which the IoT is embedded, to shape systems around societal need and ultimately to drive the development of future and emerging technologies that are responsive to the challenges confronting their adoption in everyday life.

1.1 The ~~Internet~~ data of Things

The Internet of Things (IoT) is more than a distributed array of networked devices and systems [1]. Those devices or 'things' collect and distribute data that are often, in some way, *about* the people in whose everyday lives they are embedded. Smart meters thus generate data about household members' energy consumption, smart appliances about their use by members, smart cars about their drivers' conduct on the road, etc. Research has shown that smartphones can be used to infer a user's mood, stress levels, personality type, bipolar disorder, demographics (e.g. gender, marital status, job status, age), smoking habits, overall well-being, sleep patterns, levels of exercise and types of physical activity or movement [2]. While many would not consider smartphones as IoT devices, the sensors they use to generate data furnishing such insights are very similar to many used in IoT devices. IoT devices thus generate *personal data* and do so at a scale that outstrips smartphones by several orders of magnitude (there were nearly 4 billion smartphones and over 26 billion IoT devices in the world as of 2020). Personal data is any information that relates to an identified or identifiable person [3]. It can include 'indirect' information such as IP or MAC addresses, cookie identifiers, online identifiers (hashtags, etc.), location data – really any information generated by computational devices that relates, whether directly or indirectly, to an identified

[1]School of Computer Science, University of Nottingham, UK
[2]Dyson School of Design Engineering, Imperial College, UK
[3]Department of Computer Science & Technology, Cambridge University, UK

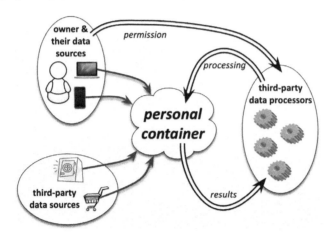

Figure 1.1   Putting citizens within the processing loop

or identifiable person. In 2015, the Federal Trade Commission, which regulates consumer privacy and the use of personal information in the United States, in reviewing the benefits and risks of the IoT reported that fewer than 10 000 households using one company's IoT home-automation product generated up to 150 million discrete data points per day [4]. That is just one IoT device in a relatively small number of homes. Little wonder, then, that the IoT has provoked widespread societal concern over the data *tsunami* it unleashes and the unprecedented insight into citizens' everyday lives that flows in its wake.

The primary concern in the works collected here is with the Data of Things or more formally, with something called Human Data Interaction (HDI). HDI is a relatively new concept, emerging within the last decade from computer science research. Nonetheless, it already has currency, becoming a key plank in DARPA's 2015 Brandeis programme and the effort to 'give data owners a way to decide how their data should be used' [5]. However, HDI is more humble in origin than the US defence department's research wing. It emerged out of digital economy research in the United Kingdom and efforts to develop a novel business-to-consumer (B2C) infrastructure enabling a new wave of personal digital services and applications [6]. The envisioned infrastructure was underpinned by the Dataware model (Figure 1.1), which posits:

- A user, by or about whom data are created.
- Data sources, for example, connected devices, which generate data about the user.
- A personal container, which holds data and is accessed via Application Programming Interfaces (APIs).
- A catalogue, which allows the user to manage access to data held by the personal container.
- Data processors, external machines that wish to purpose data.

The Dataware model describes a logical entity formed as a distributed computing system. Thus, data processing consists of a processing request (e.g. for smart meter readings) being sent to the catalogue by external processors, which is approved or rejected by the user. If approved, the catalogue issues a token to the data processor. The processor presents the token to the personal container, which then allows the processor to run the processing request on the specific data to which it has been granted access by the user (e.g. data from the smart meter). The Dataware model thus takes a distinctive approach to personal data processing. It not only makes data processing *accountable* to users and subject to user *control* but also enables data minimisation, a key requirement of data protection regulation, in limiting the distribution of data to the results of a processing operation. The data itself remain in the user's personal container.

1.2 Human data interaction

The Dataware model is just one example of how computer scientists have sought to address HDI's fundamental concern to re-engineer a currently opaque digital infrastructure. To transform it from something that people generally do not understand and are largely bystanders to data collection and use, to one that enables active participation in the processing of personal data [7]. The Dataware model was followed by the Databox (see Chapter 6), for example, and the Hub of All Things (HAT) and more recently Solid [8] offer alternate approaches to leveraging personal data while fostering accountability and control. While the latter put weaker controls on data minimisation, and in turn offer weaker protections to privacy and personal information, HDI has nevertheless driven a step-change in how we think about personal information and privacy and how this might be supported technically. HDI brings data rather than computing technologies to the forefront and would have us recognise that data are a first-class object worthy of consideration in its own right, rather than as mere 'exhaust' emanating from citizens' interactions with digital services, applications and devices. HDI seeks to shape the underlying technologies required to support human interaction with digital data including the infrastructure and analytic tools needed to render data processing – including the collection, structuring, adaptation, use, distribution, storage and disposal of data – intelligible to citizens and to provide them with resources to directly affect the flow of *their* data within the digital economy. In this, HDI aligns with the European Union's general data protection regulation (GDPR), for while 'technologically neutral', GDPR nevertheless seeks to ensure citizens 'have control of their own personal data' [3].

We recognise there are limits to this ambition. All manner of data held by state agencies and companies alike are beyond the immediate control of the individual. However, while certain carve-outs hold for data processing done in the public interest and exercise of official authority, data protection regulation assures that citizens have a spectrum of rights over processing, including the right to access, rectification, objection, restriction, portability, erasure and ultimately to be forgotten [9]. Where data are provided by the individual, whether actively through some form of reportage or passively as a by-product of interacting with digital applications, services and devices, then data protection regulations allow citizens to obtain data that relate to them in a 'structured, commonly used and machine-readable format' [3]. Regulation thus opens up the individual's pool of data and HDI seeks to put the infrastructure, tools and resources in place that enable citizens to exploit it for personal benefit. The aim, however, is not only to empower citizens disillusioned by an opaque infrastructure marked by widespread privacy infringements, data leaks and the growing trade in personal data between third parties and data aggregators over which they have no control. Equally as important, it is to drive innovation in a world dominated by a handful of players who also have the power to constrain application and service developers' access to data and thereby to distort markets in their own favour [10]. Nor does HDI seek to banish advertisers and analytics providers, and thus diminish or do away with the revenue streams that enable free applications and services at scale. What HDI aspires to – on behalf of citizens, developers and enablers alike – is to drive innovation in the use of personal data in ways that foster broad societal *trust*.

At the beating heart of HDI are three core principles, which are currently absent from the digital ecosystem.

- **Legibility**, or the ability of individuals to understand data processing. Legibility is concerned to make both the flow of data and the analytic processes to which data are subject within those flows, transparent and comprehensible to citizens.
- **Agency**, or the ability to personally control the flow of data. Agency goes beyond opting in or out of data processing to allow (but not require) individuals to access data, engage with its collection, storage and use, understand data processing and the inferences drawn from it, modify data to control representations of the self (e.g. profiles), and to withdraw from data processing.
- **Negotiability**, or the ability to collaboratively manage data processing, including limiting processing. Negotiability recognises that data often exist in a social context and is therefore 'mixed' in nature, belonging to multiple parties. This makes it necessary to support interaction between multiple parties (not just those involved in data processing but also, and for example, family members, housemates, friends, etc.) to arrive at socially negotiated outcomes (e.g. shared policies) controlling data processing.

1.2.1   Fundamental challenges

Each of these principles presents fundamental research challenges. Legibility, for example, is not simply a matter of data visualisation, not that this is particularly straightforward where large data sets are concerned. Particularly challenging for data big and small are the implications they carry for the individuals or social groups they relate to and what the data mean or 'say' about them given the particular nature of the processing to which they have been subject [11]. How citizens are to understand data processing, and especially the automated decision-making that may turn upon it, is a key challenge of our time. Will the provision of information, a là GDPR, do the job and allow citizens to determine the significance and consequences of data processing before the processing takes place? Does society need 'explainable AI' [12] or self-explicating machines that can account for their decision-making processes? Are 'counterfactuals' explaining the outcomes of automated decision-making required [13]? Whatever the answer, and arriving at one will likely as not require an innovative mix of solutions, GDPR makes it clear that the law will hold those who 'control' automated decision-making to account, not the machines they use, if and when push comes to shove [14]. Suffice to say for the time being that data processing is a complex matter compounded by the fact that data lack specific meaning until they are processed in some way, for some purpose [15]. It is critical, then, that citizens are equipped with the resources to apprehend data processing, not only as it generally applies to a population but as it applies specifically, to themselves, on particular occasions of data processing if they are to invest trust in the enterprise.

GDPR requires that the 'data subject' or the identifiable/identified person to whom data relate be informed of data processing before processing takes place where data are provided by them, or within a 'reasonable period' (typically but not exclusively within a month) where data are obtained from another source. The data subject should also be informed if their data are to be further processed for purposes other than those they were originally obtained or are to be disclosed to another recipient. These legal requirements are intended to make citizens aware that their data are being purposed by others and to ensure they can exercise the spectrum of control rights over its processing, whatever legal basis underpins it (consent is but one). If citizens are to be truly empowered, however, HDI takes the view (as reflected in Figure 1.1) that agency also requires that individuals have the capacity to act within the systems that process their data. This is not to say that individuals should be continuously engaged in the management of their personal data, the overhead would be too onerous, but that they should have the ability to do so as and when they have need. Furthermore, we take the view, as Bartlett [16] suggests, that were data processing intelligible to individuals and they could actually exercise control, including terminating processing, not only would they have a greater degree of confidence, they would also be willing to share additional data as a result. Indeed, enabling accountability and control within the systems that process citizens' data may well open up a wealth of information to innovation, should solutions be put in place that reduce data distribution to the outcomes of processing and ensure that data remain under the individual's control.

While innovators may readily see and treat personal data as a commodity, something to be exchanged in return for a service (e.g. online news, social media, live traffic maps), it has to be acknowledged that personal data relate to an identified and identifiable person and increasingly persons (in the plural). Personal data are increasingly 'mixed' by default of members living together and sharing devices (laptops and tablet computers, smart TVs, smart home voice assistants, connected cameras, doorbells, locks, thermostats, etc.). It has been suggested that this raises the spectre of members becoming 'joint data controllers' subject to the stringent accountability and non-compliance requirements of GDPR [17], a view thankfully tempered

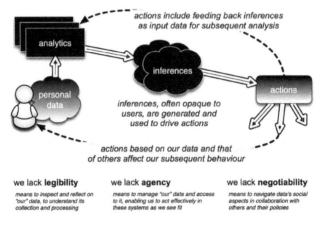

actions include feeding back inferences
as input data for subsequent analysis

analytics

inferences

personal
data

inferences, often opaque to
users, are generated and
used to drive actions

actions

actions based on our data and that
of others affect our subsequent behaviour

we lack **legibility**

means to inspect and reflect on
"our" data, to understand its
collection and processing

we lack **agency**

means to manage "our" data and access
to it, enabling us to act effectively in
these systems as we see fit

we lack **negotiability**

means to navigate data's social
aspects in collaboration with
others and their policies

Figure 1.2   Fundamental challenges for HDI

by careful consideration of GDPR's purpose and intent [18]. More pressing, from HDI's perspective, is the need to render the processing of mixed data accountable to members (again in the plural) long before the law is invoked. Data rarely exist in isolation but are situated in a lively social context that regulates who can, in practice, access data and has rights over its use [19]. These are not necessarily legal rights, though legal rights may underpin them, but rights conferred by virtue of the social relationships that hold between members (between partners, parents, children, friends of the children and so on). Data are embedded in these social relationships and often, indeed increasingly, generated within and by their ongoing conduct. It is imperative that efforts to empower individuals do not ride roughshod over the social controls that members employ to regulate one another's access to and use of data, especially as the IoT increases its production exponentially. Data processing needs to be accountable not only to the individual then, but to the other people who also have rightful claim over its use. It is not sufficient to empower the individual then, interaction mechanisms must necessarily enable members to negotiate the use of 'our' data on an ongoing basis. The need to address negotiability is a largely ignored challenge at this point in time, but crucial to any effort to enhance citizens ability to process personal data that are socially embedded and increasingly social in nature.

1.2.2   Associated challenges

Running alongside the fundamental challenges for HDI elaborated in the above section and reflected in Figure 1.2 are a number of associated challenges including the *legibility of data*, as well as the discovery of data processors, articulation of the flow of data and recipient design of data disclosure. Much as GDPR requires that data processed on the legal basis of consent be predicated on an 'informed' understanding that makes processing legible to citizens [20], there is a similar need to render data legible so citizens can make informed choices about their use. While the specific meaning of data on any occasion is dependent on the particular processes to which it is subject (e.g. parsing location data through Google Maps to reveal traffic build ups), there is a need to inform citizens as to its general meaning (e.g. that location data will reveal journeys taken and places visited, smart lock data entry and exit patterns in the home, smart TV data viewing preferences, smart watch data one's heart rate and blood pressure). Sensitising citizens to the fundamental things their data 'say' about them is a necessary precursor to meaningful engagement with the HDI ecosystem. Especially in a world where data generated by connected consumer devices are unfamiliar and citizens are unaware of what they might reveal about their 'lifestyle details' [21]. Essentially the challenge is to arm citizens with basic knowledge of their data assets and understanding of why they might be of value to data processors. This may also involve making external information (e.g. consumer trends data) visible so that users understand just what they are being asked to hand over on any occasion. This extends to specific occasions of processing and making it possible for citizens to review the results of processing in a legible way prior to their distribution so as to be able to make a truly informed choice about the purposing of their data in the digital economy.

It is also important to the growth of the digital economy that steps are taken to enable user-driven *discovery of data processors* and to help citizens extract value from their personal data. We do not assume value is essentially pecuniary in nature, at least not for citizens [22], but rather that value is heterogenous and includes social benefits and public good as well the potential utility of personalised services [23]. However, the HDI ecosystem as envisaged in the Dataware model is asymmetrical, with processing being driven by processors rather than citizens, who only have the ability to accept or reject data processing requests or to terminate them if they wish. The user is as such dealing with one-way traffic and lacks reciprocal opportunities for discovery. One way to counter this and open up the possibilities for discovery is to create what are effectively 'app stores', much like Apple and Google provide, that make data processing applications and services available to end-users. This has the virtue of leveraging a now familiar model of discovery. App stores not only provide users a gateway to applications and services, and furnish information about apps and their authors which plays an important role in their decision-making. The social nature of app stores, which allows users to rate apps and provide qualitative feedback to others, also helps build the trust between users and service providers that is essential to the discovery and adoption of new technologies. Furthermore, the possibility exists to disrupt the status quo by decentralising data processing [24]. HDI infrastructure might thus be developed in such ways as to enable sectors, and even individual companies, to provide their own apps to users as part of their data processing operations (e.g., see Chapter 6).

The development of an app store infrastructure may go some way towards *'articulating' the flow of data*. We bracket the notion as it has a technical as well as an ordinary meaning and refers to the way in which actions are 'joined together' and thus coordinated [25, 26]. The Dataware model organises interaction between its actors (users and processors) through the catalogue. However, while the catalogue permits the flow of information between users and data processors, the flow itself stands in need of articulation. What, for example, in the absence of an app store, might occasion a processing request being made, for example, and made in such a way for it to seem reasonable to a user? Such matters, mundane as they may be, require articulation both as we ordinarily understand the term and technically. Thus, a key design challenge in HDI is to support the cooperation between actors that is needed to make data flows possible and to sustain them. App stores may go some way to remedy the situation in providing a shared rationale for data processing, but there is need to go further. A user cannot tell from the catalogue such things as where in a process the processing has reached, what is going to happen to their data next, where the results of processing (which are still personal data) have been distributed and so on. Articulation of the flow of data is limited in the Dataware model and app stores alike to who wants what data for what purpose. Nonetheless, it is a key challenge that cuts across legibility, agency and negotiability, not only requiring that data flows are rendered transparent so they can be inspected by users, but that they can also be acted upon by users and the purposing of data thus be negotiated in accordance with GDPR's spectrum of control rights. Indeed, GDPR recommends that 'where possible, the controller should be able to provide remote access to a secure system which would provide the data subject with direct access to his or her personal data' [3] as a principle means of enabling citizens to exercise those rights. HDI might go further by articulating the flow of data throughout its processing.

HDI seeks to support and surpass regulation. In the mundane course of their everyday lives, citizens have much greater control over personal information than GDPR provides for, regulating access and use through physical and digital practices of *'recipient design'* [27]. What persons tell one another of how much they smoke or drink or what kinds of foodstuffs they eat and how much they weigh, for example, very much depends upon who they are telling it to. It is well known by doctors, for example, that such matters are grossly underestimated when told to them. The same applies more generally. People are selective in what they divulge about their personal lives, with the selectivity being done with respect to the relationships that hold between the parties involved. Now the Dataware model construes of the recipient as the processor, which presents a particular request for processing to the data source after it has been granted permission. How is the ubiquitous principle and indeed practice of recipient design to be respected and supported in this context? More specifically, how are users to permit selective access to their data and limit what is made available to a processor? How are they to redact information if do wish to do so, for example, or control its granularity? The ability to design information for recipients is an essential means not simply of controlling the flow of information but, in so doing, of managing the presentation of self in everyday life [28]. Wholesale disclosure would undermine individuals' ability to control how they represent themselves to others and have a corrosive effect on individuals and the fabric of social life [29]. Enabling citizens to exercise fine-grained control over the presentation of data, both to external processors and anyone else (e.g. family, friends, colleagues), is key to any effort to empower users.

Recipient design is, perhaps, the most disconcerting challenge from a technological viewpoint where data quality is increasingly prized, especially in a world where processing is driven by artificial intelligence (AI). However, data quality is not a ubiquitous requirement in everyday life. No general social expectation of full disclosure holds between persons in their interactions. That would undermine the social and moral order, producing something akin to a world in which people told the whole unvarnished truth to one another [30]. Despite technological arguments, only sometimes does data quality and accuracy matter (e.g. when meter readings are required) and such occasions are often legally enforced (e.g. by contract law). While AI brings new challenges and concerns regarding the trustworthiness of such processing – including data quality and accuracy, bias and discrimination in automated processing, the transparency and accountability of automated decision-making, and the ethics and governance of AI [12, 31] – recipient design should not be seen as a nuisance to be dispensed with. It is a tried and tested social means of managing personal information and an age-old practice that if broadly supported will enable citizens to invest trust in data processing and foster appropriation of HDI solutions at scale. Such solutions are, as yet some way off widespread adoption. While early efforts to develop 'personal data stores' are emerging onto the market, such as HAT, Solid, MyDex, Digi.me and Meeco, the potential benefit of data ownership has yet to be established [8]. There is some way to go, then, before HDI solutions become part and parcel of everyday life. Building-in the means for citizens to design data disclosure for recipients will be key to that achievement.

1.2.3   Summary

It is broadly recognised that IoT brings with it privacy and security challenges. Indeed, security is often seen and treated as a panacea to privacy concerns. The argument goes that securing connected devices from attack, including encrypting data, will protect citizens from unwarranted intrusion and thus allow them to invest *trust* in the IoT. However, this is only true to a certain extent. As Winstein [32] observes,

> Manufacturers are shipping devices as sealed-off products that will speak, encrypted, only with the manufacturer's servers over the Internet. Encryption is a great way to protect against eavesdropping from bad guys. But when it stops the devices' actual owners from listening in to make sure the device isn't tattling on them, the effect is anti-consumer.

While security is necessary, it is *not sufficient* to protect consumer privacy or the privacy of citizens more broadly. Their data are still open to the kinds of abuses that we are all familiar with in the 'walled gardens' of industry [33]. More is required, then, to protect citizens' privacy and to foster their trust in the IoT.

HDI recognises the overarching need to build *accountability and control* into a currently opaque digital infrastructure and ecosystem of applications, services and devices that enable personal data processing at scale. If citizens are to trust the IoT, they need to be able to understand data processing and be able to affect the flow and use of their data in the digital economy. HDI thus posits three fundamental engineering challenges that require *legibility, agency and negotiability* be built-in to the digital infrastructure to enable accountability and control. Legibility requires engineering digital infrastructure to surface data flows and make the analytic processes to which data are subject comprehensible to citizens. Agency

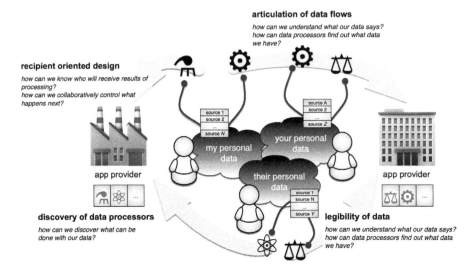

Figure 1.3   Associated challenges for HDI

requires engineering digital infrastructure to permit citizens to actively engage with data collection, storage and use, to understand data processing and the inferences drawn from it, to modify data and control representations of the self (e.g. profiles), and to withdraw from data processing. And negotiability requires engineering digital infrastructure to support collaborative data management and allow citizens to arrive at socially negotiated outcomes (e.g. shared policies) controlling data processing. As summed up in Figure 1.3, these fundamental issues implicate a range of associated challenges concerning the legibility of data, the discovery of data processors, the articulation of data flows and recipient design. The legibility of data recognises the need to arm citizens with basic knowledge of their data assets and an understanding of why they might be of value to data processors as precursor to meaningful HDI. The discovery of data processors recognises the need to enable citizens to extract value from their personal data through the discover of data applications and services that are of social, public and personal utility. The articulation of data flows recognises that data processing is distributed across various actors (citizens, data processors, third-party recipients, etc.) and that mechanisms are needed to support cooperation between them and to enable citizens to exercise their legally enforced spectrum of control rights. And recipient design recognises the need to extend support for HDI beyond legal mandate and support established social practice to enable citizens to design data disclosure for recipients, including controlling the granularity of data and redacting data, as appropriate to the relationships that hold between them.

These challenges, which recognise the need not only to empower citizens but to add value to their everyday lives, underscore the point that privacy is not a panacea to the problem of trust in its own right. As Narayanan *et al.* [34] remind us,

Privacy is always a secondary feature—while it might tip the balance between two competing products, users rarely pick a product based on privacy alone.

These comments were made nearly a decade ago but would appear to hold at the time of writing [8]. If citizens are to be truly empowered, there is not only need to build privacy and security into the IoT to foster societal trust. There is also need to enable the active participation of citizens in innovation within the digital economy. Right now, their participation is limited and largely passive, the traffic largely one-way as commercial ventures and governments alike seek to leverage personal data for their benefit. While an argument can be made that this also benefits citizens in providing free services or services that are cheaper to provide, or more efficient, or better tailored around their needs, the reality is that personal data processing is still something that is largely done to citizens, not by them or with them. Personal data are resources whose ownership is increasingly concentrated in the hands of large content providers who valorise it through increasingly sophisticated analytic techniques [35]. Against this backdrop, and in addition to calling for enhanced accountability and control, HDI seeks to disrupt the current hegemony and empower citizens to directly exploit the data of things alongside any other class of personal data for their personal benefit. As Karl Marx (perhaps surprisingly) observed [36], society's ability to generate wealth 'springs from the propensity to exchange' and is 'limited by the extent of exchange'. The one-sided nature of the current infrastructure and ecosystem clearly limits this. HDI has the potential to change the situation and unleash the extent of exchange. As Marx put it (ibid.), 'in advanced conditions, every man becomes a merchant'. While we do not envisage that citizens will sell their data, we do envisage and seek to foster an ecosystem in which individuals and smaller data processors alike can accrue value, not only the big players that increasingly dominate the field.

1.3   Contribution of collected works to HDI

The challenges posed by HDI are not settled matters but open up a range of themes for further investigation and elaboration. Each of the works collected in this book seeks to contribute to HDI's development, whether by investigating one of its substantive themes or by making methodological contributions that foster their investigation.

Given the overarching importance of accountability in a currently opaque digital world, we begin in Chapter 2 by examining the relatively recent legal requirement introduced by GDPR that data processors, or more precisely the parties who control data processing, be able to demonstrate accountability. Lachlan Urquhart and Jiahong Chen show us how accountability is at the heart of data protection regulation and elaborate the range of obligations or requirements accountability places on the 'data controller'. The authors go on to argue that just who constitutes the controller, and who therefore determines the purposes of processing, is not clear-cut in a domestic context increasingly populated by connected devices. They raise the possibility that members of the smart home may be 'joint controllers' insofar as they exploit connected devices that process the data of the others in the home. This gives rise to the possibility that household members may be required to comply with the accountability principle, despite the household exemption clause in GDPR, which raises a host of design challenges for equipping non-experts (legal or technical) with the tools, resources and know-how to enable collective accountability and control.

In Chapter 3, Peter Tolmie and Andy Crabtree examine accountability through the lens of ordinary action. In contrast to a set of legally binding obligations, accountability is here construed of as a taken-for-granted feature of ordinary action, which allows members to see and hear what others are doing and to coordinate their actions accordingly. The authors present the key results to emerge from a number of ethnographic studies conducted over a 10-year period, which elaborate privacy as accountability management and a range of common-sense methods members have designed to protect their privacy from attack in an increasingly connected world. The authors also explicate how privacy is routinely breached through the mismatch between common-sense reasoning and the operation of digital systems, and the destabilising effect of rendering ordinarily invisible activities visible and thus available to account through widespread sensing. Drawing on their empirical work, the authors show how the IoT has the potential to disrupt the ordinarily unremarkable foundations of the social and moral order and undermine societal trust, which may be repaired by building reciprocity into the digital infrastructure.

In Chapter 4, Damla Kilic and colleagues debunk the widely held myth of privacy as personal control over data disclosure. The authors introduce the 'cardboard box' study, a lightweight technology probe exploring members reasoning about privacy and data disclosure or data sharing within the home and between known parties. The study reveals that, within the home at least, privacy is not the default position for handling personal data. Rather, a great deal of data is shared by default of members living together in a shared ecology in which devices are embedded. The authors find that far from being ubiquitous, privacy is occasioned and that when it is, it plays a distinct social function that is concerned to ensure 'human security'. Privacy is thus invoked to protect the integrity and autonomy of the individual as a competent social actor. Ultimately, they find in the interplay between members that privacy and data disclosure are socially negotiated through mundane reasoning and situated practices that organise the informational boundaries of the self in everyday life. The cardboard box study sensitises us to the need to extend our gaze beyond the individual and design solutions that support the collaborative management of personal data.

In Chapter 5, Chris Norval and colleagues return us to the theme of accountability, but this time from a technical perspective, exploring how accountability might be fostered in the real world where the IoT is composed of a system-of-systems across which data processing is distributed. The authors make the case for reviewability, which they construe of as a holistic form of transparency spanning technical systems and the organisational processes they are embedded in as a whole. Reviewability involves developing logging and record-keeping mechanisms that allow systems and processes to be interrogated and assessed for legal compliance. The authors argue that reviewability is needed to enable compliance with the accountability principle and determine which parties are accountable for the different components of a system-of-systems. This also includes surfacing data flows and the different entities involved. The authors explicate the legal and organisational case for reviewability, the potential benefits of oversight for the developers of technical systems and the opportunity reviewability provides to better inform users about the specific nature of data processing operations in a distributed context.

In Chapter 6, Andy Crabtree and colleagues further explore how accountability might be built into the IoT. The authors focus on the external accountability requirement, which requires that data subjects be provided with detailed information about data processing in order that they are properly informed and can exercise control accordingly. The authors argue that GDPR has transformed accountability to the data subject into a functional requirement that should be built-in to digital products and services. The authors describe a privacy-enhancing technology called the Databox, which seeks to make data processing within the IoT accountable to users. The Databox sits at the edge of the network in the user's home and allows the individual to collate personal data from connected devices and online sources as well, insofar as APIs allow. The Databox ecology consists of an app store that allows users to download drivers to import data to the box and apps that allow them to process data on the box. If data are distributed, only the results of processing are passed on. The Databox makes it accountable who wants a user's data, what for, who the results are shared with, etc., and allows individuals to exercise direct control over processing operations.

In Chapter 7, Tom Lodge and Andy Crabtree turn our attention to application developers. The authors suggest that this particular cohort is much neglected in discourses about privacy and data protection. Nonetheless, they argue that developers require support to help them meet the Data Protection by Design and Default (DPbD) requirement imposed by GDPR. GDPR recommends that Data Protection Impact Assessments (DPIAs) be conducted to ensure DPbD. DPIAs are mandatory in cases where processing is high risk and otherwise recommended whenever personal data are processed. However, the authors recognise that many application developers do not have the knowledge or access to legal expertise that is needed to conduct DPIAs. The authors describe an integrated development environment (IDE) that supports the design of legally complaint Databox apps. The IDE does not encode DPIAs but sensitises developers to the potential need for an assessment to be carried out. The IDE thus seeks to support due diligence in the development of apps that process personal data, helping developers' reason about what personal data are involved in processing during the actual construction of apps, advising developers as to whether or not the design choices they are making occasion the need for a DPIA and making app-specific privacy information available to others, including users, for review.

In Chapter 8, Hamed Haddadi and colleagues consider moving data analytics from the cloud to the edge of the network. The authors unpack the potential benefits of decentralised and distributed data analytics. These include reducing the carbon footprint created by shipping large volumes of data to data centres, which have increased in number by over seven million in the last decade and are predicted to account for 20% of global energy consumption by 2030. Other benefits include enhanced service efficiencies (not to mention resilience) enabled by low latency interactions between locally networked components. Increasing user privacy by distributing analytic results rather than the data itself. And savings to data processing organisations, both in terms of the cost of storing and processing data and repairing the damage caused by security breaches. Distributing data analytics across millions of devices such as the Databox, rather than putting it in a single honey pot, significantly reduces the potential for attack, which has increased exponentially over recent years and has a global annual cost for business of billions. The authors outline a system architecture predicated on the Databox to distribute machine learning algorithms at scale.

In Chapter 9, Derek McAuley and colleagues focus on the application of HDI to enable human-centred network security in the home. It is broadly recognised that a great many IoT devices are deeply insecure and frequently implicated in denial-of-service attacks. The authors argue that security is poorly supported in the home, with network tools being developed to support professionals rather than ordinary people. While acknowledging the limits of user empowerment, and that the vast majority of household members do not actually want to become security experts, the authors recognise that they do have occasional need to interact with their network and the devices that hang off it to ensure its smooth running in daily life. The authors present novel security controls that exploit tangible interfaces to enable users to easily detect troubles, reboot devices, restrict access and switch between local networks. The authors also consider the role of regulation in enabling security, highlighting that security is not just about technological design but also about normative development. A supportive regulatory environment, created with the right set of legal rules and technical standards, is also needed to promote security in smart homes.

In Chapter 10, Paul Coulton and colleagues consider the adoption challenge. The authors argue that adoption and acceptability are rarely taken into consideration when developing future and emerging technologies. Rather, this concern, which is fundamental to societal uptake, is typically bolted on afterwards. This means that challenges and barriers to adoption are often only identified late in the development process, after problematic design patterns have been established. The authors point to the tsunami of data generated by IoT devices in the smart home and how, when surfaced, this disrupts users' expectations of privacy and impacts acceptability leading them to resist adoption. The authors champion an experiential approach to uncovering acceptability and adoption challenges, exploiting design fiction to concretise technological futures through something they call 'worldbuilding'. This approach puts emphasis not only on creating design artefacts that reflect future and emerging technologies, but on merging them into a coherent whole that allows users to get their hands on the future. These fictional worlds prototype potential futures and engagement with them allows potential users to elaborate acceptability and adoption challenges that may fed back at an early stage in the development cycle.

Together the chapters in this book provide the first extensive treatment of HDI and the contemporary challenges it seeks to address. As any technological endeavour, HDI does not exist in a vacuum and so the works collected here address the legal and social context in which fundamental concern with the Data of Things is situated. Thus, technological efforts to enable accountability and control are complemented by legal and social perspectives that shape our understanding of what these might amount to in practice: building reciprocity as well as reviewability into the digital infrastructure and enabling collaborative and well as individual control over data processing. It speaks also to the forgotten, the invisible, the ignored and the need to help developers build a world in which privacy can be built-in to the ecosystem of applications, services and devices by design and default. To grand and global challenges of our times that see the soaring trade in personal data impact the planet and impose rising costs on business as it grapples with the widespread problem of data security. To the need for human-centred security, designed for ordinary people and their everyday lives, not technical professionals and expertise. And it underscores the importance of tackling the adoption challenge early in the development life cycle to circumvent problems and ensure that future and emerging technologies that exploit personal data are acceptable to society. As machine learning and AI proliferate, the case and need for HDI could not be stronger.

1.4   Acknowledgements

The research reported here was supported by the Engineering and Physical Sciences Research Council [grant numbers EP/G065802/1,EP/M02315X/1, EP/N028260/1, EP/N028260/2, EP/M001636/1, EP/R03351X/1].
This chapter is based on the following original articles:

- McAuley D., Mortier R. and Goulding J. (2011) The Dataware Manifesto. *Proceedings of the 3rd International Conference on Communication Systems and Networks*, Bangalore, India, January 2011. New Jersey: IEEE, pp. 1–6. https://doi.org/10.1109/COMSNETS.2011.5716491
- Haddadi H., Mortier R., McAuley D. and Crowcroft J. (2013) Human-data interaction. *University of Cambridge Computer Laboratory Technical Report 837*. https://www.cl.cam.ac.uk/techreports/UCAM-CL-TR-837.pdf
- Crabtree A. and Mortier, R. (2015) Human Data Interaction: Historical Lessons from Social Studies and CSCW. *Proceedings of the 14th European Conference on Computer Supported Cooperative Work*, Oslo, Norway, September 2015. Cham: Springer, pp. 3–21. https://doi.org/10.1007/978-3-319-20499-4_1
- Mortier R., Haddadi H., Henderson, T., McAuley D., Crowcroft J. and Crabtree A. (2016) Huma Data Interaction. *Encyclopedia of Human-Computer Interaction*, chapter 41. https://www.interaction-design.org/literature/book/the-encyclopedia-of-human-computer-interaction-2nd-ed/human-data-interaction

References

[1]   Singh J., Millard C., Reed C., Cobbe J., Crowcroft J. 'Accountability in the IoT: systems, law, and ways forward'. *Computer*. 2018;**51**(7):54–65.

[2]   Peppet S.R. 'Regulating the internet of things: first steps towards managing discrimination, privacy, security and consent'. *Texas Law Review*. 2014;**93**(85):85–176.

[3]   European Union. 'Regulation 2016/679 General data protection regulation'. *Official Journal of the European Union*. 2016;**59**:1–149.

[4]   Federal Trade Commission. *Internet of Things: privacy and security in a connected world [online]*. 2015. Available from https://www.ftc.gov/system/files/documents/reports/federal-trade-commission-staff-report-november-2013-workshop-entitled-internet-things-privacy/150127iotrpt.pdf [Accessed 29th June 2021].

[5]   GCN. *DARPA to pursue 'revolutionary' privacy tools [online]*. 2015. Available from https://gcn.com/articles/2015/03/12/darpa-brandeis.aspx [Accessed 29th June 2021].

[6]   McAuley D., Mortier R., Goulding J. 'The dataware manifesto'. Proceedings of the 3rd International Conference on Communication Systems and Networks; Bangalore, India; 2011. pp. 1–6.

[7]   Haddadi H., Mortier R., McAuley D., Crowcroft J. *Human-data interaction. University of Cambridge computer laboratory technical report 837 [online]*. 2013. Available from https://www.cl.cam.ac.uk/techreports/UCAM-CL-TR-837.pdf [Accessed 29th June 2021].

[8]   Bolychevsky I. 'Are personal data stores the NEXT BIG THING?' *Medium [online]*. Available from https://medium.com/@shevski/are-personal-data-stores-about-to-become-the-next-big-thing-b767295ed842 [Accessed 29th June 2021].

[9]   Urquhart L., Lodge T., Crabtree A. 'Demonstrably doing accountability in the Internet of things'. *International Journal of Law and Information Technology*. 2019;**27**(1):1–27.

[10]   Falahrastegar M., Haddadi H., Uhlig S., Mortier R. 'The rise of panopticons: examining region-specific third-party web tracking'. Proceedings of the 6th International Workshop on Traffic Monitoring and Analysis; London, UK, Apr 2014; 2014. pp. 104–14.

[11]   Booth R. 'How Bristol assesses citizens' risk of harm – using an algorithm. *The Guardian'*. 2019. Available from https://www.theguardian.com/uk-news/2019/oct/15/bristol-algorithm-assess-citizens-risk-harm-guide-frontline-staff [Accessed 29th June 2021].

[12]   Royal Society. *Explainable AI: the basics [online]*. 2019. Available from https://royalsociety.org/-/media/policy/projects/explainable-ai/AI-and-interpretability-policy-briefing.pdf [Accessed 29th June 2021].

[13]   Wachter S., Mittelstadt B., Russel C. 'Counterfactual explanations without opening the blackbox: automated decisions and the GDPR'. *Harvard Journal of Law & Technology*. 2018;**31**(2):841–87.

[14]   Selbst A.D., Barocas S. 'The intuitive appeal of explainable machines'. *Fordham Law Review*. 2018;**87**(3):1085–139.

[15]   McQuillan D. 'Data science as machinic neoplatonism'. *Philosophy & Technology*. 2018;**31**(2):253–72.

[16]   Bartlett J. *The Data Dialogue*. London: Demos; 2012.

[17]   Edwards L., Flink M., Veale M., Zingales N. 'Data subjects as data controllers: a fashion(able) concept'. *Internet Policy Review [online]*. 2019. Available from https://policyreview.info/articles/news/data-subjects-data-controllers-fashionable-concept/1400 [Accessed 29th June 2021].

[18]   Janssen H., Cobbe J., Norval C., Singh J. 'Decentralised data processing: personal data stores and the GDPR'. *SSRN Electronic Journal*. 2020;**243**(2).

[19]   Zeng E., Roesner F. 'Understanding and improving security and privacy in multi-user smart homes'. Proceedings of the 28th USENIX Security Symposium; Santa Clara (CA), USA; August 2019. pp. 159–76.

[20]   Article 29 Data Protection Working Party. *Guidelines on consent under regulation 2016/679 [online]*. 2017. Available from https://ec.europa.eu/newsroom/article29/document.cfm?action=display&doc_id=51030   [Accessed 29th June 2021].

[21]   Article 29 Data Protection Working Party. *Opinion 8/2014 on the recent developments on the Internet of Things [online]*. 2014. Available from https://ec.europa.eu/justice/article-29/documentation/opinion-recommendation/files/2014/wp223_en.pdf [Accessed 29th June 2021].

[22]   PricewaterhouseCoopers. *Putting a value on data [online]*. 2019. Available from https://www.pwc.co.uk/data-analytics/documents/putting-value-on-data.pdf [Accessed 29th June 2021].

[23]   Accenture. *The era of living services [online]*. 2015. Available from https://www.fjordnet.com/media-files/2015/05/Living-Services.pdf [Accessed 29th June 2021].

[24]   National Science Foundation. *Workshop report on grand challenges in edge computing [online]*. 2016. Available from http://iot.eng.wayne.edu/edge/finalreport.php [Accessed 29th June 2021].

[25]   Schmidt K., Bannon L. 'Taking CSCW seriously: supporting articulation work'. *Computer Supported Cooperative Work: An International Journal*. 1992;**1**(1):7–40.

[26]   Strauss A. 'Work and the division of labor'. *The Sociological Quarterly*. 1985;**26**(1):1–19.

[27]   Crabtree A., Tolmie P., Knight W. 'Repacking "privacy" for a networked World'. *Computer Supported Cooperative Work*. 2017;**26**(4–6):453–88.

[28]   Goffman E. *The Presentation of Self in Everyday Life*. Edinburgh: University of Edinburgh Social Sciences Research Centre; 1956.

[29]   Marmor A. 'What is the right to privacy?' *Philosophy & Public Affairs*. 2015;**43**(1):3–26.

[30] Sacks H. 'Everyone has to lie' in Blount B., Sanches M. (eds.). *Sociocultural Dimensions of Language Use*. New York: Academic Press; 1975. pp. 57–80.

[31] European Commission. *White paper on artificial intelligence – a European approach to excellence and trust [online]*. 2020. Available from https://ec.europa.eu/info/sites/info/files/commission-white-paper-artificial-intelligence-feb2020_en.pdf [Accessed 29th June 2021].

[32] Winstein K. 'Introducing the right to eavesdrop on your things'. *Politico*. 2015. Available from https://www.politico.com/agenda/story/2015/06/internet-of-things-privacy-concerns-000107/ [Accessed 29th June 2021].

[33] Patterson D. 'Facebook data privacy scandal: a cheat sheet.' *TechRepublic*. 2020. Available from https://www.techrepublic.com/article/facebook-data-privacy-scandal-a-cheat-sheet/ [Accessed 29th June 2021].

[34] Narayanan A., Barocas S., Toubiana V., Nissenbaum H. 'A critical look at decentralised personal data architectures'. 2012.

[35] Szczepański M. 'Is data the new oil? Competition issues in the digital economy'. *European Parliamentary Research Service*. briefing PE 646.117. 2020. Available from https://www.europarl.europa.eu/RegData/etudes/BRIE/2020/646117/EPRS_BRI(2020)646117_EN.pdf [Accessed 29th June 2021].

[36] Marx K. *Economic and Philosophical Manuscripts of 1844 (trans Mulligan, M.)*. Moscow: Moscow Progress Publishers; 1932.

Chapter 2

On the principle of accountability: challenges for smart homes and cybersecurity

Lachlan Urquhart[1] and Jiahong Chen[2]

This chapter introduces the 'accountability principle' and its role in data protection (DP) governance. We focus on what accountability means in the context of cybersecurity management in smart homes, considering the EU General Data Protection Regulation (GDPR) requirements to secure personal data. This discussion sits against the backdrop of two key new developments in DP law. First, the law is moving into the home, due to narrowing of the so-called 'household exemption'. Concurrently, household occupants may now have legal responsibilities to comply with the GDPR, as they find themselves jointly responsible for compliance, as they are possibly held to determine the means and purposes of data collection with Internet of Things (IoT) device vendors. As a complex socio-technical space, we consider the interactions between accountability requirements and the competencies of this new class of 'domestic data controllers' (DDC). Specifically, we consider the value and limitations of edge-based security analytics to manage smart home cybersecurity risks, reviewing a range of prototypes and studies of their use. We also reflect on interpersonal power dynamics in the domestic setting, e.g. device control; existing social practices around privacy and security management in smart homes; and usability issues that may hamper DDCs ability to rely on such solutions. We conclude by reflecting on (1) the need for collective security management in homes and (2) the increasingly complex divisions of responsibility in smart homes between device users, account holders, IoT device/software/firmware vendors and third parties.

2.1 Introduction

Consider the following scenarios. A teenage son wants to lodge a *right to be forgotten request* with his father for compromising smart camera footage at their family

[1]Law School, University of Edinburgh, UK
[2]Horizon Digital Economy Research Institute, University of Nottingham, UK

home?[a] Or a student vacating her flat submits a *data portability* request to her flat-mate to obtain the heating schedule built up in their learning thermostat?[b] A grand-parent living with their adult children is concerned about them monitoring his diet and submits a *subject access request* to their daughter to see what the smart fridge knows? These situations may seem far-fetched, but this chapter unpacks how DP obligations between household members are increasingly being recalibrated, making these scenarios more likely in the future. This is because the law is moving into the home, due to narrowing of the so-called 'household exemption'. Concurrently, household occupants may now have legal responsibilities to comply with the GDPR, as they find themselves jointly responsible for compliance, as they are possibly held determine the means and purposes of data collection with Internet of Things (IoT) device vendors.

To focus our discussion, in this chapter, we examine one set of near-future DP problems: what the EU GDPR obligations around the *accountability principle* will require in smart homes for *cybersecurity*. This involves unpacking what cybersecurity duties household occupants may have and how they should manage these.

This chapter is composed of three primary sections.

We will begin in the introduction by setting some brief context particularly around the high-level message which is: accountability is an important element of the GDPR but changes in DP law practice mean individuals operating IoT devices in smart homes may need to find ways of providing demonstrations of accountability to data subjects, i.e. their family and friends. To unpack this, we focus on demonstrations in relation to personal data information security require-ments in the GPDR.

In Section 2.2, we provide an overview of what the accountability principle is and what it might require to be realised in practice. To do this, we first consider how it has emerged historically as a governance tool, before turning to how it is framed in Article 5(2) of the EU GDPR. We reflect on the obligations it creates for data controllers and what they need to do in order to satisfy the principle. In this section, we will focus on three elements. First, we situate accountability in the context of the GDPR more widely, considering it in conjunction with Article 24 GDPR (which unpacks the wider responsibilities of data controllers). We consider the implications of a broad reading of accountability, particularly in relation to compliance strategies for the GDPR and difficulties of prioritising different ele-ments of the legislation. We offer a set of requirements to support this. Second, we unpack who accountability is owed to and why this is important, considering accountability requirements that domestic data controllers (DDCs) need to attend to (this theme is explored in more depth in Section 2.4). Third, we reflect on what form a 'demonstration of accountability' might take (e.g. record keeping, privacy impact assessment, privacy by design, etc.). Again, this is to raise oppor-tunities controllers have and to explore what some of these might look like. We

---

[a]A recent Dutch court ruling, albeit in a social media context, has indicated such a possibility. See [1].
[b]In practice this would not work, as portability does not work this way (it does not cover inferences, i.e. the heating schedule, but just the 'raw' personal data).

conclude this section by reflecting on the role of technical measures in demonstrating accountability for compliance with GDPR security requirements in Article 32 and Article 5(1)(f).

We then turn in Section 2.3 to unpacking why we argue DDCs exist as a class of controllers, and how we have reached this position legally. In this regard, we reflect on the two aforementioned trends occurring in DP law around the narrowing of the household exemption and joint controllership broadening. We will document what each concept means in DP law in the light of recent case law which underpins these shifts. We will raise some of the implications here, particularly stressing that it leads to DDCs having responsibilities in relation to demonstrations of accountability, which we pick up on in more detail in the rest of this section.

In Section 2.4, we adopt a more exploratory perspective, aligning the first two parts to pose the question: how can DDCs in smart home demonstrate accountability to data subjects in the home? We will focus on demonstrations in relation to security obligations in the GDPR. As Article 32 talks of both *organisational and technical* measures, we will use this as an opportunity to think about demonstrations under these two broad headings, with particular attention to technical measures (but how they work within the organisation of the home). We reflect on the nature of the home as a setting for demonstrating accountability, consider the promise of smart home security technologies but also their limitations. We consider how DP law might impact the domestic social order, particularly with interpersonal relationships and concerns of control, access, permissions and power. Despite these new responsibilities, DDCs are likely to still be domestic users of technology who just happen to be in a position of authority due to hierarchies in the home or from the technology. Thus, we will conclude by questioning the differentiated responsibilities between vendors and DDCs[c] to manage accountability responsibilities.

2.2   The principle of accountability

In order to understand the accountability principle, we will briefly consider how it has emerged as a DP tool before turning its current instantiation in Article 5(2) GDPR.

2.2.1   *Trajectory from the OECD 1980 to GDPR 2016*

Despite only explicitly appearing once in the EU GDPR [3], the accountability principle has been key in DP policy for decades, particularly as a means of enforcing fundamental principles of DP law [4]. Whilst not tightly defined in

---

[c]Concept of DDCs in Flintham *et al.* [2].

formulating requirements for action, its flexibility too can be a strength, particularly as it enables more innovative technological and organisational approaches for DP compliance.

The principle has its roots in early OECD DP guidelines from 1980 [5]. These were recently updated in 2013 and simply state 'A data controller should be accountable for complying with measures which give effect to the principles stated above'.[d] The principles referred to include 'collection limitation; data quality; purpose specification; use limitation; security safeguards; openness and individual participation'.[e] Apart from the last two,[f] these are broadly similar to the principles that existed in Article 6 of the former EU Data Protection Directive 1995 and Article 5(1) of the current EU GDPR 2016.

We return to EU law below, but for now we want to briefly pick up on these final two OECD principles. They state accountability would also require measures that involve greater 'openness about developments, practice and policies with respect to personal data' and also measures to enable rights of individuals in relation to their data.[g] This would require measures for individuals to: obtain confirmation that a controller has their data; to have such data communicated within a reasonable time where that can be for a non-excessive charge, in a reasonable manner and in an intelligible form; to obtain some justification is a request is rejected; and to challenge the data, including having it erased, rectified, completed or amended.

The latter two principles broaden the scope of accountability, covering similar ground to the data subject rights around access, restriction, notification, erasure, portability and objection in Articles 15–21 GDPR. Openness broadly translates to the transparency and information provision sections in Articles 12–14 GDPR. As we discuss, strict reading of Article 5(2) GDPR relates only to compliance with Article 5(1) hence the OECD framing is broader in content than the EU. However, as we argue later, Article 5(1) needs to be read in conjunction with other GDPR provisions, such as Article 24 on broader data controller responsibilities. This in turn makes it wider (arguably requiring compliance and demonstrations of this with the entire GDPR).[h] However, a key difference between the GDPR and OECD framings of accountability is the latter does not mandate a 'demonstration' of accountability, a point we return to later.

A number of pre-GDPR endeavours have sought to clarify the scope of what accountability means. The Galway [6] and Paris [7] Projects culminating in the Madrid Resolution [8] are three high-profile multi-stakeholder attempts.[i] We draw on details from these at different times below, where they help us to understand what

---

[d]Para 14.
[e]Para 14.
[f]Paras 12 and 13.
[g]Para 12.
[h]See discussion in Urquhart *et al.* [3] on this point.
[i]Business, government, academia.

a demonstration of accountability is (Paris and Galway Projects) or who it is owed to (Madrid Resolution).

2.2.2 *Article 5(2) GDPR and the obligations it creates for data controllers*

The deceptively simple Article 5(2) merely states that 'The controller shall be responsible for, and be able to demonstrate compliance with, paragraph 1'. The principles in paragraph 1 relate to lawful processing, purpose limitation, data minimisation, storage limitation, accuracy, and integrity and confidentiality principles. Explicit inclusion of the accountability principle in the GDPR is new, where it was only implied in the Data Protection Directive 1995 [9]. Despite its short length, it raises a lot of responsibilities for controllers. First, it establishes a *substantive* responsibility for controllers to comply with the series of DP principles in Articles 5(1) (a)–(f). Second, it creates a *procedural* requirement for controllers to find ways to demonstrate their compliance with these principles [1]. The importance of accountability is thus clear in the sense that it serves as a meta-principle that defines how other principles should be observed. Despite this clarity, questions quickly begin to emerge. Is it only these compliance with these principles? What does a demonstration of accountability look like? Is this defined in the law? Who is it owed to? Are there different requirements from a demonstration depending whom it is directed to?

Furthermore, Urquhart *et al.* [1] argue that Article 5(2) needs to be read in light of wider responsibilities of data controllers detailed in Article 24 GDPR. When this is done, the scope of the provision is much wider, arguably requiring demonstrations of accountability for the entire GDPR. The text of Article 24 states:

> the nature, scope, context and purposes of processing as well as the risks of varying likelihood and severity for the rights and freedoms of natural persons, the controller shall *implement appropriate technical and organisational measures* to ensure and to be able to *demonstrate* that processing is performed in accordance with this Regulation (Article 24(1) GDPR, emphasis added).

There are many elements to unpack in Article 24, from questions of processing to risks to what measures are necessary and again, what a demonstration might necessitate. However, given Article 24 goes far beyond just the Article 5(1) principles, it could be quite overwhelming for controllers to determine which elements of the GDPR should be prioritised (especially as there is no real hierarchy within the law of what to prioritise). Conscious of this, Urquhart *et al.* [1] attempt to break down and cluster the responsibilities of controllers into a series of seven accountability requirements, as seen in Table 2.1 (which is discussed in more detail in relation to requirement 6). From a procedural and substantive perspective, a DP impact assessment (Article 40) can be a useful tool for both surfacing processing risks whilst also providing a physical document that can be a demonstration. The similarities between Articles 24, 25 (on DP by design and default) and 32 (on managing data security) are also significant, where turn to technology

Table 2.1   Accountability requirements in GDPR

Accountability requirement	Source in GDPR
1. Limiting initial data collection	Purpose limitation Article 5(1b); data minimisation Article 5(1c); storage limitation Article 5(1e)
2. Restrictions on international data transfer	Data sent outside Europe on basis of adequacy decision Articles 44 and 45; binding corporate rules Article 47; appropriate safeguards Article 46
3. Responding to the spectrum of control rights	Right to access Article 15; to rectification Article 16; to object Article 21; to restrict Article 18; to portability Article 20; to erasure Article 17; information supply chain (passing down requests for rectification, erasure, restriction) Article 19
4. Guaranteeing greater transparency rights	Transparency of information Article 12; rights to provision of information Articles 13 and 14; algorithmic profiling Article 22; record keeping Article 30
5. Ensuring lawfulness of processing	Legality based on specific grounds (Article 5(1a) and Article 6, e.g. performance of contract legitimate interest); consent requirements Article 4 (11), Article 7, Article 8 and Article 9
6. Protecting data storage and security	Accuracy of data Article 5(1d); integrity and confidentiality Article 5(1f); breach notification to authorities Article 33 and to data subject Article 34; security of processing Article 32
7. Articulating and responding to processing responsibilities	Articulating responsibilities: Data Protection Impact Assessments Article 35; certifications including seals, marks and certification bodies Articles 42 and 43; new codes of conduct Articles 40 and 41 Responding to responsibilities: DPO Articles 37 and 39; DPbD Article 25

From Urquhart *et al.* [1].

safeguards is a key policy direction. Technologists are being drawn into the regulatory fray and system architecture is an acknowledged route to address wider responsibilities of data controllers when processing personal data. As this is arguably to comply with the entirety of GDPR and demonstrate how this is done, the scope for convergence of solutions that address Articles 24, 25 and 32 here is sizable, i.e. deploying information privacy preserving architectures by default could also satisfy demonstration of controller responsibilities and good security practices.

2.2.3   Accountable to whom?

The GDPR does not state who accountability is owed to or what it needs to involve, which the former Article 29 Working Party have argued is by design, to enable flexibility of application on a case-by-case basis [10]. This mirrors the OECD position where their guidelines 'do not prescribe to whom the controller should be accountable (the "accountee"), nor what this relationship should look like' [11]. The GDPR does not constrain this either. In practice it is useful to ground who should be targeted and the Madrid Resolution stated it should be, *at least the data subject and the DP regulator*. However, in smart homes where DDCs may owe accountability to these parties, whilst themselves being users, it is less clear how this might manifest. For organisations, as we see below, they have tools at their disposal to demonstrate accountability. How these translate to the domestic, complex socio-technical context of the home, is less clear. This is to state the accountability requirements that DDCs might need to attend to (picking up on this theme in more depth in Section 2.4). How might they demonstrate accountability to a data subject? Much less a DP authority? Who else might have a vested interest? IoT technology vendors?

2.2.4   What form demonstrations of accountability might take?

As noted at the beginning, accountability is a flexible notion. The fact that what a demonstration requires is not prescribed in law means creative approaches can emerge (e.g. as Urquhart *et al.* [1] argue, Databox can be a demonstration). Nevertheless, in practice we need to pin down what a demonstrable account requires to operationalise it to consider the range of options available to controllers [1]. Raab [4] has argued that how an 'account' is framed can differ from the relatively basic level of just documenting what action has been taken by a controller, to enabling questioning of this action all the way to subjects contesting the account or even sanctions being applied if it is deemed unsatisfactory. After consulting guidance from the UK Information Commissioner's Office (ICO) [9], the European Data Protection Supervisor (EDPS) [12], and the pre-GDPR Galway [6] and Paris [7] projects, we see that demonstrations of compliance could require technical and organisational mechanisms to be used. We frame these as follows:

As the guidance on accountability is geared towards organisations, the focus is often framed as developing, as the EDPS [12] puts it, a 'culture of accountability' and not just a bureaucratic 'box ticking exercise' [13]. In the Galway [6] and Paris [7] projects they unpack what a culture or demonstrable accountability might look like, ranging from internal governance structures for organisational compliance

---

Technical measures
  DP by design and default, including use of anonymisation, pseudonymisation and end-to-end encryption; IT security risk management.

Organisational measures
  Assigning DP officers (DPOs); prior consultations; certification schemes; DPIAs; transparent policies; documentation and record keeping on processing for organisations with over 250 staff; internal compliance and audits for effectiveness of approaches; training [1].

with DP standards, to enforcement bodies, training on privacy, leadership and risk analysis.

How might this translate in a home environment where the controller is another household member, and data subjects are children, spouses, extended family and friends, trades people? We consider both in part III, with particular focus on examples and uses of edge computing-based security management. For now, we want to conclude this section by considering what the GDPR precisely states in relation to cybersecurity accountability obligations, to pinpoint what DDCs need to substantively and procedurally address.

Requirement 6 in Table 2.1 states the key dimensions of accountability for security are to 'protect data storage and security', based on 'Accuracy of data Article 5(1)(d); integrity and confidentiality Article 5(1)(f); breach notification to authorities Article 33 and to data subject Article 34; security of processing Article 32'.

Articles 33 and 34 are around breach notification, notably dependent on the nature of breaches (scale, data compromised) and 72-hour time frames for doing this. Article 5(1)(d) requires that data be accurate and up to date whilst inaccurate data be also handled swiftly ('the accuracy principle'). However, in this chapter, we focus on the technical or organisational aspects of the following two GDPR provisions:

1. Article 5(1)(f) requires 'appropriate security' with processing to guard against 'unauthorised or unlawful processing and against accidental loss, destruction or damage' with 'appropriate *technical or organisational* measures'.
2. Article 32 requires *technical and organisational* safeguards for security to be built into processing, proportionate to risks and considering the state of the art, costs and nature of processing.

When viewed alongside Articles 24 and 25, we see an increased focus on technical and organisational measures in the GDPR. For security, this could include controllers taking technical steps such as use of anonymisation; pseudonymisation; end-to-end encryption;[j] regular testing of safeguard measures; mechanisms to ensure ongoing 'confidentiality, integrity, availability and resilience' of systems; provisions giving the ability to restore access to data quickly.[k]

As we will see in Section 2.3, there is a growing role for home occupants in managing DP compliance, and thus data security. The emergence of smart home security tools could be a mechanism that satisfies elements mentioned above. However, we want to explore the organisational dimensions of domestic compliance alongside the technical measures that might assist DDCs in demonstrating accountability, as the two cannot be separated easily. Furthermore, we focus on demonstrations to data subjects, as opposed to authorities in this chapter, given the complex social issues this raises. We return to these issues of these systems, and organisational security

[j]Article 25 suggests these first few, too.
[k]Article 32(1).

management in smart homes in depth in Section 2.4, but first need to unpack why we are even talking about DDCs having a role to play here. Thus, in the next section we explain why DDCs exist as a class of controllers, and how we have reached this position legally. This involves two fundamental shifts in EU case law: a broadening of the notion of a data controller and a narrowing of the household exemption in DP law.

2.3   DP in the home?

To the extent that the principle of accountability imposes the major DP compliance duties on the data controller, it is of paramount practical importance to first identify the controller – or controllers – and then deicide the scope of their responsibilities. Ascertaining who is the *de facto* data controller, however, is not always straightforward, and the increasing prevalence of IoT devices used in spaces of various nature has brought in even more legal uncertainties, not least for the wider range of actors involved and heavier reliance on technical protocols. As will be elaborated below, the GDPR has set out several rules in order for the assignment of accountability duties to reflect the nature, risks and expectations regarding certain types of data processing activities [14]. DP law is already applying to an expanding range of technologies [15, 16], and recent case law has further accelerated this trend. Most importantly, the household exemption effectively creates a carve-out of the scope of the GDPR whereby DDCs may be exempt from demonstrating compliance with the DP principles; joint controllership, on the other hand, establishes collective accountability for data controllers who jointly exercise control over the use of data.

Both the household exemption and joint controllership are therefore important considerations for one to fulfil their duties under the principle of accountability. These two legal notions, however, have been subject to judicial and scholarly debates since the time of the Data Protection Directive. Recent case law and the entry into force of the GDPR have added further dimensions to the complex application to a domestic IoT setting. By reviewing the developments of these two concepts as well as their interactions, we aim to unpack their implications for DDCs in relation to their observance of the accountability principle.

2.3.1   The household exemption and its (in)applicability to domestic IoT

Under the exemption provided for by Article 2(2), the GDPR 'does not apply to the processing of personal data [...] by a natural person in the course of a purely personal or household activity'. Any qualified domestic use of personal data, accordingly, would not be subject to any DP principles or restrictions, including the accountability principle. Two conditions of this provision immediately stand out: 'by a natural person' and 'purely personal or household activity'.

The implication of the first condition is straightforward: This exemption applies only to individuals and not organisations, regardless of the possible household nature. Manufacturers of IoT devices or providers of IoT services are thus simply unable to claim this exemption even if the use of personal data proves indeed for purely personal purposes. For end-users of smart home technologies, there is room for a claim that DP law does not apply to them as long as the second condition is also met. This, in practice, would mean that such users, even if they would otherwise qualify as a data controller, do not need to comply, or demonstrate compliance, with any of the DP requirements. A secondary question would then arise as to whether other organisational joint controllers, if any, should be expected to demonstrate the end-user's compliance as part of their accountability duties. We will discuss that issue in further detail in Section 2.4. Here, from the perspective of the users, the connection between the household exemption and the accountability principle is rather obvious: The application of former would lead to the complete exclusion of the latter.

The much more complicated prong of the household exemption lies in the second condition, namely the purely personal nature of the processing in question. The recitals of GDPR (the non-binding statements in the preamble) as well as regulatory bodies have provided some general clarifications, but it is through the jurisprudence developed in the cases decided by the Court of Justice of the European Union (CJEU) that specific complexities exhibit themselves in particular scenarios. In a highly relevant case, *Ryneš* [17], the Court was asked whether the operation of a CCTV camera on a residential building may be considered as a 'purely personal or household activity'. The Court rejected the claim on the basis that the 'video surveillance [...] covers, [...] partially, a public space and is accordingly directed outwards from the private setting of the person processing the data in that manner' (para 33). This interpretation was followed in a later case *Asociaţia de Proprietari bloc M5A-ScaraA* [18], in which the Court decided that the installation and operation of CCTV camera filming 'the common parts of [an apartment] building in co-ownership and the approach to it' (para 49) are also subject to the GDPR.

It should be noted that in either case, the domestic *purpose* or *intention* was not questioned by the Court. In fact, the Court was fully aware that the data controller – i.e. the operator of the CCTV system – may have legitimate interests in 'the protection of the property, health and life of his family and himself' [17] (para 34) or 'ensuring the safety and protection of individuals and property' [18] (para 33). It is the operative *method* of the CCTV system that came to the central point of the Court's analysis. The fact that such a surveillance system may casually capture and store the image of individuals outside the data controller's family in an electronic format will suffice for such activities to fall outside the scope of the household exemption. The implication of this judgement for smart home owners can be profound to the extent that many IoT devices are capable, or indeed designed, to collect data from a space potential beyond the physical boundaries of one's home. Visitors, neighbours, or even passers-by may be affected by, for example, the accidental collection of data from their smartphones when they approach the sensory remit of the user's smart home system.

Also, worth pointing out is that the CJEU has never ruled in favour of a claim of the household exemption. Rather, the Court has consistently taken a highly restrictive approach to interpreting this provision. By ruling out the applicability of the exemption to various cases, the scope of this exemption is increasingly shrinking, which may have an impact on any IoT end-users hoping to benefit from this exemption. The rationale of this interpretative approach is perhaps not difficult to understand: As discussed above, triggering the household exemption would mean the GDPR ceases to apply altogether to the case concerned, which would potentially create a regulatory vacuum to the detriment of the data subject. While the Court has laid down clear rules on what would *not* count as purely personal – data accessible by an unrestricted number of people, or concerns a public space beyond the private sphere [19] (para 42) – the only cases unquestionably exempt are those explicitly provided for in Recital 18 GDPR, namely 'correspondence and the holding of addresses, or social networking and online activity undertaken within the context of such activities'.

As such, the circumstances under which a claim of the household exemption can be reasonably made by an end-user will need to be examined on a case-by-case basis. If the use of personal data in these context does not pass the threshold set out in the case law, the user would have to demonstrate compliance with the accountability principle. While the Court has never directly addressed Article 5(2) GDPR (or Article 6(2) DPD), it seems obvious that accountability suggests some form of duty of care to be assumed by the data controller even concerning merely household activities, which would entail an assessment of the technical options in the light of the interests and risks of the parties involved. As AG Jääskinen opined in *Google Spain and Google* [20], 'Article 6(2) of the Directive obliges [data controllers] to weigh the interests of the data controller, or third parties in whose interest the processing is exercised, against those of the data subject' (para 107). In *M5A-ScaraA* [18], the Court also stated that 'the proportionality of the data processing by a video surveillance device must be assessed by taking into account the specific methods of installing and operating that device' (para 50) and 'the controller must examine, for example, whether it is sufficient that the video surveillance operates only at night or outside normal working hours, and block or obscure the images taken in areas where surveillance is unnecessary' (para 51). How such considerations can be demonstrable by domestic users in practice, however, is a different and yet even more challenging issue.

2.3.2 Domestic and non-domestic joint controllership in domestic IoT

Another concept crucial to implementing the accountability requirements is joint controllership, as it defines how DP obligations are shared among a group of controllers who make co-decisions on how personal data are processed. Article 26(1) provides that 'Where two or more controllers jointly determine the purposes and means of processing, they shall be joint controllers.' The same provision goes on to require joint controllers to 'in a transparent manner determine their respective responsibilities for compliance with the obligations under this Regulation'. This definition seems to suggest that joint controllership arises from a unanimous decision by all controllers with regard to how the DP duties are split and discharged by each of them. However, the allocation of duties cannot be determined on an arbitrary or unreasonable basis. Instead, such an arrangement must 'duly reflect the respective roles and relationships of the joint controllers *vis-à-vis* the data subjects'. This has also been emphasised in the opinions issued by the Article 29 Working Party. The Working Party has specifically highlighted the importance to establish 'clear and equally effective allocation of obligations and responsibilities' [21] that genuinely reflects the legal relationship of between the joint controllers. For example, if a contract substantially gives one an entity material powers to decide how data are processed, but formally only assigns a different entity with less influence as a sole controller, such an assignment would be invalid and the former entity would remain liable as a joint controller.[1]

Apart from the scenarios involving contractual arrangements, which are clearly covered by the definition of joint controllership, the CJEU has decided on a number of more complicated cases where such a contractual relationship does not clearly exist. For example, in *Jehovan todistajat* [19], the Court decided that the Jehovah's Witnesses Community was a joint controller with its members with regard to the collection and use of personal data through door-to-door preaching. The judgement was concluded on the basis that the 'preaching activity is [...] organised, coordinated and encouraged by that community' (para 70), regardless of the lack of formal instructions issued, or actual access to the data, by the Community (paras 67, 69). The mere organisational structure facilitating the processing of personal data was considered sufficient to give rise to joint controllership.

Joint controllership may also result from activities aligned by technical protocols. The Court considered in *Fashion ID* [23] whether the operator of a website became a joint controller with Facebook by placing a 'Like' button on a webpage, which would trigger and enable Facebook to collect personal data from a visitor. This does not depend on any communications or existing legal relationship between the website and Facebook, and as such, the formation of joint controllership can be purely a matter of technical settings. Although *Fashion ID* does not concern a smart home context, the implications for domestic IoT users can be profound as the two scenarios bear some resemblances: One party controls the switch of a system, whose architecture is designed by the other party to allow the latter to collect personal data from third parties. In Chen *et al.*'s [14] words, the former possesses *operational control* and the latter *schematic control*. Data collection would not take place without the action of either party, but their cooperation does not rely on a formal mutual agreement, but simply by ways of technical configurations.

The expanding coverage of joint controllership by the CJEU means that the 'co-decision' by joint controllers does not have to take the form of contractual arrangements, but can be achieved simply with a much looser relation enabled by organisational or technical configurations. Recognising this point is especially crucial for compliance with the accountability principle because data controllers

---

[1]For a discussion on how, in a context of personal data stores, such an allocation can be specified in the terms of service, see [22].

are under a clear obligation to 'implement appropriate technical and organisational measures' (Article 24 GDPR). The nature of the joint controllership can be a critical first step in establishing what measures should be put in place to coordinate responsibilities and document compliance. In fact, the Court has noted that the joint controllers 'may be involved at different stages of that processing of personal data and to different degrees, so that the level of responsibility of each of them must be assessed with regard to all the relevant circumstances of the particular case' [23] (para 43). For example, in *Fashion ID*, the Court unequivocally pointed out that the duties to obtain consent from, and to provide information to, visitors of a website with an embedded Facebook 'Like' button fall on the operator of the website, not Facebook, even though the data are transmitted only to the latter [24] (paras 98–106). A comparison can be made with the case of domestic use of IoT technologies, where the homeowner, if held jointly responsible with an IoT service provider who collects data potentially from non-members of the family, may be under a duty to ensure there is a legitimising basis and to inform the affected parties (e.g. guests) of the details.

2.3.3 Accountability shared between domestic and non-domestic controllers

Having discussed the implications of the narrowing scope of the household exemption and the widening application of joint controllership in case law, now let us consider how these complexities would play out in observing the accountability principle in a variety of circumstances in an IoT-enabled smart home. Table 2.2 shows different combinations of the nature of the processing and the category of the controllers. It should be noted that a DDC here refers simply to an individual processing personal data with an IoT device in their home, and does not necessarily imply such uses are for domestic purposes only, who may or may not be covered by the household exemption. Likewise, a non-DDC is defined here as a controller other than a DDC, who does not have to process the data for a professional or commercial purpose.

It is noteworthy that even if a particular use of personal data is within the course of a 'purely personal or household activity', the household exemption would not apply to the non-DDC, meaning that the latter would remain responsible for the processing in question. This is because the household exemption operates essentially on a controller-specific basis. Recital 18 GDPR makes it clear that 'this Regulation applies to controllers or processors which provide the means for processing personal

Table 2.2   Data controller(s) responsible to demonstrate accountability

	DDC only	DDC and non-DDC	Non-DDC only
Purely domestic use	Nobody	Non-DDC*	N/A
Non-domestic use	DDC†	DDC and non-DDC‡	Non-DDC§

data for [...] personal or household activities.' As a result, the non-DDC may be held responsible as the sole controller in two scenarios, one where the domestic user does exercise control on the processing but is exempt from the duties due to the domestic nature of the processing (scenario *), and the other where the domestic user has no control at all (scenario §). While it is clear in the latter case that the non-DDC must demonstrate accountability concerning the full range of DP obligations, this is open to question in the former case where certain duties would have fallen on the DDC had the household exemption not applied. For example, consider the situation where a homeowner uses a smart thermostat in a guest room occupied by a visiting family guest, which sends room temperature data to the vendor's server that are accessible only to the homeowner. Assuming such data are personal data and this is a purely household use of such data, would the vendor, as a non-DDC, be placed under any primary or secondary obligations to demonstrate that, say, there is a legitimate basis on the homeowner's part to use such data, or adequate information has been given to the guest?ᵐ One interpretation of the household exemption can be that these duties would not apply at all once the exemption has been established, meaning that no demonstration of accountability would be required when it comes to such duties. However, it can be an equally valid contention that such duties do not apply, but just *to the DDC*, and the exemption does not preclude the non-DDC's duties on these matters if they have not already been fulfilled by the domestic controller. Such uncertainties would call for further regulatory or judicial guidance.

Another challenge is where it is incumbent on the DDC to demonstrate compliance with the DP principles, whether solely (scenario †) or jointly with the professional controller (scenario ‡), how their accountability can be demonstrated and assessed. The subtle differences mirrored in varying interpretations of the tensions between DDCs, non-DDCs and data subjects may remarkably affect our understanding of what is 'accountable' and what is 'demonstrable' in a domestic IoT environment. Such nuances are not merely a legal fiction but rather a relational reflection of the complex socio-technical attributes embedded in today's smart homes. As will be seen in the next section, empirical evidence has suggested this is indeed a highly sophisticated landscape. Effective policymaking as well as enforcement of the accountability principle would therefore depend on a meticulous capture of the role of various solutions in both technical and organisational terms in managing accountability. It is in this regard that we now turn to the human–computer interaction scholarship for further answers.

2.4   Accountable DDCs

In this part, we align discussions from the two previous sections to pose questions around how DDCs in smart homes can demonstrate accountability to data subjects

---

ᵐThe scenario where the homeowner processes their own personal data is not a central case to our discussion, but is subject to the same concern that the responsibilities can be unfairly shifted to the homeowner if they are classified as a joint controller for their own data. See [22, 25].

in the home. As an emerging domain, we take this opportunity to explore related literature, and pose some questions to be addressed to understand what DP law coming into the home may mean in practical terms. We are interested in both the form and challenges that may arise in creating *demonstrations of accountability*. DDCs may have to provide appropriate security (Article 5(2) GDPR) and use technical and organisational measures to support secure data management (Article 32 GPDR). What this will look like in the domestic context requires unpacking, particularly around interpersonal relationships in homes.

We focus here on technical measures, but consider how the organisational deployment setting (i.e. the home) will shape how technical measures might work or be adopted. Below, we turn to contemporary empirical and technical work from fields of human–computer interaction and usable privacy/security, to help us unpack the following lines of inquiry:

- What technical measures exist for supporting demonstrations of accountability, specifically focusing on smart home security management tools?
- What occupant privacy and security management practices exist in smart homes, particularly around interpersonal relationships?
- What socio-technical and usability problems might these tools raise with DDCs using them?
- How might these discussions intersect with GDPR compliance requirements for DDCs, particularly for demonstrations of accountability?

A fundamental tension raised by the shifts outlined above is that giving DP responsibilities to DDCs is *they lack both resources and skills of organisations* that the legal framework was designed to apply to. Thus, there can be shared responsibility with vendors of smart home technologies or even those providing smart home security management tech (depending on the architecture). *Ordinary* organisational mechanisms are unlikely to work here, e.g. will a partner be auditing the quality of their spouse's password? Will they conduct a review of breach management strategies? What might domestic processing record keeping look like here and the description of measures taken?[n]

Another is the compliance *setting*. It is not a company with organisational resources for record keeping capabilities or capacity to know when to do a DP impact assessment or hire a DPO (many normal steps seen for accountability). Instead, it is a home; space where cohabitants live their daily lives. Thus, translating regulatory concepts to this domain could feel forced. Should regulatory norms structure domestic life? Domesticating technology itself can take time [26] and designing technologies so they can be embedded in daily lives requires an appreciation of what that life looks like [27]. The same will be true for *designing technical and organisational measures for demonstrating accountability*. We need to understand how security is

[n]Article 30 GDPR – documenting details about processing, e.g. purposes of processing, categories of data and subjects, etc. but importantly, under Article 30(1)(g): 'where possible, a general description of the technical and organisational security measures referred to in Article 32(1).'

managed currently in smart homes, and thus we first consider what tools there are and the context they will need to operate in, i.e. what do occupants currently do?

2.4.1 Smart home cybersecurity management tools

Whilst traditionally (and still predominantly) the system architectures of IoT devices are centralised and cloud based, we are seeing increased use of distributed analytics and storage at the edge of networks. In terms of data handling responsibilities, managing these systems may increase the role for users and others (e.g. DDCs) at the edge of the network. This is often by design, in the case of some edge-based storage systems, such as personal information management systems (PIMS) like *Databox, HAT, MyDex*, etc.[o] It is recognised in privacy policymaking and privacy engineering communities that PIMS can help users determine how their data are used, and increase control over who has access to it [29, 30]. Similarly, distributed data analytics can enable new privacy preserving forms of federated machine learning which can address ethical and governance concerns around data harvesting, severing personal data from users and associated privacy harms stemming from big data analytics. This shift to 'small data' led systems [31, 32] can empower users, address DP compliance concerns, particularly around opacity of data flows and power asymmetries around access by third parties [1]. Nevertheless, these systems still require (sometimes high levels of) oversight and awareness around how to do this. Given varying skillsets and motivations to manage privacy and security, this could be problematic. Interface design often does not help either (as we return to in topic 3).

These systems open up scope for edge-based systems for security management to enabling smarter network monitoring and security management tools. There are a range of commercial and research-led offerings, including *Cujo* [33], *IoT Keeper* [34] and *Sense* [35]. We describe a few examples below, including both prototypes and commercial products.

- *IoT Inspector* examines device firmware for security vulnerabilities after it is uploaded to the platform, analysed and risks reported back [36, 37]. It is geared towards a range of industry stakeholders, particularly vendors, and thus could be useful for joint controllers, where responsibility lies with them, in addition to DDCs.[p]
- *Fingbox* is a consumer-orientated physical box that can be bought for the home. It monitors network activity (including open ports), conducts vulnerability analysis, blocks intruders or unknown devices and observes who is on the network.[q]
- *Wireshark* is an open source, freely available network protocol analyser that provides granular analysis on network activity by sniffing packets. It can be used for intrusion detection too [38]. For an everyday user, there may be skillset requirements in interpreting these data.

[o]See Urquhart *et al.* [28] for more details.
[p]Also targeted to corporate users, infrastructure providers, researchers and resellers.
[q]www.fing.com/products/fingbox

- *Homesnitch* is a prototype that seeks to increase transparency and control over domestic networks by classifying device behaviour. As opposed to just reporting packet flow it 'learns' about behaviour in order to report on what this might mean, e.g. 'downloading firmware, receiving a configuration change, and sending video to a remote user' [39]. This could be more contextually useful for users.

- *IoT Sentinel* is another prototype architecture where the system has a more active role in managing network security. It identifies types of devices on a network, spots any security vulnerabilities and then enforces network rules against these devices automatically. This latter step can range from isolating devices and blocking external access, filtering traffic to prevent data being exfiltrated or notifying users of issues [40].

- The *DADA system* seeks to monitor network traffic for vulnerable devices and unexpected behaviours (e.g. using Manufacturer Usage Description (MUD) profiles). It then informs users of different options to deal with vulnerable devices, e.g. to block the device from the network, etc. [41].

- *Aretha* includes an integrated training aspect for end-users, firewall management and a network disaggregator [42]. Part of the tool gave users the ability to set directives for the firewall in a user-friendly way, e.g. with a graphic user interface and in plain language. Despite this, they found there was need to simplify this to enable user adoption, coupled with difficulties in users analysing risk of safety or danger in blocked domains. The researchers posit a greater role for experts pre-formulating black lists that users can then tweak, or using presence of certain metrics to block sources, e.g. 'company reputation, jurisdiction, purpose of data collection, retention and disclosure properties'.^r This tool also offers training, visualisations and a physical presence, all helping strengthen collective user engagement with security and privacy management.

Whilst these tools show promise as technical measures for DDCs demonstrating accountability to other occupants, we also believe there are complex socio-technical considerations around their possible integration into the home. Thus, we will review some literature around current user security management practices in smart homes.

2.4.2 Security (and privacy) management in smart homes

Security does matter to smart home users. A study by Emami-Naeini *et al.* [43] found that whilst not as highly valued as price and features, both privacy and security are important factors when buying new IoT devices. Nevertheless, consumers can find it difficult to obtain information about the security and privacy credentials

---

^rThey highlight that it does a variety of things: 'the probe brought about not just a heightened awareness of privacy concerns—by being a salient and visible physical totem in their living room—but a transformative one, in which privacy management transitioned from being a solo concern anchored with the individual responsible for technology within the home, to one discussed between multiple home stakeholders. The visibility of the probe within the home inspired conversations among household members, and the visualisations provided a common ground' (p. 9).

of a product but do state they may be willing to pay a premium (between 10% and 30%) for a device with this information.[s]

In the wild, user concerns around security and privacy threats in smart homes vary. Zeng *et al.* [44] find participant concerns focused on physical security, e.g. control over smart locks enabling home access. They observed that different levels of technical knowledge shaped their awareness of types of IoT vulnerabilities, e.g. skilled users were concerned about HTTPS, less skilled about weak passwords or unsecured Wi-Fi (p. 71). They also observed this knowledge shaped how users manage risks from changing behaviour, e.g. avoiding speaking in front of Alexa to more skilled participants setting up a separate Wi-Fi networks or blocking traffic.

Looking to smart speakers, as an example smart home system, Huang *et al.* [45] unpack privacy concerns around smart speakers with respect to internal (siblings/flatmates), key for DDCs to consider. These include:

- concerns about overheard calls
- unauthorised access to contact details, calendars or reminders on speakers, due to inadequate voice authentication (e.g. it is open to all as opposed to being tied to a specific users' voice)
- speakers being exploited for unintended uses by children or visitors like unauthorised purchases.

In terms of managing these concerns, more skilled users might not link any private information with the speaker and they suggest there could be routes for customising speakers to share information users might be comfortable their peers accessing.

As Crabtree *et al.* [46] have noted, within the home, the nature of control and who accesses information is not always framed in 'privacy' terms. Often it is about managing relationships and is part of the work of living with networked systems. As they state, '"privacy" *dissolves* into a heterogeneous array of mundane practices and local concerns that are not primarily to do with the disclosure of personal data, but with managing *who* gets to access what devices, applications, and content'. However, with the emergence of DP norms within smart homes, it forces reflection on how informational privacy might be reframed, and how those norms structure domestic relationships and practices. We now turn to studies exploring security management in homes in more depth, particularly interpersonal aspects.

2.4.3   Interpersonal power dynamics in smart homes

Geeng and Roesner [47] provide valuable insights into social *power dynamics* in smart homes, particularly around the 'smart home driver', i.e. the individual who

---

[s]They argue labelling schemes might offer viable solutions in simplifying information provision.

wants to have the device in the home. Drivers have a prominent role when something goes wrong and in mediating access/control over the devices for other occupants. This can differ across the life cycle of devices, e.g. when first installing to long-term management.[t] They note that drivers are ordinarily men and had more interest in learning about using the devices, thus giving more power and agency in the home, whereas other relied on them to manage change (p. 8). Drivers may be more likely to be the DDCs, as the one managing the device and its processing in the home.

Their role can be problematic for other occupants and Zeng *et al.* [44] provide data from those who are not primary but 'incidental' users in the home. They observed incidental users might not have apps installed or even have access to functionality of devices. This ranges from less interest to restrictions from primary users to prevent them from changing settings, e.g. restricting change of thermostats. This control can take different forms, from landlords remotely observing transcripts from smart speakers or security camera footage to monitoring use of the home, e.g. parties, or even surveilling when other household members leave/arrive at the home (e.g. husband monitoring smart lock). The latter example aligns with earlier studies from Ur *et al.* [48] around impacts on family dynamics from parents observing when children arrive home through smart lock logs. Zeng *et al.* [44] conclude, 'while the people who set up smart homes, particularly early adopters, often treat the technology as a personal hobby, smart homes are fundamentally not personal technologies. As a result, any security and privacy (or other) decisions made by the primary user directly affects other residents and visitor' (p. 75).

More concerningly, this power could link into Freed *et al.*'s [49] work examining how technology is used for intimate partner violence. They observe how authorised users use functionality that they have access to in order to track, manipulate and threaten their partners. In response, they recommend use of reviews during the design process or managing default settings when systems are adopted (e.g. removing display of recent location information). Clearly, in smart homes, this could be a risk and the work of Parkin *et al.* [50] responds by developing different usability heuristics to assess risks IoT devices create for intimate partner violence. Recent work by Levy and Schneier [51] further theorises how smart home technologies can facilitate invasion of privacy in intimate relationships by augmenting the coercive power possessed by the member with explicit or implicit authority.

Mundane smart home device *account* management can also raise power issues in families. Goulden [52] explores the way firms, such as Google and Amazon construct hierarchies in the household to coordinate everyday activities. This can involve linking accounts and defining roles in the home, e.g. by attributes like age. This can enable control over others accounts and what they can do with and observe uses of devices, e.g. remove permissions or delete from family group. Goulden is concerned about the impacts on domestic family life of this type of intervention.

---

[t] For example, 'Device Selection; Device Installation; Regular Device Use; Things Go Wrong; Long-Term Device Use'.

In smart homes, data are co-constructed and relational; it often does not only identify one individual [53]. This can lead to difficulties for us in thinking about data controllership and subjects. In a home, both DDCs and data subjects may be identifiable, e.g. in traces from sensors in the home. Reconciling this issue needs further attention around the duality of how a controller can be both a steward for personal data of others in the home, alongside their own. This is further complicated when we consider the joint nature of controllership with IoT vendors, who may not have the same interests in these data. Family members would likely want to protect the data of other family members (violence and abuse notwithstanding), but, as we know, IoT vendors may seek to monetise and use those data to understand everyday life and make inferences. The power dynamic between controllers and subjects in this domain will remain messy.

Desjardins *et al.* [54] observe different relationships with data in smart homes, and how data are visualised within the home by occupants, developing how data are part of experiencing the home and daily life. They see 'IoT data not as an undefined, ephemeral, position-less, and singular mass (although it might be conceptualized this way): these data are, in fact, of a home, in a home, and part of unique domestic assemblages which are important to recognize and honour when designing for them.' This point further highlights how established labels and categories in DP law around personal data, identifiability and prescriptive responsibilities over data might not translate to the home context, where the messiness of data is part of life. Yet, with DP law entering the home DDCs will face responsibilities for other occupants. They will need to consider how what they do fits with legal terms of art, like personal data, and how they can demonstrate they are protecting data rights of others.

2.4.4   Control struggles in smart homes

Despite thinking about these near future issues, we need to unpack how control of data and devices is managed *currently* in smart homes, given accountability requires demonstrations from DDCs to subjects (i.e. between family members). Thus, it is valuable to consider what types of control issues smart homes pose for daily life.

Geeng and Roesner [47] consider some of the interpersonal tensions different stakeholders face in *controlling* domestic smart technologies. Examples include: partners disagreeing about third party access via door lock code (e.g. cleaners); roommates controlling temperature via apps, where others do not use the app; sibling locking each other's media accounts for punishment; parents and children competing for control of an Amazon Echo, e.g. with music it plays (p. 6). Physical security and safety concerns around co-occupants being able to still use resources despite lack of expertise or account control like lighting, heating and exit/entry. This is particularly important when devices stop working, e.g. in DIY smart homes.

Given the home is a shared space, co-management of devices and how groups manage security of shared resources is an important consideration we return to below. Such relational complexities are perhaps exacerbated by the heterogeneity of governance structure of smart systems, or in Singh *et al.*'s [55] words, the 'systems-of-systems' nature of IoT. Technologies can play a role, they argue, in enabling accountability by supporting control and audit of IoT systems.

Mazurek *et al.* [56] consider how access control across devices is managed in homes, exploring the complexity of creating approaches that work in practice vs how users want them to work. Whilst focused on protecting sensitive data on laptops or phones, it is interesting the lessons about shared device usage for IoT too. Designers need to enable users to create granular access controls, to enable subtle creation of guest accounts (to avoid awkwardness when sharing devices). Interestingly, they noted that in deciding about access, it went beyond *types of files* (work, music, photos, etc.) and *who* the other user was (e.g. partner, parents, friends, etc.). Instead, factors such as presence and location of both controller and those accessing files was important, as was the device type (e.g. phones more personal) and even time of day (e.g. in the evening where sleep should be occurring). These show what might shape access policies to information and how for IoT.

This is valuable to further reflect on concerns of Goulden [52] that smart homes having formalised models of control, access and roles. Here, we can see, the home is messy, and notions of accountability play out differently there, unlike in institutional security policies with strict hierarchies, safelists and permissions work more effectively. In homes, it needs to be more dynamic and contextual. In terms of how vendors might support accountability, as joint controllers, this is an area for further work on designing more adaptive forms of permissions and account management. One route forward could be from ID management protocols. Rosner and Kenneally [57] have argued in relation to IoT privacy that identity management is important to consider because it involves 'discussion of privacy as control, access management, and selective sharing'. They suggest building systems that prevent linking of identities and unobservability of users by default, in addition to value of protocols such as User Managed Access (UMA), which enable user led control of access and selective permissions.[u]

For DDCs, this could be a valuable tool but would require vendors to enable such functionality. In terms of other routes forward, we now consider the importance of engaging others in the home in security management.

2.4.5 Towards collective security management in homes?

Geeng and Roesner [47] argue that designers need to be more aware of different relationship types in homes and also consider how to make the account creation process more sensitive to multiple occupancy with shared devices. They suggest IoT designers need to incorporate 'mechanical switches and controls' for basic device functionality like switching on or off. They also suggest need for measures to manage temporary device access for short-term occupants and also for deletion/migration of data when people move out. Similarly, Zeng *et al.* [44] recognise systems

[u]https://kantarainitiative.org/confluence/display/uma/Home

should 'support multiple distinct user accounts, usability and discoverability of features are critical for secondary, less technical users', e.g. using physical controls and indicators in the home for when being recorded.

Tabassum *et al.* [58] have also looked beyond the walls of the home, to consider how use of smart devices is shared with others outside and the nature of this shared management. Factors such as security are critical for enabling others to access devices to deal, with motivations like helping manage deliveries or emergencies when occupants are away. Enabling remote access to the home with smart locks or safety of pets and older people is another example. However, they noted that this has to be underpinned by trust in the community they are sharing access with and because of this, often it was full access given to external parties, as opposed to more nuanced forms. Here, we can see that DDCs might not just be parties within the home but managing data flows as an external party.

Similarly, Watson *et al.* [59] reflect on collective management of cybersecurity for a range of resources (devices, social media, streaming accounts, etc.). Whilst not specifically for smart homes, a key concern raised is those inside the group posing threats to group as a whole, in part due individual to poor security practices compromising the group as a whole. Whilst in practice, the participants hold each other accountable for shared resources, 'group security is only as strong as the individual with the weakest security behaviours, which can be inequitable and lead to resentment'. Thus, each member has responsibility, even if unsupervised by others to do their best, and they can risk losing access to these resources. In contrast to papers above flagging concerns around hierarchies, they suggest need for tools to address this weakest link element, and to allow 'group members with higher S&P awareness, motivation and knowledge' to act as stewards for more vulnerable members.

Whilst this may be pragmatic, as we see above, vesting too much control in one party can lead to other risks, and impacts for the domestic social order. With DDCs navigating responsibilities, clearly there will be questions around to what extent collective management makes sense (e.g. in flat shares) vs one party managing security on behalf of everyone (e.g. with a family or elderly user). However, this should not just be because of the assumptions that a smart device driver will do this, or because of the affordances of a system around accounts.

Irrespective of if there is individual or collective control over devices in the home, one issue remains around the usability of systems. Adoption of technical solutions for accountability, such as the security systems mentioned above, need to be usable. In the enterprise context, there can be a perception that users are to blame for security not being managed effectively, but adopting user-centric design principles or communicating how to use a system properly could address these [60]. Dourish *et al.* [61] examined system security manifests in everyday life for users. They focus on the disconnect between user goals and security goals can often leave users unsure how best to secure their systems. They state security for ubiquitous computing environments needs to be 'manageable and understandable to end users'.

There are attempts to support user preferences around privacy practices for IoT with privacy assistants. Colnago *et al.* [62] qualitative study of user needs from privacy assistants showed different user preferences around degrees of automation, control and frequency of notifications. They advocate systems be built with modularity and configurability of autonomy for users to tweak systems individually. Part of this is assistants providing external recommendations, which is preferred to recommendations based on past behaviour, although the systems might need to provide choice over what recommended sources are used (again enabling tweaking by the user).

Nevertheless, this may change over time. Jakobi *et al.* [63] found the level of information users seek whilst managing smart homes differs over time. At the beginning, there is a desire for more granular information and feedback on current and past behaviour. As years passed, this reduced to wanting information when systems 'not working, needed their attention, or required active maintenance'. How Article 5(2) requirements may require more long-term oversight might not intersect with domestic practice. Thus, there is scope for the law to disrupt how users might ordinarily live with smart technologies. In attempting to subject the home to regulatory norms, like accountability, this may impact how systems are integrated into daily life by requiring mechanisms that prolong system oversight and may even disrupt the social order.

2.4.6   *Differentiated responsibilities*

We have seen the narrowing of the household exemption and joint controllership arrangements emerging, leading DP law to enter the home.

DDCs managing data collection in the home are still reliant on data processing architectures defined by others. This is unlike the normal situation for a controller where they design and define the nature of processing. Clearly, vendors of IoT devices, or those providing security management tools have a role to play in shaping how DDCs manage data domestically. They may even be joint controllers, depending on if they process personal data too, e.g. via analytics, cloud storage, etc.

In any case, if they are joint controllers, they too are implicated in the need to help demonstrate accountability with GDPR. As this section has shown, the provision of security management tools themselves could help to provide technical measures required. We conclude by thinking about how accountability obligations for security might be shared by vendors and DDCs.

There is a clear role for vendors in helping DDCs manage data processing in the home. Two key areas that have emerged are around improving quality of account management tools. Current approaches do not reflect the context of use and complexities of permissions, accounts and access. Another is around ensuring that there is usability of security tools. Whilst there are promising approaches emerging, increased engagement with DDCs and users is necessary to see the competencies, skillsets and challenges they face in using these systems. Some are technical, where users may lack those skills; others may want more control. Vendors should do more in integrating such systems into their offerings, including using user-centric design principles to shape what this looks like. Such a supportive role results not just from the fact that vendors tend to be better resourced and skilled in managing security threats, but also more importantly, they are in a unique position to have native, usable tools built into their products to achieve and demonstrate compliance. There is also an economic case to be made here, considering how vendors may be held jointly liable for data breaches caused by security incidents [64]. Broadly speaking, one can even argue what accountability means for vendors is two-fold: To be able to demonstrate their own compliance, and to be able to demonstrate usable solutions provided to DDCs to facilitate their compliance.

With or without the support from vendors, there is also a clear role for DDCs in demonstrating accountability. On one hand, this may be as simple as adopting the use of technical measures, systems like Aretha, DADA, IoTSentinel, and relying on this as a demonstration of what they are doing to secure the home. However, as discussed, the home is a complex organisational space for these technologies to be used. They also have to integrate with how security of IoT devices is currently managed in the home. This includes thinking about interpersonal relationships, control, power asymmetries and guarding against abuses of such power. Ordinarily, such practices would not be mediated by legal requirements and further work will be necessary to see how DP law might restructure the social order of the home, by introducing new formally defined accountability norms.

2.5   Conclusion

In conclusion, within this chapter, we began by exploring the nature of the accountability principle and thinking about security compliance obligations in GDPR. We then charted two fundamental shifts in recent EU DP case law: the narrowing of the household exemption in DP law and the broadening of notions of joint data controllership. The consequence of this is a new class of DDC with responsibilities to other home occupants when processing their personal data. To contextualise this shift, we considered the implications for accountability in smart homes, and how home occupants who find themselves as DDCs might demonstrate compliance with security requirements of GDPR. We focused on the organisational setting of the home, as a site of smart technology use, and the types of technical tools available to DDCs that could provide a demonstration of accountability. However, we also raised complex questions that need to be addressed in order for DDCs to do this effectively. These ranged from unpacking the nature of interpersonal relations in the home around power, control and access; how technical tools might intersect with current security concerns and practices; and the differentiated nature of responsibility between joint controllers, the vendors of smart home technologies and the DDCs.

2.6   Acknowledgements

The research reported here was supported by the Engineering and Physical Sciences Research Council [grant numbers EP/R03351X/1, EP/M02315X/1, EP/T022493/1]. This chapter is based on the following original works:

- Urquhart, L., Lodge, T., Crabtree, A. "Demonstrably Doing Accountability in the Internet of Things". *International Journal of Law and Information Technology*. 2019; 27(1): pp. 1-27
- Chen, J., Edwards, L., Urquhart, L., McAuley, D. "Who Is Responsible for Data Processing in Smart Homes? Reconsidering Joint Controllership and the Household Exemption". *International Data Privacy Law*. 2020; 10(4): pp. 279-293
- Urquhart, L., Chen, J. "Stuck in the Middle with U(sers): Domestic Data Controllers and Demonstration of Accountability in Smart Homes". *Proceedings of the ETHICOMP* 2020*; Logroño, June 2020 (Logroño, Universidad de La Rioja, 2020)

References

[1] BBC. *Grandmother ordered to delete Facebook photos under GDPR*. 2020. Available from www.bbc.co.uk/news/technology-52758787 [Accessed 13 Jun 2020].

[2] Goulden M., Price D., Urquhart L., Flintham M. (eds.) 'Domesticating data: socio-legal perspectives on smart homes and good data design' in Daly A., Devitt S.K., Mann M. (eds.). *Good Data*. Amsterdam: Institute of Network Cultures; 2019.

[3] Urquhart L., Lodge T., Crabtree A. 'Demonstrably doing accountability in the Internet of things'. *International Journal of Law and Information Technology*. 2019;**27**(1):1–27.

[4] Raab C. (eds.) 'The meaning of "accountability" in the information privacy context' in Guagnin D., Hempel L., Ilten C., Kroener I., Neyland D., Postigo H. (eds.). *Managing Privacy through Accountability*. London: Palgrave Macmillan; 2012.

[5] OECD. *OECD guidelines on the protection of privacy and transborder flows of personal data [online]*. 1980. Available from https://read.oecd-ilibrary.org/science-and-technology/oecd-guidelines-on-the-protection-of-privacy-and-transborder-flows-of-personal-data_9789264196391-en [Accessed 13 Jun 2020].

[6] Centre for Information Policy Leadership. *Data protection accountability: the essential elements [online]*. 2009. Available from www.informationpolicycentre.com/uploads/5/7/1/0/57104281/data_protection_accountability-the_essential_elements__discussion_document_october_2009_.pdf [Accessed 13 Jun 2020].

[7] Centre for Information Policy Leadership. *Demonstrating and measuring accountability [online]*. 2010. Available from www.informationpolicycentre.com/uploads/5/7/1/0/57104281/demonstrating_and_measuring_accountability_a_discussion_document__accountability_phase_ii-the_paris_project_october_2010_.pdf [Accessed 13 Jun 2020].

[8]   International Conference of Data Protection and Privacy Commissioners. *International standards on the protection of personal data and privacy: the madrid resolution [online]*. 2009. Available from http://privacyconferenc e2011.org/htmls/adoptedResolutions/2009_Madrid/2009_M1.pdf [Accessed 13 Jun 2020].

[9]   Information Commissioner's Office. *Accountability and governance [online]*. 2019. Available from https://ico.org.uk/for-organisations/guide-to-data-pro-tection/guide-to-the-general-data-protection-regulation-gdpr/accountability-and-governance/ [Accessed 13 Jun 2020].

[10]   Article 29 Data Protection Working Party. 'Opinion 3/2010 on the principle of accountability'. 2010.

[11]   Alhadeff J., Van Alsenoy B., Dumortier J. 'The accountability principle in data protection regulation: origin, development and future directions' in Guagnin D., Hempel L., Ilten C., Kroener I., Neyland D., Postigo H. (eds.). *Managing Privacy through Accountability*. London: Palgrave Macmillan; 2012.

[12]   European Data Protection Supervisor. *Our role as an advisor [online]*. 2016. Available from https://edps.europa.eu/data-protection/our-role-advisor_en [Accessed 13 Jun 2020].

[13]   European Data Protection Supervisor. *The accountability principle in the new GDPR: speech by giovanni buttarelli given at the european court of justice, luxembourg [online]*. 2016. Available from https://edps.europa.eu/data-pro-tection/our-work/publications/speeches/accountability-principle-new-gdpr-0_en [Accessed 13 Jun 2020].

[14]   Chen J., Edwards L., Urquhart L., McAuley D. 'Who is responsible for data processing in smart homes? Reconsidering joint controllership and the house-hold exemption'. *International Data Privacy Law*. 2021;**10**(4):279–93.

[15]   Purtova N. 'The law of everything: broad concept of personal data and future of EU data protection law'. *Law, Innovation and Technology*. 2018;**10**(1):40–81.

[16]   Gellert R. 'Personal data's ever-expanding scope in smart environments and possible path(s) for regulating emerging digital technologies'. *International Data Privacy Law*. 2021;**11**:1–13.

[17]   Case C-212/13. *Ryneš*. OJ C 46/6; 2014.

[18]   Case C-708/18. *Asociaţia de Proprietari bloc M5A-ScaraA*. OJ C 54/8; 2019.

[19]   Case C-25/17. *Jehovan todistajat*. OJ C 319/7; 2018.

[20]   Case C-131/12. *Google Spain and Google*. OJ C 212/4; 2014.

[21]   Article 29 Data Protection Working Party. 'Opinion 1/2010 on the concepts of controller and processor'. 2010.

[22]   Janssen H., Cobbe J., Norval C., Singh J. 'Decentralized data process-ing: personal data stores and the GDPR'. *International Data Privacy Law*. 2021;**10**(4):356–84.

[23]   Case C-210/16. *Wirtschaftsakademie Schleswig-Holstein*. OJ C 268/3; 2018.

[24]   Case C-40/17. *Fashion ID*. OJ C 319/2; 2019.

[25]   Edwards L., Finck M., Vaele M., Zingales N. *Data subjects as data con-trollers: a fashion(able) concept? [online]* 2019. Available from https://

policyreview.info/articles/news/data-subjects-data-controllers-fashionable-concept/1400 [Accessed 9 Dec 2019].

[26] Silverstone R., Hirsch E. *Consuming Technologies: Media and Information in Domestic Spaces*. Routledge; 1992.

[27] Tolmie P., Pycock J., Diggins T., MacLean A., Karsenty A. 'Unremarkable computing'. CHI '02: Proceedings of the SIGCHI Conference on Human Factors in Computing Systems; 2020.

[28] Urquhart L., Sailaja N., McAuley D. 'Realising the right to data portability for the domestic Internet of things'. *Personal and Ubiquitous Computing*. 2018;**22**(2):317–32.

[29] European Data Protection Supervisor. EDPS opinion on personal information management systems. 2016. Available from https://edps.europa.eu/data-protection/our-work/publications/opinions/personal-information-management-systems_en [Accessed 13 Jun 2020].

[30] The Royal Society. Protecting privacy in practice: the current use, development and limits of privacy enhancing technologies in data analysis. 2019. Available from https://royalsociety.org/-/media/policy/projects/privacy-enhancing-technologies/privacy-enhancing-technologies-report.pdf [Accessed 13 Jun 2020].

[31] McAuley D., Mortier R., Goulding J. 'The dataware manifesto'. *Proceedings of 2011 Third International Conference on Communication Systems and Networks (COMSNETS 2011)*; 2011.

[32] Mortier R. *On the edge of human-data interaction in the DATABOX [online]*. 2019. Available from http://iot.ed.ac.uk/files/2019/05/mortier-opt.pdf [Accessed 13 Jun 2020].

[33] CUJO LLC. *CUJO AI. 2020 [online]*. Available from https://cujo.com/ [Accessed 13 Jun 2020].

[34] Haffeez I., Antikanien M., Ding A.Y., Tarkoma S. *IoT-KEEPER: securing IoT communications in edge networks [online]*. 2018. Available from https://arxiv.org/abs/1810.08415 [Accessed 13 Jun 2020].

[35] F-Secure. *F-Secure SENSE [online]*. 2020. Available from www.f-secure.com/gb-en/home/products/sense [Accessed 13 Jun 2020].

[36] SEC Technologies GmbH. *IoT inspector [online]*. 2020. Available from www.iot-inspector.com/ [Accessed 13 Jun 2020].

[37] Apthorpe N., Reisman D., Sundaresan S., Narayanan A., Feamster N. *Spying on the smart home: privacy attacks and defenses on encrypted IoT traffic [online]*. 2017. Available from https://arxiv.org/abs/1708.05044 [Accessed 13 Jun 2020].

[38] Banerjee U., Vashishtha A., Saxena M. 'Evaluation of the capabilities of WireShark as a tool for intrusion detection'. *International Journal of Computer Applications*. 2010;**6**(7):1–5.

[39] O'Connor T., Mohamed R., Miettinen M., Enck W., Reaves B., Sadeghi A.-R. 'HomeSnitch: behavior transparency and control for smart home IoT devices'. WiSec '19: Proceedings of the 12th Conference on Security and Privacy in Wireless and Mobile Networks; Miami, Floria; 2019.

[40] Miettinen M., Marchal S., Haffeez I., Asokan N., Sadeghi A.-R., Tarkoma S. *IoT sentinel: automated device-type identification for security enforcement in IoT [online]*. 2016. Available from https://arxiv.org/abs/1611.04880 [Accessed 13 Jun 2020].

[41] McAuley D. *Lessons from home [online]*. 2019. Available from www.internet-of-everything.fr/wp-content/uploads/2019/06/Derek-McAuley-Defence-Against-the-Dark-Artefacts-Lessons-from-home.pdf [Accessed 13 Jun 2020].

[42] Seymour W., Kraemer M.J., Binns R., Van Kleek M. *Informing the design of privacy-empowering tools for the connected home [online]*. 2020. Available from https://arxiv.org/abs/2001.09077 [Accessed 13 Jun 2020].

[43] Emami-Naeini P., Dixon H., Agarwal Y., Cranor L.F. 'Exploring how privacy and security factor into IoT device purchase behavior'. CHI '19: Proceedings of the 2019 CHI Conference on Human Factors in Computing Systems; 2019.

[44] Zeng E., Mare S., Roesner F. 'End user security and privacy concerns with smart homes'. Proceedings of the Thirteenth Symposium on Usable Privacy and Security (SOUPS 2017); Santa Clara, CA; 2017.

[45] Huang Y., Obada-Obieh B., Beznosov K. 'Amazon vs. My Brother: how users of shared smart speakers perceive and cope with privacy risks'. CHI '20: Proceedings of the 2020 CHI Conference on Human Factors in Computing Systems; Honolulu, HI; 2020.

[46] Crabtree A., Tolmie P., Knight W. 'Repacking "Privacy" for a networked world'. *Computer Supported Cooperative Work*. 2017;**26**(4–6):453–88.

[47] Geeng C., Roesner F. 'Who's in control?: interactions in multi-user smart homes'. CHI '19: Proceedings of the 2019 CHI Conference on Human Factors in Computing Systems; 2019.

[48] Ur B., Jung J., Schechter S. 'Intruders versus intrusiveness: teens' and parents' perspectives on home-entryway surveillance'. UbiComp '14: Proceedings of the 2014 ACM International Joint Conference on Pervasive and Ubiquitous Computing; Seattle, Washington; 2014.

[49] Freed D., Palmer J., Minchala D., Levy K., Ristenpart T., Dell N. '"A stalker's paradise": how intimate partner abusers exploit technology'. CHI '18: Proceedings of the 2018 CHI Conference on Human Factors in Computing Systems; Montreal QC, Canada; 2018.

[50] Parkin S., Patel T., Lopez-Neira I., Tanczer L. Usability analysis of shared device ecosystem security: informing support for survivors of IoT-facilitated tech-abuse'. *NSPW '19: Proceedings of the New Security Paradigms Workshop*; San Carlos, Costa Rica; 2019.

[51] Levy K., Schneier B. 'Privacy threats in intimate relationships'. *Journal of Cybersecurity*. 2020;**6**(1):1–13.

[52] Goulden M. '"Delete the family": platform families and the colonisation of the smart home'. *Information, Communication & Society*. 2021;**24**(1):903–20.

[53] Goulden M., Tolmie P., Mortier R., Lodge T., Pietilainen A.-K., Teixeira R. 'Living with interpersonal data: observability and accountability in the age of pervasive ICT'. *New Media & Society*. 2018;**20**(4):1580–99.

[54] Desjardins A., Biggs H.R., Key C., Viny J.E. 'IoT data in the home: observing entanglements and drawing new encounters'. CHI '20: Proceedings of the 2020 CHI Conference on Human Factors in Computing Systems; Honolulu, HI; 2020.

[55] Singh J., Millard C., Reed C., Cobbe J., Crowcroft J. 'Accountability in the IoT: systems, law, and ways forward'. *Computer*. 2018;**51**(7):54–65.

[56] Mazurek M.L., Arsenault J.P., Bresee J., Gupta N., Ion I., Johns C. 'Access control for home data sharing: attitudes, needs and practices'. CHI '10: Proceedings of the SIGCHI Conference on Human Factors in Computing Systems; Atlanta, Georgia; 2010.

[57] Rosner G., Kenneally E. *Clearly opaque: privacy risks of the internet of things. 2018 [online]*. Available from www.iotprivacyforum.org/wp-content/uploads/2018/06/Clearly-Opaque-Privacy-Risks-of-the-Internet-of-Things.pdf [Accessed 13 Jun 2020].

[58] Tabassum M., Kropczynski J., Wisniewski P., Lipford H.R. 'Smart home beyond the home: a case for community-based access control'. CHI '20: Proceedings of the 2020 CHI Conference on Human Factors in Computing Systems; Honolulu, HI; 2020.

[59] Watson H., Moju-Igbene E., Kumari A., Das S. '"We hold each other accountable": unpacking how social groups approach cybersecurity and privacy together'. CHI '20: Proceedings of the 2020 CHI Conference on Human Factors in Computing Systems; 2020.

[60] Adams A., Sasse M.A. 'Users are not the enemy'. *Communications of the ACM*. 1999;**42**(12):40–6.

[61] Dourish P., Grinter R.E., Delgado de la Flor J., Joseph M. 'Security in the wild: user strategies for managing security as an everyday, practical problem'. *Personal and Ubiquitous Computing*. 2004;**8**(6):391–401.

[62] Colnago J., Feng Y., Palanivel T., Pearman S., Ung M., Acquisti A. 'Informing the design of a personalized privacy assistant for the internet of things'. CHI '20: Proceedings of the 2020 CHI Conference on Human Factors in Computing Systems; Honolulu, HI; 2020.

[63] Jakobi T., Stevens G., Castelli N., Ogonowski C., Schaub F., Vindice N. 'Evolving needs in IoT Control and accountability: a longitudinal study on smart home intelligibility'. Proceedings of the ACM on Interactive; Mobile, Wearable and Ubiquitous Technologies; 2018.

[64] Mahieu R., Van Hoboken J., Asghari H. 'Responsibility for data protection in a networked world: on the question of the controller, "effective and complete protection" and its application to data access rights in europe'. *JIPITEC*. 2019;**10**:85–105.

Chapter 3

Accountability in ordinary action

Peter Tolmie[1] and Andy Crabtree[2]

This chapter explores the notion of accountability in ordinary action and how it applies to our understanding of privacy. It reflects findings from a range of ethnographic studies in the home that highlight that privacy is a matter of accountability management. This is organised through common-sense methods that exploit physical resources alongside digital methods of cohort management to control the disclosure of information. The studies also highlight how and why privacy breaches occur and that digital innovation poses particular threats to privacy by rendering ordinarily invisible activities visible and open to account. This development undermines members' competence, autonomy and trust in the digital world.

3.1 Introduction

As we saw in the previous chapter, the legal concept of accountability is essentially concerned with demonstrable compliance with the law. This contrasts with accountability in ordinary action, which refers to the 'observable and reportable' character of human action in everyday life [1]. If you cast an eye around you, it takes no great effort to observe and report what the people you see are *doing*. You may see people out on the street 'walking along the road', 'crossing the road', 'driving cars', 'parking', 'talking on their phone', 'going into a shop', 'coming out of a shop', etc. In an office, you may see people 'reading e-mail', 'writing a document', 'taking a phone call', 'having a meeting', 'processing an order', 'checking the status of an account', 'having a coffee break', etc. In a factory, you may see people 'checking the machine settings', 'stacking the orders', 'loading the van', etc. On a train, you may see people 'reading a newspaper', 'looking at the messages on their phone', 'texting someone', 'looking out the window', 'checking tickets', etc. Wherever we look we find that human action is observable and reportable by and to *members* [2]. This is in contrast to strangers such as, for example, a Western tourist visiting an ethnic hill tribe in Laos or Myanmar who may find that many aspects of everyday

[1]Information Systems and New Media, University of Siegen, Germany
[2]School of Computer Science, University of Nottingham, UK

life are opaque, especially if they do not speak the local language. As members, we can often see and hear at-a-glance what those around us are doing and if not, we know that an account can be provided that will render their actions intelligible. Accountability is an unremarkable fact of everyday life and *that* we know and rely on it not only to see, recognise and understand what is going around us but, just as importantly, to coordinate our actions accordingly *is* a taken-for-granted feature of our competence as members of the social settings we inhabit. This includes digital settings. Accountability in ordinary action is, in short, the glue of social life.

Despite the ubiquity and pervasiveness of ordinary, naturally occurring account-ability, it has largely been ignored in the digital domain, perhaps because of its utter mundanity [3]. One persistent, if relatively small thread of interest relates to how computing systems might make visible to their users 'what they are doing' as a resource for human–computer interaction. This notion can be traced back to the work of Dourish [4–6], Dourish and Button [7], Belloti [8], and Belloti and Edwards [9] and has resurfaced more recently in the context of AI, where it has been framed within a growing body of work on the 'transparency' of algorithms and algorithmic decision-making [10]. There has been some discussion in the design literature regarding notions of 'personal accountability', especially in relation to matters such as sustainability and energy consumption [11], but the focus here is on persons' adherence to overt moral agendas rather than accountability in ordinary action. There has also been some work regarding what is termed 'accountability theory' [12], which focuses on how people consider themselves to be accountable to others for certain actions and how this can then be fateful for the things they do and the decisions they make, including how they use technology. Recent work examines how the use of digital technologies impacts upon the accountability of people in the workplace [13], though this is more focused on the risks posed by digital technology for rendering workers open to formal account for their work practices to manage-ment. Some specific studies examine natural accountability in terms of how routine activities are treated as unremarkable [14–17], and how digitally mediated activities are routinely made accountable to the 'gambits of compliance' [18] implicated in organised conduct [19–22]. And, as we have explicated at some length elsewhere [23, 24], there is some treatment of how accountability is handled as a matter of policy by users in the privacy and data sharing literature. What is absent from all of this is a discussion of how naturally occurring accountability impacts our under-standing of privacy and data sharing.

What is typically missed by the design literature is the *indexical* relationship between natural accountability and the *reflexive* production of the social and moral order [1]. What we mean by this is that in speaking and/or performing some action (e.g., taking one's place in a queue, waiting to catch a driver's eye before crossing a busy road, turning the indicator on before making a turn in a car, waving at a friend in an airport lobby, etc.) we are not only making what we are doing observable and reportable to others, we are also *at the same time* ordering what we are doing, where the 'we' refers to not only to ourselves but to the others who are party to what is being done. There is, then, a reflexive relationship between natural accountability and the production of social and moral order and one only need try walking to the front of a queue to witness it in action. It is not that there is naturally accountable action on the one hand and the social and moral order on the other. The two are entwined, they are *locally* and *mutually constitutive* [25], which means that in ignoring natural accountability, in taking it for granted and passing it by due to its utter mundanity, we also ignore the *real-world, real-time social organisation* of naturally accountable phenomenon, analogue and digital alike.

What we want to do here is consider the findings from a range of field studies conducted over a 10-year period and what they reveal about the observable and reportable, naturally accountable organisation of people's digital privacy and data sharing practices in a domestic context. The studies focused on the mundane use of wireless networks in the home and how online activity is constituted as an ordinary part of everyday life [14], how people interact with and account for data generated by connected devices [26] and how they understand and construe of privacy in a massively networked world [23, 24]. The studies were conducted as part of a number of funded projects including the EU project 'User-Centric Networking', the EPSRC-funded projects 'Homework' and the 'Hub of All Things' and the EPSRC Fellowship 'Privacy by Design: Building Accountability into the Internet of Things'. As catalogued in the papers referenced above, participants in the studies came from a wide variety of demographic backgrounds. This gave us an opportunity to explore the naturally accountable organisation of members' mundane interactions with domestic networks, devices and data from different perspectives, with people from different walks of life, living in different circumstances, with different occupations and interests, across rural, urban and suburban environments in both the United Kingdom and France.

Abstractly, various concepts of privacy posit axioms that essentially revolve around the *disclosure* of personal information or 'data'. Often cited definitions thus inform us that privacy is the ability to *control* the disclosure of personal information [27], to create and manage *interpersonal boundaries* [28] and to employ *contextual norms* to regulate the ad hoc flow of personal information between people [29]. Concretely, the studies make it visible that privacy ordinarily and accountably revolves around managing a polymorphous array of mundane activities in which the digital is embedded in the ongoing conduct of manifold human relationships. Within this lively context, the disclosure or sharing of personal data is accountably organised in terms of managing members' access to devices, applications and content through situated practices, procedures or methods that exploit the local ecology, device visibility and recipient design. The studies make it perspicuous that members' concern with privacy is a concern to manage their accountability in the digital world and that manifest in data sharing practices is an evolving *calculus of accountability* employed to manage the potential attack surface the digital creates in everyday life. That the digital poses a threat to privacy and therefore undermines *societal trust* in the digital is broadly acknowledged. Much less well-known and understood is how and why this happens and what kinds of steps beyond demonstrable compliance with the law might need to be taken to remedy the situation.

3.2   The naturally accountable organisation of digital privacy in the home

Managing digital privacy is intimately bound up with the observability and report-ability of one's digital activities and how other people might be able to *see* them in the first place. Developers and security analysts alike recommend passwords as the first line of defense to protect oneself from prying eyes. Yet there is a more funda-mental naturally accountable organisation to privacy in the real world, as one of our participants, Paul (not his real name), tells us:

> **Paul:** I'm not particularly fussed about setting up passwords and things. I mean there's no threat of network hijacking here. We live in the middle of the countryside, miles away from another house, it's just not an issue.

So, as Paul makes accountable, one of the simplest and most ubiquitous ways to constrain access and protect privacy is by controlling access to the environments in which our digital activities occur, i.e., controlling access to the places in which digital devices are kept.

Paul's was not the only example of password suspension for devices considered inaccessible that we encountered in our studies. It was commonplace for devices that always stayed in the home, such as desktop PCs, tablets and media servers. The reasoning generally bound up with this is that the people who have rights of access to the network and the devices on it are the people who have rights of access to the environment in which those devices are located. This point was underscored by Christine, a 63-year-old reflexologist who runs her practice from home:

> **Christine**: I'm big on making sure that the whole house isn't open to their view. I'm forever closing doors and shutting things off. I make sure eve-rything is clear that I consider sensitive. When I used to be in that smaller room particularly, I did not want my laptop there open while I was about to start a treatment.
> **Fieldworker**: So that window into your digital world you prefer to have closed to clients as well?
> **Christine**: Closed off. Absolutely. Absolutely. And obviously I have to make sure that I don't leave information about previous clients lying around for clients to see.
> **Fieldworker**: So it's both professional and personal reasons kind of wrapped in together?
> **Christine**: Well absolutely because you know, I could be sued if people felt it was a breach of data protection. So I have to be aware of that. I don't have anything lying around that in any way gives any window into anything. I don't keep my purse or my phone in the room with me either.
> **Fieldworker**: OK, and with regard to the network, if you had clients back-ing up, where one was waiting for another one to go, would you give them access to the network?

Christine: No. Absolutely not. No, no. I wouldn't even give them access to the television unless Brian's [her husband] in the room watching it!

This vignette elaborates the fairly blanket operation of a situated privacy practice designed to minimise the risk of the incidental sharing of personal information of any kind – analogue or digital – with visitors to the house where the relationship is confined to business. Despite the account being directed towards breaches of data protection, Christine is also closing doors and generally constraining the movements of her clients. It is not just data relating to other clients but also of her own personal life she is keeping from view. What this makes particularly clear, however, is that *physical barriers* such as doors (and curtains, and hedges, etc.) are the principal gateway controlling access to personal information.

Privacy is also managed through device visibility, which is not only controlled through physical barriers but by members proximity to screens. This is observably and reportably the case for participants who want to share very specific content where that content is a feature of activities and repositories described as private. Here Evelyn, a 21-year-old student, is talking about how she might occasionally share content with others around her on Tumblr:

Evelyn: I don't like anybody seeing what's going on on Tumblr. Occasionally I'll show Susan [her sister] a picture or a gif of a cat. But I don't.
Fieldworker: You show it to her?
Evelyn: Yeah.
Fieldworker: Rather than you let her watch you doing the posting?
Evelyn: Yeah. Being on a phone it's a smaller screen so there is less over-sight. I tend to keep it quite close to me anyway. So I'm fine with browsing Tumblr when, like, I'm sitting on a chair downstairs and there are people walking about, or when we're about to watch something.

Evelyn can and does manage to keep what she is doing private by relying on the size of the screen. However, the way she *positions* the screen in relation to herself and others is not incidental. Indeed, insofar as screens are positioned not to disclose content then there is a mutual orientation to that content that it is not for general consumption. This, of course, is common practice, found in all kinds of settings. Dourish *et al.* [30] found, for example, that computer screens are often positioned such that visitors to an office cannot see them, and Klasnja *et al.* [31] found that people try to preserve their privacy when using devices in public places by 'finding a seat against the wall' or 'tilting or dimming the screen'.

Members have a mutually understood right to keep things from view that they routinely trade upon, such that, what might at first sight be viewed as guarded behaviour is nothing of the sort, but rather an everyday method for making manifest the status of particular kinds of personal data as 'not to be shared'. So, as a matter of method, privacy can be and is managed by controlling how one physically enables others in the environment to see one's devices. There are a number of permutations whereby this can be brought about. It might be that the recipient is in an adjacent position and it is just a matter of locating the thing to be shared and then re-angling the device so that they can see it. It may also be the case that the device is not mobile, in which case sharing may involve calling the recipient over to the device. Locating the data may also be something that is done prior to sharing it or may be done once the recipient is actually co-present. But, however it occurs, privacy and data disclosure are routinely managed through the social positioning of devices and content in interaction.

Now none of this is to say that passwords are not used. It is simply to recognise what we all take for granted: that privacy is principally managed through the methodical use of physical barriers to control members' access to the places where devices are located; and by controlling the access to devices themselves through their social positioning and making content selectively available to others by allowing them in various ways to see screens. That said, our participants did have 'occasion' to use passwords, as Mike and Alice elaborate:

> **Mike**: The PC upstairs occasionally has a password. It usually doesn't. It's in the back room. The last time I put a code on was when we had a decorator in to do that room. I've done it once or twice when we've had guests staying.
> **Alice**: Yeah, when my nephew comes, 'cause he just logs into everything.
> **Fieldworker:** It kind of depends on the guest?
> **Mike**: Yeah.
> **Fieldworker**: 'cause you see it as a potential risk?
> **Mike**: Yeah.
> **Fieldworker**: What would be a potential risk?
> **Mike**: Basically, er, adult material on there. So potential embarrassment I guess.
> **Mike**: With the decorator guy, it was more the general principle. There's personal information on there.
> **Alice**: Bank details and stuff, so we don't want them.
> **Mike**: Yeah, whereas if it was like family staying there, it's more like the scenario where they just use the PC for something and stumble across a folder I'd rather they don't stumble across.

It would be easy to render what Mike is saying here as being that he and Alice use passwords to ensure data privacy. They do, of course, want to protect their 'bank details and stuff', but there is more to it than that. Insofar as they do use passwords to ensure data privacy, then they do so on a *selective basis*, rather than as a blanket policy. This will no doubt cause security advisors to throw their hands in the air. However, it is accountably the case that what drives the use of passwords is the *social relationships* that hold between members. Be it 'the decorator guy', 'guests', 'my nephew', 'family', etc., who someone is, what relationship holds between them and those they are visiting in the home and why they are visiting determines the use of passwords. We, therefore, found that family members, friends, friends of the kids and baby-sitters were routinely *given* passwords to access networks, devices and applications, whereas tradesmen and the customers and clients of home-workers were not. In cases where visiting was premised upon purely professional relation-ships, we found that access was more heavily controlled, with participants entering passwords into visitors' devices if necessary. Some even monitored visitor's behav-iour, 'sticking around' to ensure they did not do anything they did not want them to do.

However, what is notable about Mike and Alice's occasioned use of pass-words is that it is also driven by an accountable concern with risk, not in terms of data privacy but *to members*, e.g., to the nephew who just logs into everything and might be exposed to adult material, or to the family staying in Mike and Alice's backroom, who might be embarrassed by such material, just as Mike and Alice might be embarrassed by them seeing it. Our studies are shot through with this accountable concern with risk, which is why we hesitate to render the occa-sioned use of passwords as a matter of data privacy. Rather, privacy is a gloss for a host of situated practices designed *by* members to manage the risks that the digital poses *to* members. We thus find that commonplace practices such as the setting of passwords is as much about protecting children from harmful content, as it is about protecting data from harmful actions. Equally commonplace, but more rarely recognised, are the situated practices for managing the manifold risks of accountability in the digital world and what can therefore be observed and reported about oneself.

3.2.1   Privacy as accountability management

Passwords are an obvious means of managing accountability – if one's devices can-not be accessed, what one does online cannot be rendered observable and reportable and thus be opened up to account. However, it is in the nature of living with other people that devices are accessible to them. Joe and Carrie tell us something of what organises device access:

> **Joe**: My wife might use my phone if it's handy, or I might use hers, you know. It's not a big deal for us. But my daughter [who is 17] has got a PIN number on hers, and I think my son [who is 21] has as well. He's got his locked.
> **Fieldworker**:You don't know the PINs?
> **Joe**: No, no. They have all their feeds coming in, Snapchat and Twitter and god knows what.
> **Carrie**: We consider their stuff as private. We don't need to nose in.

As Joe and Carrie make perspicuous, managing accountability is not sim-ply a matter of putting passwords in place, but very much turns on appropriate relationship-relevant behaviour and thus on *cohort-relevant access*. While mem-bers of the 'husband and wife' or 'partner' cohort, such as Joe and Carrie, may routinely access one another's personal devices, they do not necessarily access devices belonging to members of the 'children' cohort (whether members do or do not very much depends on the children's age and the expectations that go along with that). It is also the case that, while members of the 'partner' cohort may routinely access one another's devices, they do not have blanket access. They may use a partner's phone to call someone if it is handy to do so, but accessing other applications is an occasioned matter, e.g., they might read a social media post because their partner has asked their opinion of it, or read out loud a text message that has just arrived because their partner is busy doing something else. Perhaps surprisingly, the restricted nature of cohort-relevant access is not principally driven by a concern with privacy – many a partner told us they had 'nothing to hide' from one another – but with social relevance. Simply put, what one does online is not seen or treated as *relevant* to one's partner by default. Privacy only becomes a concern when cohort-relevant access is disregarded, which would ordinarily be an accountable matter (e.g., what are you doing?) and be dysfunctional and even dangerous if it persisted [32].

An equally obvious means of managing one's accountability is to clear caches, cookies and browser history and/or use private browsing modes.

> **Fieldworker**: Do you clear caches, cookies or search histories?
>
> **Kit**: The only time I've done it is when it's like Tim's birthday and I try to do things secretly so he doesn't know. I put private browsing on and I – I've asked him before and he told me how to empty things.
>
> **Tim**: Clear the cache, yeah. Yeah the only other times I could see mild embarrassment is if you've gone out and I've got Netflix to myself and then I'll be like, right, good car chase film – when do I ever get to watch good car chase films? But then obviously it comes up, doesn't it, you know, like next time you go on Netflix, you've been watching …
>
> **Kit**: Oh! Hmmm.
>
> **Tim**: So you can log onto Netflix and delete these things.
>
> **Fieldworker**: And do you?
>
> **Tim**: No I don't actually. Well, if I did, I wouldn't tell you, but I don't. But I definitely wouldn't answer that honestly if I did.

As Tim somewhat amusingly makes visible in this vignette, owning up to clearing caches and histories can be a thorny issue, but rendering one's on online behaviour invisible and thus unaccountable to other members of the home is not done merely to mask embarrassment, mild or otherwise. As noted above, there is a strong presumption of cohort-relevance built into our online activities and this warrants the occasional use of procedures to ensure the confidentiality not only of *what* we do, but *who* we do it with or for. So, while these procedures can be used to protect one's privacy, they are also quite often used for the benefit of others (e.g., to avoid special occasions and surprises alike being spoiled).

Cohort-relevance drives *cohort separation* to ensure that one is only accountable to those one needs to be accountable to, and nowhere is this more pronounced than on social media.

> **Fieldworker**: And the Facebook friends are, er, who?

Chloe: People I know. Basically, most of my family, and my friends and a few people that I know from school who asked me so I just accepted 'cause I know them. But if it's anybody I don't know I won't accept.
Fieldworker: And do they overlap with your Twitter people? Do you have the same Facebook friends that you're following on Twitter or following you?
Chloe: No.
Fieldworker: No connection between them at all?
Chloe: No, my social life has nothing to do with my Twitter life. Twitter life is Internet life. Facebook life is social life.

As Chloe makes clear, it is common practice amongst people who employ multiple social media channels to use them to facilitate the separation of cohorts and to reflexively enable, as a matter of method, the management of friend and follower relationships. Along with this, they can manage the relationship-based tailoring of personal content to particular channels and cohorts. The methodical separation of cohorts is bound up with an abiding practical concern to avoid having to endlessly account for one's online activity to the people one knows best in everyday life, such as one's friends and family. Members do not seek to dispense with accountability entirely, only to manage *just who* they might be accountable to and for what, so they exploit different channels to design personal content for different categories of recipient. Recipient design even includes adopting pseudonyms, which not only averts the potential need to account for turning down friend or follower requests from people one is routinely accountable to in other ways, but carries the advantage that there will be less chance of sharing personal data with people one would not ordinarily wish to share it with. While this is common practice there is, we note, no stability in the choice of channels (e.g., that Twitter is used for a certain kind of cohort and Facebook for another). Nor is there any stability in the purposes for which different channels are used (what one person uses Twitter for another may use Facebook or any other social media channel for instead). What we do see, regardless of matters of personal choice, is that different channels are *tied* in practice to different cohorts and the particular kinds of relationship that hold between their members.

Against this background, data is shared on the basis of an assumed and accountable *right of disclosure*, which is commonly understood by recipients and further limits the potential impact of posting personal data online.

Samantha: I wouldn't mind somebody seeing something that I was sending, but I'd be uncomfortable about somebody seeing something that Tom [her brother] had sent me.
Fieldworker: OK. Why's that?
Samantha: It would feel like more of a breach of privacy, because it's something he's sending specifically to me. Often it is just like photos of him and Rick [his partner], or food that he's made or things that he's seen that reminded him of me, and things like that. It would feel much weirder for somebody to see what he was sending me.
Fieldworker: Why would it feel weird? What would feel wrong about it?

Samantha: Well Tom is a very private person and I wouldn't like to share stuff with other people that he's sent specifically to me without having asked his permission to do so.

Fieldworker: OK. So you need the right to be able to share it you feel? And you wouldn't just have that right automatically to share it?

Samantha: No.

Fieldworker: OK. Does that go for other content that you receive from other people on social media?

Samantha: Yeah, I don't share stuff like that because, as I said, it's something that's been sent specifically to me and I wouldn't share it without asking somebody if they were OK with that.

Something that Samantha makes evident is that one's accountability for data that has been shared with you by other people is not necessarily handled in the same way that you would handle your own data. There are chains of accountability to be considered, such that the onward sharing of data is organised around one's right to share it. This right may be presumptive, or someone may quite literally be given a legal right to share data. However, the presumptive right largely obtains in mundane interaction, even when the recipient knows that the data shared with them may well have been shared with others. Indeed, while Samantha often discussed Tom's social media posts with family members, she was not given to showing them the actual messages he sent her, that would feel like a breach of privacy.

3.2.2   Breaching privacy

Members routinely manage their privacy through situated practices that have become common-sense ways of managing their accountability in the digital world. Thus, we find that members observe cohort-relevant access as much (if not more) than they use passwords to control interpersonal use of devices and their content. They implement cohort separation and tailor personal content to the members of particular cohorts through the use of dedicated communication channels, limiting unintended disclosure and personal exposure through the use of multiple channels and identities. Data is shared under a presumed right of disclosure that limits onward distribution. That said, as attested to by a host of studies [33–40], the digital world frequently manages to breach one's accountability and privacy. What we want to do now is consider some of the ways in which that routinely happens.

An increasingly diverse array of everyday activities is now geared towards interaction with parties and organisations online. These parties may, in principle, be located anywhere and be oriented to either as known members of various cohorts or unknown or unknowable, beyond what common-sense assumptions may be made about them and their interests. This has an important impact upon people's sense of accountability, as data sharing is predicated on the vital interplay of mutually assumed rights and expectations accorded to the specific relationships in play. In short, if there is no established relationship because a party is unknown or unknowable, then the grounds of mutual accountability are hard to assess, which in turn informs a generic data sharing policy:

Christine: There was a hideous picture [once], but if it was something that I considered to be *that* sensitive I wouldn't use it. If I'm not happy to share it, then it doesn't go anywhere.

Alice: I wouldn't put anything on that I wasn't happy for anybody to see. Managing real private stuff is – stuff shouldn't exist, that's the level of it: it doesn't get written down; it doesn't get put in a photo; it doesn't exist. Definitely do not put online.

As Christine and Alice make clear, the sensitivity of data and the risk of personal exposure furnishes a general account for not sharing something. Nonetheless, people often share things online that they subsequently regret. The literature is replete with examples of postings on social media that have escaped the control of their authors and resulted in embarrassment. So, while many people, like Christine and Alice, entertain a generic data sharing policy, there is evidently an inherent tension between that policy and actual occasions of data sharing. The tension is often referred to in terms of the 'privacy paradox', which privacy expert Daniel Solove [41] dismisses as a myth on the basis of 'a series of improper generalisations from people's behaviour'. We concur, but this does not dispense with the inherent tension between general data sharing policies and specific occasions of data sharing, which can and do lead to privacy breaches. The difficulty lies not in the seemingly paradoxical relationship between members' reasoning and their behaviour (what they say versus what they do), but in the *mismatch between members' reasoning and the operation of digital systems.*

This mismatch is made perspicuous when we consider the mundane challenges of managing accountability in a digital world where members are inherently connected, socially as well as technologically.

Michel: One of the reasons why Carrie is not so sensitive about posting family photos on Facebook is because pretty well the only network who get to see that are family and friends. Whereas with me, the network who can actually see that includes work colleagues, some of whom I don't even know very well. I mean, we've had photos of me in fancy dress for instance on Facebook and it's become clear that other people have had access to those things!

Fieldworker: So it's other people's stuff that you're in and they've put up?

Michel: It's never stuff that I share myself, no, 'cause I don't do that kind of stuff.

Carrie: I do, of fancy dress (laughs). Have you seen that one (Carrie holds up her iPad to Michel, and then turns it to show the fieldworker).

Fieldworker: (Laughs at photo of them both in fancy dress).

Michel: (Laughs).

Carrie: It's stuff like that he doesn't want me to put on.

Michel: This is the problem for me. I can control it all I like myself, but I have no control over what other people do.

Here, we can see that Michel expresses his frustration with the limited resources he has available for controlling what kinds of things get shared with whom on Facebook, and his frustration reveals the extent to which managing accountability through friend and follower relationships is a blunt instrument. The issue here is not so much to do with the fact that other people can post data about you, or data that involves you, but is more to do with how to manage distinctions between people who have access to that data. The distinctions that hold between 'family' and 'friends' may be relatively straightforward to make but those that hold between 'friends' and 'work colleagues' are certainly more blurred, where the latter may also include the former as well as people one does not know very well, if at all. Differences in relationship are accompanied by differences in accountability, and this applies even when one is a member of the same cohort. Consider the accountability that holds within the family between one's partner and children, for example, and with it the different rights and obligations that hold between different members of the same cohort. The digital world rides roughshod over such differences and pushes people into what amount to *generic data sharing mechanisms*, which assume that all people in the same bucket (e.g., friend or follower) are essentially the same. They are not. Furthermore, there is no way to express or reflect the nuances in human reasoning and human practice where members manage *just what* is made visible and *just who* it is made visible to. Nor is there any way to reflect the range of common-sense methods that exploit place, physical barriers and proximity to control *just when* things are said, *just where* they are said, *just how* they are said and so on. Generic digital data sharing mechanisms inhibit embodied methods of recipient design. So, in the digital world, where the operation of these methods is restricted by technical mechanisms, members must live with the consequences and have to manage breaches as they occur.

The mismatch between human reasoning and the operation of digital systems is further underscored by members efforts to account for privacy breaches. Members do not stop reasoning about why things happen just because they are encountered in the digital domain. They hold the digital accountable and attempt to find reasonable, ordinary, everyday explanations for the things they see and experience there. Now, to presume that digital systems reason in the way that human beings do, and to hold them intersubjectively accountable on those terms, is admittedly problematic. However, it does not prevent members from reasoning about the digital in this way and it does not mean that this way of reasoning is inconsequential for how members proceed.

> **Sara:** There's one thing that worried me. Do you remember that time – my family's Jewish, and my uncle sometimes posts things, just once or twice, about searching for family in the Ukraine and stuff – and I was starting to find a shop selling everything Jewish coming up advertising on my page. So they've obviously made a connection that somewhere in the family there is somebody Jewish, and they've advertised that to me so that means obviously that it's visible to somebody. It makes you very aware that people are watching what you're doing. It's like I was explaining to Hannah

[Sara's teenage daughter] the other day. She was getting ads for pregnancy tests and she says, why am I getting this stuff. I said it's targeted because you're a teenage girl. And she said, but I've never gone on any site like that, I've never looked at anything. I said it doesn't matter, they can tell by the type of sites that you do go on to – they can put you within an age group and sex group and so you're targeted. She really doesn't understand that even so. She says I go on gaming sites, I could be a boy. Yeah, you could, but even so the indications that you give are a flag to somebody.

Sara invites us to consider two distinct but interrelated matters here. The first reflects widespread societal concern that personal data is accessed and used by parties who are not party to our online interactions, i.e., a third party, and an anonymous one at that. The second matter for consideration is that Sara does not understand how her data has been acquired by a third party, because she has not knowingly shared her data with somebody outside her online interactions. The same applies to Sara's daughter as well, just as it does to many millions and indeed billions of people. So, Sara makes it visible that *what counts as data sharing* in the digital world is deeply problematic. From a members' perspective, data sharing in the digital ecosystem is evidently opaque. This lack of accountability – of observability and reportability – and with it the ability to see, recognise and understand what is happening goes beyond what we have been saying about the crudity of tools for managing relationships online and the way they pre-configure sharing on a generic basis. We can see now that this goes beyond digital systems obliging members to engage in generic rather than situated reasoning about data sharing, thereby disrupting the ordinary grounds of accountability. They also do not necessarily count as sharing what members *recognise* as sharing practices and do not make themselves evidently accountable for handling what is shared in the same way. This, of course, goes to the core of understanding what counts as data, and, more than this, what digital systems can do with personal data, as opposed to what other *people* can do with it, where intersubjective reasoning and ordinary accountability can be assumed to hold.

This mismatch between human reasoning and digital operations is further evidenced in the occasioned sharing of data.

Sylvie: I tried for a while having people graded by their friendship status. So I'd have like real true friends, and then I had my work friends who would ask me to be their friend but I felt kind of like socially awkward saying no on Facebook, so I had them as acquaintances. It got really confusing, you know. Someone might graduate from being an acquaintance to an actual friend but they still work with you, and then they come into work and say, 'Oh I saw that picture of you at the park, it was really cute' and everyone else goes, 'What picture? I didn't see that on Facebook.' So I've given up on that. It just got really hard.

Sylvie's experience with Facebook makes it perspicuous that data sharing in the digital world is essentially marked by *a lack of reciprocity*, which is key to ordinary accountability. Reciprocity means that the world 'as I see it for all practical purposes' (in contrast to theoretical, political, ideological or religious purposes, etc.), is the world 'as you see it for all practical purposes'. If this were not the case, I would not be able to see what you were doing (e.g., waiting to cross a busy road) and to coordinate my actions accordingly (e.g., to slow my vehicle and wave you safely across regardless of whatever theoretical, political, ideological or religious thoughts might be running through either of our heads). Now this is obviously not the case for Sylvie and her friends, be they 'real true friends', work friends, actual friends or acquaintances. The practices she devised for sharing data and managing her accountability were not practices that *others* were able to recognise and organise their own interactions around in response. Of course, people were being embarrassed by awkward revelations long before digital technology arrived on the scene. However, the interesting thing here is that the source of trouble is not so much the content itself, as the lack of *intersubjective understanding* of the practices involved in the management of digital content: how might Sylvie's Facebook friends have *known* that she was adopting a practice of organising them in such a fine-grained fashion, when there is nothing within the digital domain that makes her situated practices observable and reportable? There is no reciprocity of perspectives. This is not only problematic for members like Sylvie, who are concerned to manage the day-to-day sharing of data and their concomitant accountability, it is also, as Sara highlighted for us above, a source of widespread complaint. Thus, a general lack of reciprocity in the digital world not only renders invisible the situated practices members devise and use to manage data sharing, thereby enabling privacy breaches, it *also* masks the practices of others who might access their data without their knowledge.

The operation of digital systems poses further challenges to members' efforts to manage their accountability by *rendering the ordinarily invisible visible*. As the digital reaches further into our physical and social environment, it increasingly renders members accountable for things that are outside of their control, surfacing information about members' activities that they would usually expect to remain out of view and creating circumstances where they are obliged to account for things for which accounts would never ordinarily be sought.

> **Susannah**: (Reading a time series graph of motion and humidity sensor data from the bathroom). So what are we saying? We're saying the 5th, that was Mary being off, and the 6th was you being at home. Oooh, what did you do?
> **Frank**: I didn't do anything.
> **Susannah**: You did. At 12 o'clock. Look at that.
> **Frank**: Where? Nothing.
> **Susannah**: No, here.
> **Frank**: I could have been up late, 'cause I've had this headache thing. I've been a bit poorly – oh give me sympathy – so that's probably me getting up late isn't it. Having a late shower. It's high for along time. I don't remember having that long a shower.

> **Susannah**: Yeah, but you could have had a shower and then you could have had a shave.

It is a brute fact of life, as Frank can testify, that the cohort most likely to call members to account for their activities is their family and those with whom they have the most intimate relationships (parents, siblings, partners, etc.). Now, it is of course the case that member's bathroom practices can be called to account as an ordinary feature of everyday life in all sorts of ways: toothbrushes may be left in the 'wrong' place or the toothpaste squeezed in the 'wrong' way; towels may be left in a heap on the floor; all of the hot water may have been used up and so on. Members may also make their own bathroom practices visible to others: calling out to say they are about to have a shower, so that others do not turn on taps and make the shower run suddenly hot or cold; saying where one likes to keep their towel because someone keeps moving it; calling out their weight from the bathroom because they have just stood on the scales and it has gone down; etc. All of this is a normal and a naturally accountable part of the daily round. However, the presence of a new digital window onto what members do, created by an increasing array of sensor-based devices, stands outside ordinary everyday reasoning. This is especially the case with respect to how knowledge of one's activities might be made visible and the concomitant possibility of needing to provide an account for them. This has the scope to cause serious trouble, disrupting in a pejorative way the foundations of everyday life.

Let us hover for a moment longer in the sensor-equipped bathroom of the imminent future to underscore the seriousness of rendering the ordinarily invisible visible.

> **Susannah:** I'm aware that there's evidence that Sally's gone for a wee when she's spent most of her life trying to. At the moment, she's defining her space, and David [their son] is defining his space. So now there's evidence, now I can see into these spaces, so there's a sense of invasion. I can now look and find out who went for a wee, when, and where they went.

As Susannah makes perspicuous, rendering the ordinarily invisible visible creates a sense of invasion, allowing one to now look and find who did what, when and where. This is problematic in various respects. It obviously breaches members' privacy, but there is more to it than that. The issue is not simply that the digital furnishes Susannah with evidence that Sally has gone for a wee. Parents often have cause and need to observe and remark on their children's toilet habits. But it is when their habits cease to merit observation and report, when they become *unremarkable*, that matters. Then the child may be said to have mastered the art and demonstrated their competence in the ordinary affairs of everyday life. Just to be clear, it is not that the child can go for a wee on its own that marks their competence, but their ability to do so without occasioning the need to pass, or for others to pass, remark during or after the event. That everyday activities and accomplishments *are* unremarkable is not just a practical matter, but a moral one essentially concerned with the orderly nature of our conduct. So, when a technology is introduced into the world that makes whatever mundane, unremarkable things members are doing visible and open to account, it breaches fundamental expectations about how social life is organised. Susannah's sense of invasion is not about Sally's privacy per se, then. It is not to do with the fact that she can see that Sally has had a wee, but apodictically in doing so that she puts Sally's competence and with it her growing sense of independence at risk. Furthermore, accountability cuts both ways, which is to say that it is not only the data subject who is rendered potentially accountable. Members who disclose their knowledge of ordinarily invisible activities are just as likely to find themselves accountable for why they have taken an interest in them in the first place. Thus, in rendering the ordinarily invisible visible and open to account, the digital world *disrupts the unremarkable foundations of everyday life*, not only impacting members' privacy but in doing so their competence or ability to conduct their everyday affairs in an unremarkably orderly manner, thereby undermining their autonomy.

3.3   Discussion

Privacy is routinely breached in the digital world not because there is a mismatch between what members say and what members do, but because of the mismatch between members' reasoning and situated practices on the one hand, and the operation of digital systems on the other. In the analogue world, members exploit an array of embodied practices to manage their accountability. This is done by carefully designing data disclosure for particular recipients, i.e., controlling *just what* is made visible and *just who* it is made visible to through a range of common-sense methods. These methods exploit place, physical barriers and proximity to control *just when* things are said, *just where* they are said, *just how* they are said and so on. However, in the digital world, the operation of these methods is restricted by generic data sharing mechanisms that designate members as friends or followers, for example, without respect to the nuances that hold within a cohort let alone between them. Then there is the fact that what counts as data sharing in the digital world is deeply problematic. Digital systems do not necessarily count as sharing what members recognise as sharing and do not make themselves accountable for the handling of what is shared in the same way. There is also a lack of reciprocity in the digital world, which renders invisible the situated practices members devise and use to manage data sharing. More than this, it masks the practices of others who might access their data without their knowledge. We can add to this how the digital increasingly renders the ordinarily invisible visible, thereby disrupting the unremarkable foundations of everyday life. Put these things together and it becomes perspicuous how and why privacy breaches occur. We have seen that privacy is not simply a matter of controlling one's accountability, but that doing so is essential to members' autonomy and their ability to conduct their everyday affairs in an orderly manner, unhindered without due cause by others. Little wonder then that the digital undermines *societal trust* at scale.

It might be said that it is blindingly obvious that privacy is essential to members' autonomy, but that merely begs the question why, then, have we built a destabilising infrastructure into the fabric of everyday life? The answer is no doubt complex and turns as much on accident or at least the lack of foresight as it does intent, but it is the question of trust that occupies us here. This ordinary language concept has been, and will no doubt continue to be, subject to heterogeneous treatments. Thus, trust is commonly understood as an attitude and matter of choice as much as it is to do with assessing risk, all of which runs alongside domain considerations such as 'trust and the family' or 'trust and political systems'. The social theorist Pierre Bourdieu [42] construed of trust as 'habitus', a defining feature of how members perceive and orient to the social world, whereas Luhmann [43] sees trust as performing a sociological function. Gambetta's rational choice theory [44] is concerned with the 'conditions under which trust is justified', and Coleman's [45] influential modification of this theory focuses upon trust as a calculated and calculable risk 'taken about the performance of others'. We take the rather mundane view that trust is a 'background condition' of ordinary action [46], something that members for the most part have no need to call into question. As Watson [47] notes,

> When the trust condition is not in place, participants experience bewilderment, confusion, frustration or indignation, or they attempt to make sense of or normalize the events in different terms – as a joke, or hoax, a deliberate provocation, obtuseness or whatever.

Now this *attempt to normalise* situations in which trust is breached is key to members' efforts to incorporate the digital world into ordinary action. The attempt consists of exploiting an evolving calculus of accountability to manage the 'attack surface' the digital creates in breaching privacy and disrupting the unremarkable foundations of everyday life.

The notion of the attack surface in a digital context is usually invoked with respect to security, which emphasises the management of unauthorised access to hardware, software, firmware and networks as a general panacea to privacy concerns [48]. Technically the attack surface is understood as the sum of the different points in a computational environment where an unauthorised party might get into that environment and get data out [49]. This contrasts with the attack surface in everyday life, which we might understand as the sum of the points in a computational environment where ordinary action can be made observable and reportable. The human attack surface is increasing exponentially with the emergence of sensor-based devices in everyday life and the so-called 'Internet of Things' or IoT. As we have seen, the IoT surfaces information about ordinary action members would usually expect to remain out of view, creating circumstances where they are obliged to account for things that they would never ordinarily have to account for. The attack surface in the connected home consists not just of desktops, laptops, tablets and smartphones, but an increasing number of smart products [50] including wearables, household appliances, embedded devices and fast-moving consumer goods that are starting to be wrapped in increasingly intelligent packaging [51]. We are on the cusp of an explosive increase in the domestic attack surface. Industry analysts [52] predict that 29.3 billion devices will be connected to IP networks by 2023, that the share of machine-to-machine (IoT) connections will grow to 50% in the same period, that the consumer segment will account for 75% of total devices and connections, and that connected home applications will account for the 'largest share' of these.

Right now, members are managing to protect themselves in circumstances where the attack surface is constituted by an average of ten connected devices per household [53]. They do so by physically controlling who has access to the places where digital devices are situated and by exploiting physical barriers, people's proximity and the positioning of devices to manage the availability and visibility of personal information. We have also seen that the social relationships that hold between members is a primary determinant of digital access controls, with the use of passwords being driven as much by a concern to manage cohort-dependent risks and protect others from exposure to inappropriate digital content as it is to protect personal data from harm. We have further seen that members exploit cohort-relevant access controls to manage the interpersonal use of personal devices, effect cohort separation (e.g., through the use of bespoke social media channels and identities) to manage their accountability in sharing personal information online, and handle data shared by others under a presumptive right of disclosure that restricts sharing and onwards distribution. In these ways, i.e., through situated practices, members attempt to normalise the effects of a destabilising infrastructure on everyday life. These practices are constitutive of a *calculus of accountability* – a set of common-sense methods rooted in ordinary action that are evolving to enable members to manage the observability and reportability of their online activities. Time and again, the reasoning driving this evolving body of practice amounts to avoiding real-world accountability for the things done online in order to carefully manage just who it is one might be accountable to and in what ways. This reasoning is imbued with a strong (moral) preference that one's actions are found to be naturally accountable and therefore ordinary and unremarkable features of everyday life. The evolving calculus governing privacy and data sharing in the digital world thus seeks to *constrain* the accountability of persons and their digitally mediated interactions to being seen in this way.

We find, then, that members manage their accountability locally by managing access to their devices and data. In this way, they can control just who can see what and what might therefore be treated as a topic of remark or conversation. The practices involved in doing this are utterly taken for granted and routine. Thus, when people keep things from view, the fact they are doing this is in no way treated as remarkable, but rather as a naturally accountable feature of ordinary action in its own right. When it comes to the sharing of personal data online, members also orient to what is or is not made visible and to whom and seek to manage that accordingly. However, what is different in the online world is the relatively crude tools available for managing just who the information will be shared with and what kinds of accounts can be shaped within and around the content of the data being shared. We find, then, that members take great care over the management of cohorts, identities and the visibility of the digital self, methodically employing multiple social media channels to limit the impact of the digital on their accountability and the accountability of their actions. And, we find in these situated practices that managing the potential attack surface is increasingly becoming a matter of routine. That members are, on a daily basis, and in a great many cases, able to exploit the calculus of accountability to bring about their online activities and digitally mediated interactions as naturally accountable, ordinary and unremarkable features of everyday life.

That members are finding ways to normalise a destabilising infrastructure and manage the attack surface created by the digital on their accountability and integrity as autonomous human beings, is no reason to be complacent or to assume that digital systems are already good enough and that it is simply a matter of time before people come up to speed with innovation in the ecosystem. For all that people evidently can make do with what the digital world provides them, it is also evident that it is routinely encountered as a troublesome place that breaches the calculus of accountability. Privacy breaches are commonplace, and members have common cause to complain about the paucity of generic data sharing mechanisms and their inability to enable intersubjective understanding of their own situated data management practices or the practices of others. Add to that the potential for new technology to render members accountable for matters that might ordinarily be expected to remain out of view and be normally and naturally unremarkable, and the capacity for the digital not only to breach the calculus of accountability but also the social and moral order with it, and it becomes apparent that members' trust in the digital world hangs by a rather more tenuous thread.

As Watson [47] elaborates, trust is a necessary background condition of mutually intelligible courses of action, by which he means that the parties to ordinary action must understand that they are engaged in the same practice, must be competent to perform that practice, must actually perform it competently and assume this also of others, and that all parties to ordinary action must therefore be oriented to the same 'rules of engagement' so to speak. As we have seen, competence in a practice is a socially organised, moral matter that turns on ordinary action's unremarkable character and, more specifically, on members being able to bring their activities about in that way, i.e., accountably as naturally occurring, perceivedly normal, ordinarily unremarkable courses of action [1]. We have also seen that technologies that disrupt the ordinarily unremarkable grounds of everyday activities in rendering the ordinarily invisible visible, break the rules of engagement by violating the grounds upon which mutually intelligibility stands. They not only open up ordinarily unremarkable activities to unwarranted account but throw members' competence and autonomy into question by doing so. So, technologies that breach the ordinarily unremarkable grounds of everyday activities are not only disruptive of specific courses of action, they are disruptive of members' trust in the workings of the social and moral order itself.

There is need to proceed with care as the attack surface expands in everyday life. Key to this endeavour is the recognition that there is more to the sharing of personal data than data. It is, of course, still important to articulate what data is being shared, especially with respect to underlying and evolving technological platforms. New data protection regulations and the interest in making algorithms accountable suggest elements of this are already in hand. However, it is also important to transcend generic mechanisms and support the haecceities of data sharing to enable people to manage just where, just when and just who gets access to their data, and to determine just what gets used, what it gets used for and by whom, whether incidentally or purposefully on a case-by-case basis. This implies that the digital ecosystem needs to provide ways of supporting the sharing of data that move beyond pre-specifying data access policies and sharing permissions. Providing more granularity by giving lots of sub-cohort options [54], for example, will not fix the fundamental problem, because people do not know in advance what every instance of sharing involves and such 'rules' (like any others) are 'merely advisory to action' [55].

Building trust into the digital world requires that members be furnished with resources that support the calculus of accountability and thus enable the attack surface to be managed and contained. While cybersecurity measures may be a necessary part of the mix, they are not sufficient and efforts are also required to build a reciprocity of perspectives into the digital ecosystem. Reciprocity is key to accountability – to the observability and reportability of ordinary action and to its coordination. Without it, it is not possible to see, recognise and understand what another party is doing and to respond accordingly. Reciprocity thus enables members to engage in mutually intelligible courses of action and interaction. This has been markedly lacking in the digital world for a long time [56]. Resources are particularly required to enable intersubjective understanding of members' situated data sharing practices and third-party access to and use of members' data. Reciprocity is not a precursor to action and interaction, but something that is written into its DNA and runs throughout. It cannot be reduced to privacy notices, checkboxes and informed consent, but must be enabled as an accountable feature of ordinary action *within* the digital world and the unfolding, ongoing flow of members' digitally mediated interactions.

3.4   Conclusion

We began this chapter by saying that accountability in ordinary action refers to its observable and reportable character and thus to the mundane fact that members can usually see and hear at-a-glance what is going on around them. We also said that ordinary accountability is a taken-for-granted feature of our competence as members: that it not only allows us to see, recognise and understand what is going around us but that, in so doing, it enables us to coordinate our actions accordingly. On this basis, we said that ordinary accountability is the glue of social life, reflexively constitutive of the social and moral order. In unpacking how privacy is socially and morally organised we have seen that it is essentially a matter of *managing one's accountability*. Members especially seek to avoid real-world accountability for the things they do online in order to control just who they might be accountable to and in what ways. This involves the careful management of cohorts, identities and the visibility of the digital self online. Over the course of these mundane accomplishments, we have seen that members have devised common-sense methods that enable a calculus of accountability that is designed to manage the attack surface created by the digital's incorporation into everyday life. This is growing exponentially with the introduction of the IoT and threatens to render ordinarily invisible activities observable and reportable at scale.

Now, it be might asked why, if ordinary action is observable and reportable and *the fact that it is so* is essential to the social and moral organisation of everyday life, introducing a technology that renders everyday activities observable and reportable is problematic? The answer, as we have seen, lies in the taken-for-granted nature of ordinary action. It resides in the fact that ordinary action is and is supposed to be *unremarkable*. Member's competence turns on their ability to bring about ordinary action *as* an unremarkable achievement [57]. Imagine a world in which we were constantly asking of one another 'what are you doing?' and 'why?' in the course of going about the ordinary business of everyday life. It is not simply a nuisance to have one's ordinarily unremarkable achievements *opened up* to account. It is consequential. This is not simply because it breaches our privacy but that, in so doing, it interferes with our ability as members to conduct our daily business in a competent fashion. Increasing the potential attack surface and rendering the ordinarily invisible visible at scale thus impinges on members' autonomy, disrupts the workings of the social and moral order, and threatens the fragile trust members have managed to invest, to date, in being able, for the most part, to manage their accountability in the digital world. Given the potential impact of the IoT on everyday life, great care needs to be taken in the emerging digital ecosystem to complement innovation by providing members with the resources they need to manage their accountability. Building-in reciprocity is key.

Reciprocity means that ordinary action is mutually intelligible, that the ways in which members manage their accountability are tied up with intersubjective reasoning about how others will apprehend and understand their actions. In other words, a reciprocity of views is essential for accountability to hold. Our studies make clear that breaches of privacy turn on a lack of reciprocity, making the effective management of accountability difficult. The problem is not so much one of *what* is shared as one of *how* it is shared. Generic data sharing mechanisms are simply not capable of supporting the nuanced situated practices that accountability management turns upon. Building-in reciprocity frames technical development in a different way to current trends in computing, which emphasise pre-specifying privacy policies and sharing permissions, both manually and increasingly automatically through the introduction of privacy assistants and AI. However, reciprocity is not a *precursor* to ordinary action but runs throughout it. Reciprocity thus needs to be engineered into the infrastructure of the digital world to enable intersubjective understanding within the *unfolding, ongoing flow* of ordinary action. Building-in reciprocity is not only a matter of making members aware of what is going on in the digital world and of making machine-to-machine interactions observable and reportable. Members also need to be able to understand how those interactions render them accountable. And they need to be furnished with the resources to manage their accountability online and in the analogue world as connected devices become increasingly embedded in the fabric of everyday life. Right now, that is something the digital is poorly equipped to do.

3.5 Acknowledgements

This research was funded by the EU FP7-ICT Programme (Grant Agreement ID:611001) and the Engineering and Physical Sciences Research Council (grants

EP/F0642776/1, EP/K039911/1, EP/M001636/1). This chapter is based on the following original works:

- Crabtree A., Mortier R., Rodden T. and Tolmie P. [10] 'Unremarkable networking: the home network as part of everyday life'. *Proceedings of the ACM Conference on Designing Interactive System*, Newcastle, UK, 11–15 [28] New York: ACM Press, pp. 554–563. https://doi.org/10.1145/2317956.2318039
- Tolmie P., Crabtree A., Rodden T., Colley J, and Luger E. [53] '"This has to be the cats" – personal data legibility in networked sensing systems'. *Proceedings of the ACM Conference on Computer Supported Cooperative Work*, San Francisco (CA), USA, 27 February – 2 March 2016. New York: ACM Press, pp. 491–502. https://doi.org/10.1145/2818048.2819992
- Crabtree A., Tolmie P. and Knight W. [8] Repacking 'rivacy' for a networked world. *Computer Supported Cooperative Work: The Journal of Collaborative Computing and Work Practices*, vol. 26(4-6), pp. 453–488. https://doi.org/10.1007/s10606-017-9276-y
- Tolmie P. and Crabtree A. (2018) The practical politics of sharing personal data. *Personal and Ubiquitous Computing*, vol. 22, pp. 203–315. https://doi.org/10.1007/s00779-017-1071-8

References

[1]   Gambetta D. 'Can we trust trust?' in Gambetta D. (ed.). *Trust: Making and Breaking Co-operative Relations*. **1998**. Oxford: Basil Blackwell; 1988. pp. 213–37.
[2]   Garfinkel H. 'A conception of, and experiments with, "trust" as a condition for stable concerted actions' in Harvey O.J. (ed.). *Motivation and Social Interaction*. New York: Ronald Press; 1963. pp. 187–238.
[3]   Page X., Knijnenburg B., Kobsa A. 'What a tangled web we weave: lying backfires in location-sharing social media'. Proceedings of the ACM Conference on Computer Supported Cooperative Work; San Antonio, TX, USA, February 2013; 2013–273–84.
[4]   Cognizant. *Rise of the smart product economy [online]*. May 2015. Available from   www.cognizant.com/InsightsWhitepapers/the-rise-of-the-smart-product-economy-codex1249.pdf [Accessed 11 Nov 2020].
[5]   Crabtree A., Rodden T., Tolmie P., *et al.* 'House rules: the collaborative nature of policy in domestic'. *Personal and Ubiquitous Computing*. 2015;**19**(1):203–15.
[6]   Dourish P. 'Culture and control in a media space'. Proceedings of the European Conference on Computer-Supported Cooperative Work; Milan, Italy, September; 1993. pp. 125–37.
[7]   Dourish P. 'Seeking a foundation for context-aware'. *Human–Computer Interaction*. 2001;**16**(2–4):229–41.

[8] Crabtree A., Tolmie P., Knight W. 'Repacking "privacy" for a networked world'. *Computer Supported Cooperative Work*. 2017;**26**(4-6):453–88.

[9] Abdul A., Vermeulen J., Wang D., Lim B.Y., Kankanhalli M. 'Trends and trajectories for explainable, accountable and intelligible systems: an HCI research agenda'. Proceedings of the SIGCHI Conference on Human Factors in Computing Systems; Montreal, Canada, April 2018; 2018.

[10] Tolmie P., Benford S., Flintham M., *et al.* 'Act natural – instructions, compliance and accountability in ambulatory experiences'. Proceedings of the SIGCHI Conference on Human Factors in Computing Systems; Austin (TX), USA, May; 2012. pp. 1519–28.

[11] Garfinkel H., Sacks H. 'On formal structures of practical action' in McKinney J.C., Tiryakian E.A. (eds.). *Theoretical Sociology: Perspectives and Developments*. New York: Appleton-Century-Crofts; 1970. pp. 338–266.

[12] Vance A., Lowry P.B., Eggett D. 'A new approach to the problem of access policy violations: increasing perceptions of accountability through the user interface'. *MIS Quarterly*. 2015;**39**(2):345–66.

[13] Karr-Wisniewski P., Wilson D., Richter-Lipford H. 'A new social order: mechanisms for social network site boundary regulation'. Proceedings of the Americas Conference on Information System; Detroit, MI, USA, August 2011; 2011.

[14] Bourdieu P. *Outline of a Theory of Practice*. Cambridge: Cambridge University Press; 1977.

[15] Dourish P., Grinter R.E., Delgado de la Flor J., Joseph M. 'Security in the wild: user strategies for managing security as an everyday, practical problem'. *Personal and Ubiquitous Computing*. 2004;**8**(6):391–401.

[16] Lampinen A., Tamminen S., Oulasvirta A. 'All my people right here, right now: management of group co-presence on a social networking site'. Proceedings of the Conference on Supporting Group Work; Sanibel Island, FL, USA, May 2009; 2009. pp. 281–90.

[17] Solove D.J. *The myth of the privacy paradox*. **3**; 2020. Available from https://scholarship.law.gwu.edu/faculty_publications.

[18] Altman I. *The Environment and Social Behaviour: Privacy, Personal Space, Territory and Crowding*. Monterey: Brooks Cole; 1975.

[19] Cisco. *Annual internet report (2018–2023) white paper [online]*. 9 March 2020. Available from www.cisco.com/c/en/us/solutions/collateral/executive-perspectives/annual-internet-report/white-paper-c11-741490.html [Accessed 11 Nov 2020].

[20] Dourish P. 'Accounting for system behaviour: representation, reflection and resourceful action' in Kyng M., Mathiassen L. (eds.). *Computers and Design in Context*. Cambridge, MA: MIT Press; 1997. pp. 145–70.

[21] Ghaani M., Cozzolino C.A., Castelli G., Farris S. 'An overview of the intelligent packaging technologies in the food sector'. *Trends in Food Science & Technology*. 2016;**51**(10):1–11.

[22]   Stutzman F., Hartzog W. 'Boundary regulation in social media'. Proceedings of the ACM Conference on Computer Supported Cooperative Work; Seattle, WA, USA, February 2012; 2012. pp. 769–78.

[23]   Coleman J.S. *Foundations of Social Theory*. Cambridge (MA): Harvard University, Belknap Press; 1990.

[24]   Tolmie P., Crabtree A. 'The practical politics of sharing personal data'. *Personal and Ubiquitous Computing*. 2018;**22**(2):293–315.

[25]   Rosenquist M. *Navigating the Digital Age*. Chicago, IL: Caxton Business and Legal Inc; 2015.

[26]   Tolmie P., Pycock J., Diggins T., MacLean A., Karsenty A. 'Unremarkable computing'. Proceedings of the SIGCHI Conference on Human factors in Computing Systems; Minneapolis, MN, USA, April; 2002. pp. 399–406.

[27]   Westin A. *Privacy and Freedom*. New York: Atheneum; 1967.

[28]   Crabtree A., Mortier R., Rodden T., Tolmie P. 'Unremarkable networking: the home network as part of everyday life'. Proceedings of ACM Conference on Designing Interactive Systems; Newcastle, UK, June; 2012. pp. 554–63.

[29]   Luhmann N. *Trust and Power*. Chichester: Wiley; 1975.

[30]   Dourish P. 'Process descriptions as organisational accounting devices: the dual use of workflow technologies'. Proceedings of the ACM Conference on Supporting Group Work; Boulder, CO, USA, September; 2001.

[31]   Humbert M., Trubert B., Huguenin K. 'A survey on interdependent privacy'. *ACM Computing Surveys*. 2020;**52**(6):1–40.

[32]   Dourish P., Button G. 'On "Technomethodology": foundational relationships between ethnomethodology and system design'. *Human–Computer Interaction*. 1998;**13**(4):395–432.

[33]   Heath C., Luff P. 'Disembodied conduct: communication through video in a multi-media office environment'. Proceedings of the SIGCHI Conference on Human Factors in Computing Systems; Louisiana, LA, USA, April; 1991. pp. 99–103.

[34]   Klasnja P., Consolvo S., Jung J., *et al*. 'When I am on Wi-Fi, "I am fearless" – privacy concerns and practices in everyday WiFi use'. Proceedings of the SIGCHI Conference on Human Factors in Computing Systems; Boston, MA, USA, April; 2009. pp. 1993–2002.

[35]   Nissenbaum H. 'Privacy as contextual integrity'. *Washington Law Review*. 2004;**79**(30):101–39.

[36]   OWASP. *Attack surface analysis cheat sheet [online]*. 2021. Available from   www.owasp.org/index.php/Attack_Surface_Analysis_Cheat_Sheet [Accessed 11 Nov 2020].

[37]   Sacks H. 'Doing "being ordinary"' in Jefferson G. (ed.). *Lectures on Conversation*. Oxford: Blackwell; 1992. pp. 215–21.

[38]   Sleeper M., Cranshaw J., Kelley P.G., *et al*. 'I read my Twitter the next morning and was astonished – a conversational perspective on Twitter regrets'. Proceedings of the SIGCHI Conference on Human Factors in Computing Systems; Paris, France, April; 2013. pp. 3277–86.

[39]   Watson J., Besmer A., Richter Lipford H. '+Your circles: sharing behavior on Google+'. Proceedings of Symposium on Usable Privacy and Security; Washington, DC, USA, July; 2012.

[40]   Wisniewski P., Lipford H., Wilson D. 'Fighting for my Space: coping mechanisms for SNS boundary regulation'. Proceedings of the SIGCHI Conference on Human Factors in Computing Systems; Austin, TX, USA, May; 2012. pp. 609–18.

[41]   Sharrock W., Watson R. 'Autonomy among social theories: the incarnation of social structures' in Fielding N. (ed.). *Actions and Structure: Research Methods and Social Theory*. London: Sage; 1988. pp. 54–67.

[42]   Aviva. *Tech nation: number of internet-connected devices grows to 10 per home [online]*. 15 January 2020. Available from www.aviva.com/newsroom/news-releases/2020/01/tech-nation-number-of-internet-connected-devices-grows-to-10-per-home [Accessed 11 Nov 2020].

[43]   Kristiansen K.H., Valeur-Meller M.A., Dombrowski L., Holten Moller N.L. 'Accountability in the blue-collar data-driven workplace'. Proceedings of the SIGCHI Conference on Human Factors in Computing Systems; Montreal, Canada, April; 2018.

[44]   Freed D., Palmer J., Minchala D., Levy K., Ristenpart T., Dell N. 'A stalker's paradise – how intimate partner abusers exploit technology'. Proceedings of the SIGCHI Conference on Human Factors in Computing Systems; Montreal, Canada, April; 2018.

[45]   Bellotti V., Edwards K. 'Intelligibility and accountability: human considerations in context-aware systems'. *Human–Computer Interaction*. 2001;**16**(2–4):193–212.

[46]   Furniss D., Blandford A., Mayer A. 'Unremarkable errors: low-level disturbances in infusion pump use'. Proceedings of the 25th BCS Conference on Human Computer Interaction; Newcastle, UK, July; 2011. pp. 197–204.

[47]   Watson R. 'Constitutive practices and Garfinkel's notion of trust: revisited'. *Journal of Classical Sociology*. 2009;**9**(4):475–99.

[48]   Patil S., Norcie G., Kapadia A., Lee A.J. 'Reasons, rewards, regrets: privacy considerations in location sharing as an interactive practice'. Proceedings of the Symposium on Usable Privacy and Security; Washington, DC, USA, July; 2012.

[49]   Newman M.W., Ducheneaut N., Edwards W.K., Sedivy J.Z., Smith T.F. 'Supporting the unremarkable: experiences with the obje display mirror'. *Personal and Ubiquitous Computing*. 2007;**11**(7):523–36.

[50]   Bittner E. 'The concept of organisation'. *Social Research*. 1965;**32**:239–55.

[51]   Garfinkel H. *Studies in Ethnomethodology*. Englewood Cliffs, NJ: Prentice-Hall; 1967.

[52]   Bellotti V. 'Design for privacy in multimedia computing and communications environments' in Agre P., Rotenberg M. (eds.). *Technology and Privacy: The New Landscape*. Cambridge, MA: MIT Press; 1997. pp. 62–98.

[53]   Tolmie P., Crabtree A., Rodden T., Colley J., Luger E. "This has to be the cats" - personal data legibility in networked sensing systems. Proceedings of

the ACM Conference on Computer Supported Cooperative Work and Social Computing; San Francisco, CA, USA, February 2016; 2016. pp. 491–502.

[54]   Hardstone G., Hartswood M., Procter R., Slack R., Voss A., Rees G. 'Supporting informality: team working and integrated care records'. Proceedings of the 2004 ACM Conference on Computer Supported Cooperative Work; Chicago, IL, USA, November; 2004. pp. 142–51.

[55]   Zimmerman D. 'The practicalities of rule use' in Douglas J.D. (ed.). *Understanding Everyday Life: Toward the Reconstruction of Sociological Knowledge*. Chicago, IL: Aldine Publishing Company; 1970. pp. 221–38.

[56]   Guo Y., Jones M., Cowan B., Beale R. 'Take it personally: personal accountability and energy consumption in domestic households'. CHI '13 Extended Abstracts on Human Factors in Computing Systems; Paris, France, April; 2013. pp. 1467–72.

[57]   Pollner M. *Mundane Reason: Reality in Everyday and Sociological Discourse*. Cambridge: Cambridge University Press; 1985.

Chapter 4

The socially negotiated management of personal data in everyday life

Damla Kilic[1], Lewis Cameron[2], Glenn McGarry[1],
Murray Goulden[2], and Andy Crabtree[1]

Abstract

This chapter explores and unpacks the socially negotiated management of personal data in everyday life, particularly in a domestic context. It presents a study of the mundane reasoning involved in arriving at data sharing decisions and reveals that privacy is not the default for data management in the home; that when informational privacy is occasioned, it is socially negotiated and determined by members in the plural rather than by individuals alone; and that informational privacy plays a social function concerned with human security and the safety and integrity of members in a connected world.

4.1 Introduction

In the previous chapter, we saw how accountability is key to data privacy and the disclosure of personal information or 'data'. In this chapter, we will explore and elaborate how accountability extends beyond the individual and is key to the socially negotiated management of personal data in everyday life, and particularly though by no means exclusively in the home. The European Commission's Article 29 Data Protection Working Party (A29WP) [1] explains the Internet of Things or IoT as follows:

> an infrastructure in which billions of sensors embedded in common, everyday devices – 'things' as such, or things linked to other objects or individuals – are designed to record, process, store and transfer data and, as they are associated with unique identifiers, interact with other devices or systems using networking capabilities.

[1]School of Computer Science, University of Nottingham, UK
[2]School of Sociology and Social Policy, University of Nottingham, UK

The interesting thing about the IoT is that data from smart metres, connected lights, kettles, toasters, thermostats, door locks, etc. break the traditional user–device–data relationship, as the data are derived from the actions and interactions of setting members in the plural. IoT data are then are not only personal data, insofar as they reveal what A29WP calls 'inhabitants lifestyle details' (ibid.), but are also *interpersonal* [2] in nature and irreducibly social. Even those who live alone rarely do so in complete isolation and host an array of visitors and guests who may be subject to and even have access to connected devices and their data.

It might be thought that data privacy is especially important in a social context where technology creates a significant challenge to what the sociologist Erving Goffman called the 'territories of the self' [3]. However, we are deliberately cautious about applying the term uncritically in exploring the interpersonal nature of the IoT. Our discomfort lies in the assumption, usually implicit in privacy-focused discussions, that it is the withholding of information from others which should form the underlying principle of data management, including data generated by connected devices that can provide unprecedented insight into our behaviour [4]. Rather this underlying principle is far less absolutist in our view, for in a lively social context, particularly in the context of everyday life in the shared home, what is at stake is not simply the privacy of individuals but the *moral ordering of the social unit* that inhabits the home, no matter its particularly constitution. This means that not only is a great deal of IoT data interpersonal in nature but that its management is interpersonal too, and thus a matter of *negotiation* between multiple parties in a dynamic socio-technical environment.

Below we present the findings of the 'cardboard box' study, a lightweight technology probe [5] and proxy designed to explore the social acceptability of a privacy enhancing technology called the Databox (see Chapter 6). The study makes it perspicuous that privacy is *not* the default position within the home between members and that personal data of all kinds is often shared by default of their living together in a mutually visible and available ecology of activities, practices and devices that enable access to personal and indeed intimate and even highly sensitive information about one another. This is not to say that members have unfettered access to one another's personal devices or data, but that withholding information from one another is not an underlying principle of data management in domestic life. On the contrary, withholding information has to be warranted in some way whether, as seen in Chapter 3, the information is simply not relevant to others or there is clear need for cohort separation. This, in turn, makes it visible that when privacy is occasioned, it performs a distinct *social function* within domestic life, which is essentially concerned with human security and the safety and integrity of members rather than devices and data per se. Accountability lies at the centre of this moral ordering of data sharing and the socially negotiated management of personal data in everyday life and makes it observable and reportable that informational privacy is a socially defined and constituted matter, not as commonly presumed a matter of individual control.

Figure 4.1   The Databox proxy (see [6] for all cards)

4.2   The cardboard box study

The Databox proxy (Figure 4.1) consists of two cardboard boxes, two decks of cards and a set of guidelines explaining what the boxes signify and what participants are supposed to do with the cards – rules of the game as it were – which were affixed to the boxes. While the real Databox is a single unit, two cardboard boxes were required to reflect its functionality and allow participants to reason about data sharing decisions. Thus, one box (a red box on the left of Figure 4.1) was labelled Keep My Data Private and the other box (a blue box) was labelled Others Can Access My Data. The first (green) deck of ideation cards (running across the middle of Figure 4.1) presented *24 types of data* that might be found in the current and future connected home (see Figure 4.2 for an overview of the data types); the second (yellow) deck, *data processing requests* that might be made by *third-party* apps and make use of that data to deliver a service to users (see [6] for further details). We focus only on the first deck of cards in this chapter. The rules instructed participants that if they wanted to keep their data private, they should place the cards from deck one in the red box labelled Keep My Data Private. However, if they wished to share the data with *anyone they knew*, either a family member, friend or some other personal acquaintance, then they should place the cards from deck one in the blue box labelled Others Can Access My Data. We were not especially interested in which cards ended up in which box, but rather in the *mundane reasoning* [7] that provided for their placement. We, therefore, asked participants to articulate their decision-making, whether to the researcher or other family members or both, to give voice to taken for granted issues of personal data sharing and privacy, current and prospective, in their homes.

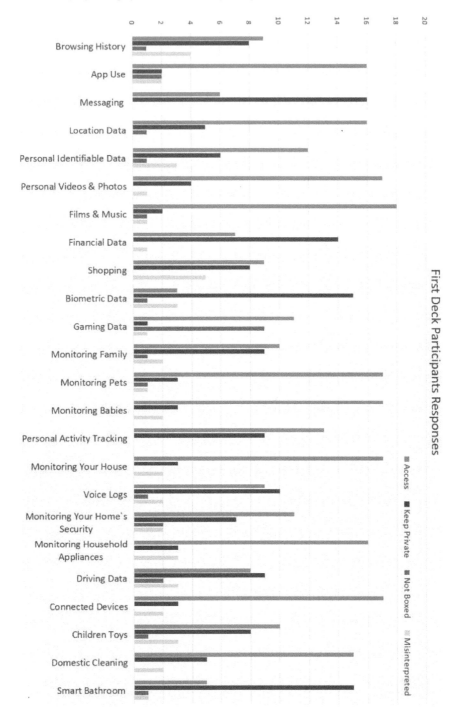

Figure 4.2   Overall responses to deck one data cards (see [6] for all responses)

We recruited 22 households distributed around the United Kingdom via our social networks to take part in this study, providing us with 38 participants. Household composition varied and included families with children, couples, housemates and people who lived alone. Demographically, our participants were of varying ages, had a variety of occupational backgrounds and differing household situations. We make no claim as to the representativeness of this sample but rather, in keeping with the technology probe methodology, set aside a concern with the logic of quantitative science and statistics in favour of the insights gained in designing and deploying a 'throw-away' artefact as a 'method to help us determine which kinds of technologies would be interesting to pursue' [5]. The studies took place in participant's homes at a date and time of their choosing, lasted between 50 minutes and 2 hours and were recorded on audio, which was subsequently transcribed and anonymised. Analysis of the data involved obtaining a gross overview of participants' reaction to each card by quantifying their responses in terms of how many of them wanted to share or keep the data private; see Figure 4.2 overleaf, the blue bars indicate how many participants would share data with others they knew, the red bars indicate how many wanted to keep the data private, the grey bars indicate cards that were not boxed and the yellow bars indicate cards that were misinterpreted and responses discounted. We then drilled down into the transcripts to understand the reasoning that accounted for these response patterns.

4.2.1 Findings

As the blue bars in Figure 4.2 make perspicuous, perhaps surprisingly for those wedded to the presumption of privacy, the majority of data cards were treated as referencing types of data that participants would allow *others to access*. This data include data about the apps they use, location data showing places visited, location data for family monitoring, location data for monitoring pets, personally identifiable data (birth certificates, passports, driving licenses, etc.), personal videos and photos, film and music collections, shopping data, gaming data, data about a baby's breathing and temperature, physical activity data, data about environmental conditions in the home, data from household security devices (e.g., smart doors and locks), data about household appliances, data about devices connected to the home network, data from smart toys and data about cleaning practices and routines. It is important to appreciate that these are not individual decisions, but *joint or collective* decisions arrived at by members (in the plural) through mundane reasoning about the actual or potential relevance of different types of data to *their* everyday lives. As Figure 4.2 makes visible, not all types of data were seen as actually or potentially relevant, and participants views on browsing data, voice log data from interactions with conversational agents (Alexa, etc.) and driving data were closely all contested. Furthermore, messages (SMS, email or social media), financial data, biometric data and smart bathroom data were strongly viewed as data that should be kept private even within the home.

As the transcripts made perspicuous, several discrete orders of mundane reasoning were invoked by participants in arriving at socially negotiated decisions to allow others to access personal data or to keep it private. There is simply too much transcript data to deal with here (547 pages and 170 000 words), so we provide summative accounts of these different orders of reasoning and use italics to reflect the practical issues invoked by members in their decision-making to substantiate them. The specific cards that occasioned this reasoning, ranging from browsing history (card 1) to smart bathroom data (card 24) in Figure 4.2, are referenced in brackets (e.g., C1, 2, 3, etc.).

While many of the data cards focused on potential futures, such as bathrooms with smart mirrors, showers, toilets, products and packaging, the transcripts made it apparent that in questioning data sharing we were not dealing with purely hypothetical situations. It was plain to see that participants *already share data* with one another in the course of their everyday lives and the social context in which they reside was often invoked to account for access decisions. Indeed, it became apparent that domestic life consists for many participants of a shared and mutually visible ecology of activities, practices, devices and data. Thus, access decisions were reasoned about in terms of *living together* (C23) and *already sharing information* (C24) that *anyone can see* (C20, C21), where anyone means *everybody here* including *family and friends* (C5, C6). Participants routinely *shared devices* (C1), used *family share* (C2), *synced data* across devices (C3), used *common devices* (C6), *joint accounts* (C8) and *shared* sources of data (C9). As Sara and David put it, for example (C1),

> **Sarah:** The iPad, its open to anyone isn't it? Because we both have the log in.
>
> **David:** Oh and family.
>
> **Sarah:** And the laptop.
>
> **Interviewer:** So it's a shared device. What about your personal machines?
>
> **Sarah:** We both have access to each other's. It's not intentionally shared, it just is shared.

Whether to occasionally *share messages* (C3), *monitor one another's whereabouts, coordinate people and events, enhance personal safety* (C4), *track and find each other* (C12), *calculate* each other's share of the energy bill (C19), etc., sharing data with others was for participants accountably something *you usually do, don't you* (C4). Data sharing also extended beyond the immediate confines of the home to other social actors, such as the *dog walker* (C18), *work colleagues* (C15) and *local community groups* (C16), reflecting participants broader interests, engagement and relationships with others. Access decisions were thus predicated on the relevance of data to oneself-and-others. While there is some *element of choice* in this (C6), e.g., the particular messages or photos one shares, participants nevertheless saw the sociality of domestic life as largely prohibiting data being treated as wholly private (C1, C3, C4, C7, C8, C21). Rather data was seen and reasoned about as something that is already shared *by default of living with others*, something that sits within a lively social context and is of *intersubjective relevance and utility*.

Social utility or the intersubjective usefulness of data is a key driver of data sharing, and this order of reasoning permeated considerations of a future home increasingly saturated by connected devices and smart products. Participants thus saw the potential to exploit IoT data to *monitor* family members (C11, C12, C13, C14, C19, C22) in carrying out their parental responsibilities, using data to *see where* their children are (C12), to understand such things as how much time they *spend playing games* (C11), how they are *learning and progressing* and to *curtail non-beneficial play* (C22). As one couple put it in considering household appliance data, for example (C19),

> **Tai:** I don't mind share it within our family. I don't know, probably the fridge would be aware Raakel [her daughter] opens the fridge two times, three times, five times or more per day, I don't know.
>
> **Amir:** You can make statistic of it. You can be aware of what choices she picking up from the fridge. You can understand and analyse as well. You can see which brands she loves or not. You can do many thing with these. I think again this is also very useful thing to share.

Like Tai and Amir, IoT data was seen as a potential useful resource by parents, something that could *help not hinder* (C14) them in fulfilling their responsibilities, and in manifold ways help them *prioritise children's health and well-being* (C14).

Indeed, participants reasoned that distinct *social virtues attach to accountability*. They recognised that while IoT data could be used to hold people to account, the ability to *check up* on and *see what is going on* in the home (C21, C23, C24) was not necessarily a bad thing. IoT data would *be like having a witness* (C17), which in turn might *enhance safety* (C4, C19, C21), as the following vignette illustrates (C16):

> **Hana:** It's like I have this app, yeah, but they don't.
>
> **Interviewer:** This is no … think smart devices in your home, for example, for lights.
>
> **Nakia:** We can share because do you remember? One day I forgot to close gas. We should share and they should know.
>
> **Aziz:** What she says, if we could track it that she forgot to switch the gas off – I think it is good to share because we are living in a house that we all care about, yeah, and we all need to know what conditions are in the house.

Participants reasoned that sharing IoT data would allow other members to *look at issues* within the home (C19), and even render connected devices and appliances accountable. Indeed, such data might even provide *evidence* and *proof* (C16) of faulty appliances and devices, and in turn be a useful resource for rendering landlords accountable.

Our participants also reasoned in various ways that generally they *have nothing to hide*, at least within the home between members. Participants said that they *wouldn't mind or wouldn't be bothered* about sharing data with other members (C1, C11, C16, C20) and that they had no issues with sharing data (C2, C19) as there was *nothing untoward* in it (C1), *nothing personal or private* about it (C2, C16), nothing *dodgy* that *warrants hiding* (C1), *no secret* (C7), just *harmless information* (C13), indeed just crap – sudoku scores, music, lights on, lights off, etc. (C2) – that others could *not do anything with* (C2) and posed *no existential threat* (C7, C21). As one participant put it when asked about allowing others to access her driving data, for example (C20),

> **Interviewer:** Would you be worried about him [husband] judging your driving, or your family judging your driving?
>
> **Sue:** I just don't think anyone would be bothered. So I wouldn't really mind.

Furthermore, participants reasoned that it is *too much effort* (C24) to keep data private from one another, that one would really have to have *something to hide* (C21) and *good reason* to hide it (C8) to want to go to the trouble of doing that and that a great deal of data in the connected home doesn't belong to a single person *unless you live alone* anyway (C18). There is, then, *no reason not to share* data (C19) and *no permission* is required to share it *between us* (C22).

Decisions to share data thus stood on the perceived harmlessness of data and what is effectively shared ownership or at least *shared rights and privileges* over it concurred by default of living together. These are not blanket rights and privileges, however. They are not equally distributed, as Sofi, a teenage girl, makes perspicuous in conversation with her parents (C17):

> **Sofi:** Alexa and Siri? I like using Siri.
>
> **Dani:** Do you mind if I hear those conversations between you and Siri?
>
> **Sofi:** No!
>
> **Ibrahim:** Why not?
>
> **Sofi:** This is my data.
>
> **Dani:** This is too much personal?
>
> **Ibrahim:** You have to explain us why? We want to know it.
>
> **Sofi:** No. No. No.
>
> **Interviewer:** I guess you are using them for personal purposes?
>
> **Sofi:** Yes. This is private.

As Sofi's conversation with her parents makes visible, accessing data is subject to the practical politics of sharing and the relationships that hold between household members, their ages and stages of life. So while small children have little, if any, say in data sharing, teenagers like their parents certainly do, and we found similar disagreements in shared households where members were not related or members of a family. The relationships that hold between household members drive the socially negotiated management of personal data in everyday life and warrant both the sharing of data and the occasional need to render it 'private'.

Accountability lies at the heart of the socially negotiated management of personal data in everyday life and the *occasioned invocation of privacy*. We found then that while participants were generally willing to share data, they sought to avoid making data available that would enable the others they live with to *have a moan* at them (C2) or data that would make them feel *uncomfortable or embarrassed* (C10), breach *secrecy* (C17) and spoil *surprises* (C9, C12, C19). Participants sought to avoid being held to account by specific parties, often their partners or parents, with respect to specific activities, including what they watch on TV (C7), their finances (C8), gaming (C11), exercise (C15), voice logs of things searched for online (C17), use of the central heating, (C19), domestic cleaning (C23) and bathroom and product usage (C24). Privacy decisions were driven by consideration of the *granularity of data*, e.g., seeing that £100 had been spent was not the same as seeing that £100 had been spent *on sweeties*, which was seen to undermine strategic ambiguity or more prosaically *the option of telling white lies* (C20).

A particular concern with accountability centred on *identity or impression management*, which was of particular issue to teenagers, housemates and where the sharing of personal data with others beyond the immediate confines of the home was concerned. Participants did not want others to apprehend *sensitive issues* (C1), including bodily functions, sexual fetishes, political views, personality traits, personal interests and future plans. It is notable that privacy decisions were not simply accounted for here tautologically, but in terms of the potential for data to be taken *out of context* (C1, C15) and to be *misconstrued* (C17). Participants were sensitive to the fact that data enables others to make *assumptions* (C17) about them and they wished to avoid giving others the *wrong impression* about themselves (C1) and *damaging their relationships* to boot (C17). Participants therefore sought to manage their identity and other people's impression of them in the face of the constant *creeping intrusion* of data into *every nook and cranny* of their lives (C23). As one participant put it with respect to the smart bathroom (C24), for example,

> **Tom:** It's like smart watches and Fitbits and all the rest of it. Everything has got to be measured. For what reason I do not know. Dickens wrote to this in the 19th century with Thomas Gradgrind, who wanted to measure everything. It was this kind of hard empiricism that everything should be measured and quantified. Whether you know the value of these things is another matter.

Participants thus made privacy decisions to protect their identity and manage other people's impression of them in a fundamental bid to *preserve agency and autonomy*, which was seen to be increasingly threatened by an increasing array of connected devices. This applied to others as much as the individual, with participants treating *children as sacred* (C22) and eschewing unfettered data access on the basis that it undermines personal *choice* and thus *compromises the foundations of liberty* (C8).

The different orders of reasoning involved in, and shaping, the socially negotiated management of data in everyday life thus exhibit fundamental concern with *human security* and the safety and integrity of household members. We have seen that data is already shared within the home between household members by default of living together. It is of social utility, and there are evident virtues to accountability, that promote the health, well-being and safety of members. We have also seen that while members generally have nothing to hide, and indeed have shared rights and privileges over data sharing, they are not blind to the potential dangers of accountability. Privacy is thus invoked, as detailed in Chapter 3, to manage accountability, and also as we have seen here for purposes of identity and impression management in the face of the increased production of personal data in everyday life. Privacy thus performs a distinct *social function*. It is not a default principle of personal data management in everyday life, but an occasioned means of managing threats to members' interpersonal relationships and ultimately their agency and autonomy. It is also a socially negotiated function, arrived at locally in consideration of the relationships that hold between household members, the responsibilities and expectations that incumbents have, and the rights and privileges that attach to their ages and stages of life. In short, members do not have a ubiquitous right to privacy, it is occasioned by the need to avoid harm to the social fabric and preserve human security in world in which accountability, agency and autonomy are increasingly threatened by widespread data production.

4.3   Discussion

We are not, of course, the first to recognise the potential of the IoT to harm household members.

> One woman had turned on her air-conditioner, but said it then switched off without her touching it. Another said the code numbers of the digital lock at her front door changed every day and she could not figure out why. Still another told … that she kept hearing the doorbell ring, but no one was there. Their stories are part of a new pattern of behaviour in domestic abuse cases tied to the rise of smart home technology. Internet-connected locks, speakers, thermostats, lights and cameras that have been marketed as the newest conveniences are now also being used as a means for harassment, monitoring, revenge and control. [8]

The IoT is becoming part and parcel of the domestic abuser's arsenal and has the ability to enable harms at a scale. In the United Kingdom, for example, the Office for National Statistics puts the home at the centre of 'intimate personal violence', including some two million victims of domestic abuse in which the digital plays an increasing role [9]. While research concerning smart technology and domestic violence is limited as yet, there is a growing body of work on Digital Domestic Violence (DDV) where attention has largely centred on DDV between partners before, during and after relationship breakdowns. Moncur *et al*. [10], for example, examined the role of digital technologies during breakdowns across different types of relationship (married, civil partnership, co-habiting, same sex, etc.) and highlighted the heightened issues of identity management and harassment. Others elaborated a range of digital practices that enable harassment and abuse, including trolling [11], sharing intimate data without consent [12], sexting, stalking and snooping [13], social media surveillance [14], and monitoring and controlling personal data, including financial and social media accounts [15]. Sitting alongside social media platforms, mobile phones including location tracking currently play a prominent role in DDV [16, 17].

Digital forms of abuse often co-exist with and facilitate non-digital forms of abuse [18], and DDV thus enables a 'continuum' of intrusive practices [19] that span physical boundaries and centre on maintaining an abuser's power and control. The digital enables domestic violence and abuse to transcend 'borders and boundaries' in new ways [20] and allows instantaneous and constant access to victims. The role of smart home technologies in enabling DDV is currently poorly understood, but the sensory functions inherent to many IoT devices and applications, tied to their ability to 'actuate' or perform automated actions, ought to raise alarm bells. Although DDV is now criminalised in many countries, guidelines currently focus on non-smart forms of abuse, e.g., evidence of abuse over the Internet, digital technology and social media platforms [21] despite evidence of smart home technologies being used in DDV cases [8]. This rift between statutory guidelines and real world, real-time practice suggests there is urgent need to address the gap [20] and for research and regulation to catch up with developments in the smart home.

4.3.1   The impact of the IoT on everyday life

Domestic abuse sits at the extreme albeit disturbingly commonplace end of the spectrum of harms enabled by digital technology and marks the point where negotiation between members is replaced by the tyranny of one over another. The breakdown of negotiation underscores the mundane fact that our increasingly data-mediated interpersonal relationships rely on *joint* decision-making rather than diktat and how devastating the consequences are when this is no longer the case. However, it is not only the pernicious effects of domestic violence that will be enabled by the IoT. As highlighted in Chapter 3, the impact is more prosaic, destabilising the unremarkable foundations of everyday life in rendering the ordinarily invisible visible and subject to account. As the sociologist Georg Simmel [22] observed over a century ago,

> If there were such a thing as complete reciprocal transparency, the relationships of human beings to each other would be modified in a quite unimaginable fashion.

Contemporary sociologists have elaborated how digital technologies enable 'social surveillance' [23] and create an 'interpersonal panopticism' [24]. An obvious example is provided smart toys targeted at children, which provide such unambiguous opportunities for remote monitoring that many have now been banned in Germany, scarred by its recent history of mass surveillance and concomitant abuse [25]. Google's location sharing service provides an example of interpersonal panopticism. While it may ease coordination between parents trying to manage work and childcare commitments, it also creates an expectation of sharing, such that at a later date, when such just-in-time logistics are no longer required, attempting to withdraw sharing permissions may come to be viewed with suspicion by the other party.

However, while there is great temptation to see the IoT under the auspices of 'surveillance capitalism' in general [26], there is a danger in importing surveillance theories into the home. Social surveillance, for example, involves the *intentional* broadcasting of selective information about the self [23]. Smart home data, by contrast, is generated without user deliberation, simply through the ongoing conduct of everyday life in the sensed spaces of the home. User consent to this process is not on the basis of its consumption by others, but rather to inform services: when the heating should come on, what goods to reorder, what films the user might like based on past viewings, etc. More troubling is the risk of what we might call 'data incontinence' or the unfettered availability of personal information amongst members, which is not well captured by a surveillance focus. Examples of data incontinence include a father discovering his daughter's pregnancy from store card data [27] or a husband's affair revealed to his wife by his Uber app [28], discoveries that were *accidental*, yet nonetheless consequential.

The introduction of pervasive sensing into the home, the production of interpersonal data and the algorithmic processing of that data for purposes of automation raises the question of how members and digital technologies alike might manage the tension between withholding and disclosing personal and even sensitive information. As sociologist Erving Goffman might put it, in being data incontinent within the boundaries of the home, the IoT begs fundamental questions as to how we might manage the 'territories of the self' [3]. In Goffman's analysis, these territorial preserves are spaces over which individuals hold dominion, and negotiation over their boundaries is a central aspect of the organisation of social life.

> here the issue is not whether a preserve is exclusively maintained, or shared, or given up entirely, but rather the role the individual is allowed in determining what happens to his claim. (ibid.)

Data incontinence breaks the ability of members to negotiate 'informational boundaries' between one another and threatens to undermine the reciprocal senses of self that hold between them fundamentally and for the worse, ultimately resulting in 'deep bewilderment' and 'acute distrust' of their surroundings.

Furthermore, members are likely to detect that they are 'being watched' by domestic devices that can be used to harm self and others alike. To borrow again from Goffman,

> The household ceases to be a place where there is the easy fulfillment of a thousand mutually anticipated proper acts. It ceases to be a solid front organised by a stable set of persons against the world, entrenched and buffered by a stable set of friends … The home, where wounds were meant to be licked, becomes precisely where they are inflicted. Boundaries are broken. The family is turned inside out.

This dystopian future arises not so much because data incontinence enables social surveillance and interpersonal panopticism, but because it rides roughshod over the 'tacit collaboration' that sustains informational boundaries and interpersonal data management. Simmel [22] suggested this tacit collaboration turns upon the *norm of discretion*, which not only respects the right of others to conceal information but also expects that members purposefully avoid actions that facilitate unwarranted disclosure and exposure. This might, for example, be something as simple as averting one's eyes from a family member's email left open on a shared device and in manifold ways ignoring data to which other members may lay claim. It is not, then, that the informational boundaries of the self are necessarily managed by the individual in withholding or disclosing information, but socially through the operation of the norm of discretion, which governs the observability and reportability of personal information in an interpersonal context. And it is not so much that members have nothing to hide from one another, but that it is hiding in plain view with the sharing of personal data being managed through a tacit social practice that renders it unremarkable and which is an essential constituent of the socially negotiated management of personal data sharing in everyday life.

4.3.2 Designing for the collaborative management of privacy

So how might we design for discretion and build an IoT that avoids creating widespread threats to human security through the excessive accountability enabled by a panoply of connected devices? How do we balance the social utility and virtues of accountability that accompany the digital with the fundamental need for identity and impression management in an incontinent or inherently porous and destabilising socio-technical environment? The technical field of 'interdependent privacy' [29] pulls together various ideas that recognise the social nature of a great deal of personal data including notions of 'multiple-subject privacy' [30], 'multi-party privacy' [31], 'peer privacy' [32], 'networked privacy' [33], 'group privacy' [34] and 'collective privacy' [35]. These various concepts of privacy have subtly different meanings but coalesce around two key thematics. One, *the impact of data sharing on others* where, for example, data affect not only the person who shares them but also others implicated in or related to them [33], including the disclosure of an individual's private information by peers [32], or the actions of persons around an individual (friends, family, etc.) that affect the individual's privacy [34]. Two, *the collaborative management of personal data*, where more than one party controls the availability of data [31], the members of a group collectively manage data access [35], and no single person has the right to control how the data is shared [30]. The latter has led to a focus on *collaborative access control* and the development of technical mechanisms that allow users to specify privacy preferences and negotiate shared privacy poli-cies[36–40]. These efforts follow existing regulatory attempts to manage online harms in largely focusing on online social networks and are largely constrained to the sharing of photographs on online social networks (OSN) at the current moment in time. They are complemented by a related thread of work that coalesces around the *detection and resolution of conflicts* between user's privacy preferences and policies. This includes automated voting strategies [41] and agent-based negotia-tion protocols that exploit measures of the relationship strength or 'intimacy' [42] and 'reciprocity' [43] that hold between users, derived from their online activity and interactions. There is also a growing body of work on differential privacy, though these solutions do not focus directly on interdependent privacy as yet [29].

While interdependent privacy is to be commended for recognising the social nature of a great deal of data in the digital world, the solutions it puts forward are nonetheless problematic in a domestic context. Many people would easily recognise the absurdity, for example, of being asked to specify privacy preferences and poli-cies for the family photo collection. This is not to say that family members do not discuss and regulate the sharing of family photos. Only that they do not and would not do so by using technical mechanisms to specify individual preferences and nego-tiate shared policies or rely on automated measures and indeed metrics of intimacy and reciprocity, let alone voting, to resolving conflicts between them. The root of the problem here is that interdependent privacy assumes that all parties are equal or have equal rights and privileges. This may be the case online in social networks amongst persons who may genuinely be called peers, but it is not the case in the home, where rights and privileges are *differentially distributed*. Any 'competent wide-awake' member [44] knows that all kind of rights and privileges, including those involved in accessing and sharing data, are distributed differently and *unequally* amongst small children, teens, adults, the aged and infirm. As noted previously, privacy is not a ubiquitous right in the home, only some people have it and then only some of the time, as much is already shared by default of living together and hiding information turns as much on social consideration of human security implications and the norm of discretion as it does on individual decision-making.

While recognising the social character of data, interdependent privacy falls vic-tim to the solipsistic fallacy that underpins common (mis)understandings of privacy, i.e., that it is essentially concerned with the ability of individuals to withhold or disclose personal information [45–48], in contrast to it being a socially negotiated and defined function where the right and privilege is bestowed on members by mem-bers as circumstances dictate. Thus, the growing independence of the child warrants an increased respect for privacy, subject to parental discretion, whereas old age, infirmity and incapacity may warrant the reverse. Privacy is defined within a lively social context in which members are not simply to be understood as individuals-in-a-group within which rights and privileges are equally distributed but of a dis-crete social unit necessarily defined by different expectations, rights and privileges that attach to members relationships, responsibilities, ages and stages of life. The shortcomings of interdependent privacy are a consequence of the group conception of the social and reminiscent of early debate in the field of Computer-Supported

Cooperative Work, which found such a conception deeply problematic. At the nub of the debate is the recognition that members are not merely individuals situated in groups, but persons who are 'mutually dependent' upon one another [49]. It is not, then, sufficient to design for the individual as a member of a group, designing for discretion also requires solutions that respect the *mutual dependence* of members in arriving at privacy or data sharing decisions.

4.3.3 Respecting mutual dependence

Designing for discretion takes us beyond a concern with recipient design as discussed in Chapter 3, to also consider the *social dynamics* that shape the situated withholding and disclosure of personal data. As philosopher Andrei Marmor observes [50], while privacy is necessary to ensure members have a reasonable measure of control over ways in which information about them is disclosed and how they therefore present themselves to others, nobody has a right to absolute control. This may come as a shock to privacy advocates, though as ethicist and moral philosopher J.J. Thompson pointed out many years before [51], none of us has a right over any fact about oneself to the effect that fact shall not be known by any other. If there is any violation of a person's right to privacy in someone knowing something about them, it must derive from the way in which the information has been obtained not the information itself. Thus,

> our ability to control the ways in which we present ourselves to others is inherently limited. And of course, that is not necessarily a bad thing. Nobody should have too much control over the way they present themselves to others, as that would make manipulation, dishonesty, and, generally, lack of authenticity all too easy. [50]

The limited nature of individual control focuses attention on the *interplay between members* in determining what happens to anyone's claim over the informational boundaries of the self. While it is important, as Goffman notes, that the individual has a role in determining their claim over the treatment of data that implicates them, it is *not their say alone*. It is not Sofi's insistence that data about her conversations with Siri are private that makes them private, for example, but that her parents silently acquiesce to her wishes as being appropriate to a teenager. Within a domestic context at least, the informational boundaries of the self are social through and through, arrived at through negotiation, whether explicit, tacit or a mixture of the two.

The socially defined and constituted nature of privacy is reflected to some extent in Helen Nissenbaum's influential concept of privacy as 'contextual integrity' [52], where privacy is seen to be governed by shared norms and values that regulate the flow of information. Sandra Petronio's communicative theory of privacy management [53] extends Nissenbaum's framework and adds rules to the mix to manage the 'dialectical tension' that inevitably arises in the interplay between members in determining claims over the treatment of personal information. Norms, values and rules provide for the layman and the analyst alike a generic, common-sense framework organising everyday life (see the work of the eminent sociologist Talcott Parsons [54] for prime example). However, in the social sciences, this common-sense framework has long been understood to be a problematic [55]. Simply put, there is a 'praxiological gap' between norms, values and rules *and their enactment* in everyday life. As Rawls [56] puts it with respect to rules, for example, they cannot tell you how to follow them, that would entail an infinite regress, and as vom Lehn [57] explains norms and values do not, in practice, provide a general framework guiding ordinary action but are instead ad hoc resources invoked, made relevant and used selectively by members as local circumstances dictate. The norm of discretion rather underscores the point.

We should exercise caution when turning to theories of privacy then, even those that orient us to its socially defined and constituted nature. Of particular concern is the in-built tendency to represent an overly simplistic and mechanistic view of the social such, for example, that the interplay between members and flow of information is seen to be regulated through general norms, values, rules, etc., rather than *situated and occasioned practices* of negotiation. Socio-logical theories of privacy render members 'cultural dopes' [58] acting in compliance with pre-established courses of action provided by a model of a common culture, even if that culture is quite restricted (e.g., to an organisation or institution of a particular type, including 'the family'). Typically, these models treat the common-sense rationalities of judgement implicated in determining who gets to control the informational boundaries of the self as 'epiphenomenal' or culturally determined, and thus ignore the practical action and practical reasoning or mundane competencies involved in interpreting and applying generic frameworks in and across the temporal succession of 'here and now' situations of choice (ibid.). The praxiological gap is a nuisance, an inconvenience to be dispensed with, modelled out of existence or at least into mute submission. Nonetheless, it is the case that members *together* negotiate the informational boundaries of the self and do so through an unacknowledged array even battery of situated and occasioned practices informed by common-sense rationalities of judgement.

Thus, and as the cardboard box study makes perspicuous, we find that the socially negotiated management of personal data in everyday life is shot through with mundane reasoning that organises the informational boundaries of the self. We find then that data is not private but shared by default of members living together, and that the mundane business of living together furnishes members with an order of reasoning to negotiate the informational boundaries of the self. We find that the value of sharing data lies in its social utility and that in manifold was this order of mundane reasoning is strongly implicated in negotiating the informational boundaries of the self. And we also find that existing common-sense rationalities of judgement allow for prospective rationalities predicated on the discernible virtues of accountability and that this order of reasoning is also important to the social shaping of the informational boundaries of the self. The cardboard box study elaborates a temporal succession of 'here and now' situations of choice organised through discrete orders of mundane reason that constitute common-sense rationalities of judgement. It makes visible that the principle risk of the IoT is not that it breaches common-sense frameworks of privacy as posited by generic socio-logical models – as Marmor reminds us, it is not the changing environment that is problematic per se [50] – but that it potentially undermines the socially negotiated management of personal data in everyday life.

Marmor elaborates the point in inviting us to imagine, as philosophers are won't to do, that we live in an environment in which the flow of information is inherently unpredictable, an environment in which the walls are effectively made of glass and the things we do and say can be seen and heard by those around us.

> Whether physically possible or not, this would seem to be a horrific world to live in. Why? For one thing, we would lose the ability to do some things that we really need to do in seclusion … [However], what we mainly lose in a Panopticon world … is something that is essential for **shaping our interactions with others**; it is, first and foremost, **our social lives that would be severely compromised, not necessarily or primarily our inner or private world**. [50]

The primary risk of the IoT in a domestic context is not to members privacy but to their social being. Indeed, the porous nature of the IoT undermines members ability to construct a sense of one another as discrete social beings. Data incontinence fundamentally interferes not only with the intersubjective management of the boundaries of the self, but reflexively in the co-construction of the self as a social object, and specifically as a human being possessed of its own distinct social identity, having its own socially negotiated and defined responsibilities, rights, privileges and the rest. This is why the IoT destabilises the unremarkable foundations of everyday life, rendering anything and everything available to account and creating deep bewilderment and acute distrust in such porous surroundings to boot. The issue, to be clear, is not about the occasional need for privacy and what an individual does not want others to see, but about *what others do not want to see*. It is about 'micro-publics' in the home and what members want to see of one other's conduct. Privacy is a means of managing that. Any technology that disrupts members ability to negotiate and socially shape the informational boundaries of the self, and to thereby manage *one another's privacy*, is bound to run into trouble then. While disruption is widely seen as a positive thing in current technological circles, it will be far less welcome in the home. For while privacy is not a default in domestic life, it nevertheless plays a social function and allows members – in the plural – to avert harms to the self in socially negotiating its informational boundaries and thereby ensuring its safety and integrity as a discrete social being.

4.4 Conclusion

Common views of privacy see it as an individual function centred on the power of the individual to control the withholding and disclosure of personal information. The IoT purportedly threatens the individual's privacy in rendering ordinarily invisible activities visible and available to account. In short, the IoT makes it possible for us to see things of one another that we could not see before, and the individual has no power to control this. This, however, is a mistaken point of view. The presuppositions are wrong. The individual never had the power to control the withholding and disclosure of personal information in the first place, at least not in a domestic context and arguably anywhere else in society. The 'individuation' of privacy is a myth of modernity. The cardboard box study makes it perspicuous (a) that informational privacy is not a default in the home, as a great deal of data is shared by virtue of the fact that members live together; (b) that when informational privacy is occasioned, it is socially negotiated and determined through differentially distributed rights and privileges and (c) that informational privacy plays a social function, ensuring human security and the safety and integrity of the self as a discrete social being. It is the potential of the IoT to disrupt the social fabric of domestic life, and particularly the ability of members to socially manage privacy, rather than to impede the exercise of the individual's mythical powers, that is of real concern. In short, it is not *I* who defines my informational privacy but *we*. The IoT needs to be designed in such a way that acknowledges and respects the social. The current emphasis on the individual is not conducive to that achievement.

4.5   Acknowledgements

The research reported here was funded by the University of Nottingham, which awarded Murray Goulden a Research Fellowship, and the Engineering and Physical Sciences Research Council (grants EP/M001636/1, EP/N028260/1, EP/N028260/2). This chapter is based on the following original works:

- Kilic D., Crabtree A., McGarry G., Goulden G. 'The cardboard box study: understanding collaborative data management in the connected home.' Working paper (November 2020), https://drive.google.com/file/d/1qrnn6bsUpvP5yDg G0mgehMGaYu8e0rd5/view?usp=sharing

References

[1]   A29WP WP223. *Opinion 8/2014 on the recent developments on the internet of things [online]*. 2014. Available from https://ec.europa.eu/justice/article-29/documentation/opinion-recommendation/files/2014/wp223_en.pdf [Accessed 16 Dec 2020].

[2]   Goulden M., Tolmie P., Mortier R., Lodge T., Pietilainen A.-K., Teixeira R. 'Living with interpersonal data: observability and accountability in the age of pervasive ICT'. *New Media & Society*. 2018;**20**(4):1580–99.

[3]   Goffman E. *Relations in Public: Microstudies of the Public Order*. New York: Basic Books; 1971.

[4]   Federal Trade Commission. *FTC staff report 'internet of things: privacy and security in a connected world [online]*. Available from www.ftc.gov/system/

files/documents/reports/federal-trade-commission-staff-report-november-2013-workshop-entitled-internet-things-privacy/150127iotrpt.pdf [Accessed 16 Dec 2020].

[5] Hutchinson H., Mackay W., Westerlund B., *et al*. 'Technology probes: inspiring design for and with families'. *Proceedings of the SIGCHI Conference on Human Factors in Computing System*; New York: ACM Press; 2003. pp. 17–24.

[6] Kilic D. *The cardboard box study [online]*. 2019. Available from https://drive.google.com/open?id=1TKEBPN9HNa6WMmnrAVAb3gZ00Na4qT0e [Accessed 12 Dec 2020].

[7] Pollner M. *Mundane Reason: Reality in Everyday and Sociological Discourse*. Cambridge University Press; 1987.

[8] Bowles N. 'Thermostats, locks and lights: digital tools of domestic abuse'. *The New York Times*. Available from www.nytimes.com/2018/06/23/technology/smart-home-devices-domestic-abuse.html [Accessed 16 Dec 2020].

[9] Office for National Statistics. *Violent crime and sexual offences – intimate personal violence and serious sexual assault [online]*. 2016. Available from www.ons.gov.uk/peoplepopulationandcommunity/crimeandjustice/compendium/focusonviolentcrimeandsexualoffences/2015-02-12/chapter4violentcrimeandsexualoffencesintimatepersonalviolenceandserioussexualassault [Accessed 16 Dec 2020].

[10] Moncur W., Gibson L., Herron D. 'The role of digital technologies during relationship breakdowns'. *Proceedings of the ACM Conference on Computer Supported Cooperative Work and Social Computing*; New York: ACM Press; 2016. pp. 371–82.

[11] Finn J. 'A survey of online harassment at a university campus'. *Journal of Interpersonal Violence*. 2004;**19**(4):468–83.

[12] Powell A., Henry N. 'Beyond "revenge pornography"' in Powell A., Henry N. (eds.). *Sexual Violence in a Digital Age*. London: Springer; 2017. pp. 117–52.

[13] Reed L.A., Tolman R.M., Ward L.M. 'Snooping and sexting: digital media as a context for dating aggression and abuse among college students'. *Violence Against Women*. 2016;**22**(13):1556–76.

[14] Lyndon A., Bonds-Raacke J., Cratty A.D. 'College students' Facebook stalking of ex-partners'. *Cyberpsychology, Behavior, and Social Networking*. 2011;**14**(12):711–16.

[15] Leitão R. 'Technology-facilitated intimate partner abuse: a qualitative analysis of data from online domestic abuse forums'. *Human–Computer Interaction*. 2021;**36**(3):203–42.

[16] Freed D., Palmer J., Minchala D., Levy K., T R., Dell N. 'A stalker's paradise – how intimate partner abusers exploit technology'. *Proceedings of the SIGCHI Conference on Human Factors in Computing Systems*; New York: ACM Press; 2018. p. 667.

[17] Stark E. *Coercive Control: The Entrapment of Women in Personal Life*. Oxford University Press; 2009.

[18] Dimond J.P., Fiesler C., Bruckman A.S. 'Domestic violence and information communication technologies'. *Interacting with Computers.* 2011;**23**(5):413–21.

[19] Vera-Gray F. *Men's Intrusion, Women's Embodiment: A Critical Analysis of Street Harassment.* London: Routledge; 2016.

[20] Harris B.A., Woodlock D. 'Digital coercive control: insights from two landmark domestic violence studies'. *The British Journal of Criminology.* 2019;**59**(3):530–50.

[21] Home Office. *Statutory Guidance Framework: Controlling or Coercive Behaviour in an Intimate or Family Relationship [online].* 2015. Available from https://assets.publishing.service.gov.uk/government/uploads/system/uploads/attachment_data/file/482528/Controlling_or_coercive_behaviour_-_statutory_guidance.pdf [Accessed 16 Dec 2020].

[22] Simmel G. 'The sociology of secrecy and of secret societies'. *American Journal of Sociology.* 1906;**11**(4):441–98.

[23] Marwick A. 'The public domain: surveillance in everyday life'. *Surveillance & Society.* 2012;**9**(4):378–93.

[24] Manning J., Stern D.M. 'Heteronormative bodies, queer futures: toward a theory of interpersonal panopticism'. *Information, Communication & Society.* 2018;**21**(2):208–23.

[25] Oltermann P. 'German parents told to destroy doll that can spy on children'. *The Guardian,* 17 February 2017. Available from www.theguardian.com/world/2017/feb/17/german-parents-told-to-destroy-my-friend-cayla-doll-spy-on-children [Accessed 16 Dec 2020].

[26] Zuboff S. *The Age of Surveillance Capitalism: The Fight for a Human Future at the New Frontier of Power.* London: Profile Books; 2019.

[27] Hill K. 'How target figured out a teen girl was pregnant before her father did'. *Forbes.* Available from www.forbes.com/sites/kashmirhill/2012/02/16/how-target-figured-out-a-teen-girl-was-pregnant-before-her-father-did/?sh=63e1f27b6668 [Accessed 16 Dec 2020].

[28] Agence France-Presse. 'Cheating frenchman sues uber for unmasking affair'. *The Guardian.* Available from www.theguardian.com/technology/2017/feb/13/cheating-frenchman-sues-uber-for-unmasking-affair [Accessed 16 Dec 2020].

[29] Humbert M., Trubert B., Huguenin K. 'A survey on interdependent privacy'. *ACM Computing Surveys.* 2019;**52**(6):122.

[30] Gnesi S., Matteucci I., Moiso C., Mori O., Petrocchi M., Vescovi M. 'My data, your data, our data: managing privacy preferences in multiple subjects personal data'. *Proceedings of the Annual Privacy Forum;* Cham: Springer; 2014. pp. 154–71.

[31] Thomas K., Grier C., Nicol D. 'Unfriendly: multi-party privacy risks in social networks'. Proceedings of the International Symposium on Privacy Enhancing Technologies Symposium; 2010. pp. 236–52.

[32] Chen J., Ping J.W., Xu Y., Tan B.C.Y. 'Information privacy concern about peer disclosure in online social networks'. *IEEE Transactions on Engineering Management*. 2015;**62**(3):311–24.

[33] Boyd D. 'Networked privacy'. *Surveillance & Society*. 2012;**10**(3&4):348–50.

[34] Radaelli L., Sapiezynski P., Houssiau F., Shmueli E., de Montjoye Y.A. 'Quantifying surveillance in the networked age: node-based intrusions and group privacy'. *ArXiv*. 2018.

[35] Squicciarini A.C., Shehab M., Paci F. 'Collective privacy management in social networks'. *Proceedings of the 18th International Conference on World Wide Web*; New York: ACM Press; 2009. pp. 521–30.

[36] Guo Y., Zhang L., Chen X. 'Collaborative privacy management: mobile privacy beyond your own devices'. *Proceedings of the ACM MobiCom Workshop on Security and Privacy in Mobile Environments*; New York: ACM Press; 2014. pp. 25–30.

[37] Hu H., Ahn G.-J., Jorgensen J. 'Multiparty access control for online social networks: model and mechanisms'. *IEEE Transactions on Knowledge and Data Engineering*. 2013;**25**(7):1614–27.

[38] Ilia P., Carminati B., Ferrari E., Fragopoulou P., Ioannidis S. 'SAMPAC: socially-aware collaborative multi-party access control'. *Proceedings of the 7th ACM Conference on Data and Application Security*; New York: ACM Press; 2017. pp. 71–82.

[39] Mehregan P., Fong P. 'Policy negotiation for co-owned resources in relationship-based access control'. Proceedings of the 21st ACM Symposium on Access Control Models and Technologies; 2016. pp. 125–36.

[40] Wishart R., Corapi D., Marinovic S., Sloman M. 'Collaborative privacy policy authoring in a social networking context'. Proceedings of the IEEE International Symposium on Policies for Distributed Systems and Networks; New Jersey; 2010. pp. 1–8.

[41] Hu H., Ahn G.J. 'Multiparty authorization framework for data sharing in online social networks'. *Proceedings of the IFIP Annual Conference on Data Applications Security and Privacy*; Heidelberg: Springer; 2011. pp. 29–43.

[42] Such J.M., Rovatsos M. 'Privacy policy negotiation in social media'. *ACM Transactions on Autonomous and Adaptive Systems*. 2016;**11**(1):1–29.

[43] Keküllüoğlu D., Kökciyan N., Yolum P. 'Strategies for privacy negotiation in online social networks'. *Proceedings of the 1st International Workshop on AI for Privacy and Security*; New York: ACM Press; 2016. pp. 1–8.

[44] Bittner E. 'Objectivity and Realism in Sociology' In Psathas G. (ed.). *Phenomenological Sociology: Issues and Applications*; 1973. pp. 109–25.

[45] Altman I. *The Environment and Social Behaviour: Privacy, Personal Space, Territory and Crowding*. Monterey: Brooks Cole; 1975.

[46] Palen L., Dourish P. 'Unpacking 'privacy' for a networked world'. *Proceedings of the CHI Conference on Human Factors in Computing Systems*; New York: ACM Press; 2003. pp. 129–36.

[47] Warren S.D., Brandeis L.D. 'The right to privacy'. *Harvard Law Review*. 1890;**4**(5):193–220.

[48] Westin A. *Privacy and Freedom*. New York: Atheneum; 1967.

[49] Schmidt K., Bannon L. 'Taking CSCW seriously: supporting articulation work'. *Computer Supported Cooperative Work*. 1992;**1**(1):7–40.

[50] Marmor A. 'What is the right to privacy?' *Philosophy & Public Affairs*. 2015;**43**(1):3–26.

[51] Thomson J.J. 'The right to privacy'. *Philosophy and Public Affairs*. 1975;**4**(4):295–314.

[52] Nissenbaum H. 'Privacy as contextual integrity'. *Washington law review*. 2004;**79**(1):119–58.

[53] Petronio S. 'Communication privacy management theory: what do we know about family privacy regulation?' *Journal of Family Theory & Review*. 2010;**2**(3):175–96.

[54] Parsons T. *The Structure of Social Action*. New York: Free Press; 1968.

[55] Garfinkel H., Sacks H. 'On Formal Structures of Practical Action' in McKinney J.D., Teryakian E.A. (eds.). *Theoretical Sociology: Sociology: Perspectives and Development*. New York: Appleton-Century Crofts; 1970. pp. 337–66.

[56] Rawls A. in Garfinkel H. (ed.) *Introduction Ethnomethodology's Program: Working Out Durkheim's Aphorism*. Lanham, Maryland, Rowman: Littlefield Publishers; 2002.

[57] vom Lehn D. 'From Garfinkel's 'experiments in miniature' to the ethnomethodological analysis of interaction'. *Human Studies*. 2019;**42**(2):305–26.

[58] Garfinkel H. *Studies in Ethnomethodology, Englewood Cliffs*. New Jersey: Prentice Hall; 1967.

Chapter 5
Towards an accountable Internet of Things: a call for reviewability

Chris Norval[1], Jennifer Cobbe[1], and Jatinder Singh[1]

As the Internet of Things (IoT) becomes increasingly ubiquitous, concerns are being raised about how IoT systems are being built and deployed. Connected devices will generate vast quantities of data, which drive algorithmic systems and result in real-world consequences. Things will go wrong, and when they do, how do we identify what happened, why they happened and who is responsible? Given the complexity of such systems, where do we even begin?

This chapter outlines aspects of accountability as they relate to IoT, in the context of the increasingly interconnected and data-driven nature of such systems. Specifically, we argue the urgent need for mechanisms (legal, technical and organisational) *that facilitate the review of IoT systems*. Such mechanisms work to support accountability by enabling the relevant stakeholders to better understand, assess, interrogate and challenge the connected environments that increasingly pervade our world.

5.1 Introduction

Our physical environments are becoming increasingly interconnected, automated and data-driven as grand visions of the Internet of Things (IoT) move closer to becoming realised. The IoT involves a range of devices interacting and collaborating to achieve particular goals [1]. We already see examples of the IoT being deployed, including within homes and vehicles [2–4], and across towns and cities [2, 4–8]. The claimed benefits afforded by so-called 'smart' devices have led to considerable interest, with one estimate suggesting that the number of IoT devices could grow from 8 billion in 2019 to 41 billion by 2027 [9].

There is, however, more to the IoT than just these smart devices. The IoT comprises a socio-technical ecosystem of components, systems and organisations involving both technical and human elements. In these interconnected IoT environments

[1]Compliant and Accountable Systems Group, Department of Computer Science and Technology, University of Cambridge, UK

data flow drives everything, in that the flow of data between, through and across systems and organisations works to both integrate them and deliver the overarching functionality [10]. An IoT deployment will often include vast quantities of data coming from a range of local and external sources, including from sensor readings, online services and user inputs, in addition to the data flows that occur across technical components (at various levels of technical abstraction) which drive particular functionalities. These data streams help to form wider algorithmic systems (which include degrees of automation, and may leverage the use of machine learning (ML) models), from which real-world consequences result.

These interactions introduce important socio-technical considerations regarding the wider contexts in which these IoT systems are built and deployed. As these ecosystems become ever more pervasive and complex, a range of devices, manufacturers, data sources, models and online service providers may be involved in automated outcomes, that can have impact at scale. Decisions made by people (e.g. vendors, developers, users and others) about which systems and services to build, deploy and connect with, how these operate, their broader aims and incentives and so forth, all serve to determine these data flows, with a direct impact on system functionality. Moreover, the complexity of these ecosystems means that systems can exhibit emergent properties and behaviours, acting in ways that are not explained by the features of their component parts when considered individually. This raises important questions for how these systems should be governed, and what happens when things inevitably go wrong.

5.1.1   *Accountability*

Algorithmic and data-driven technologies have come under increasing scrutiny in recent years. Reports of high-profile data misuse have increasingly made such systems the subject of legal and regulatory attention [11, 12], leading to calls for *more accountability* in the socio-technical systems that surround us. Put simply, accountability involves apportioning responsibility for a particular occurrence and determining from and to whom any explanation for that occurrence is owed [13]. However, this can prove challenging in an IoT context.

Accountability is often discussed in relation to a single organisation, or in a systems-context as discrete systems, where the actors (individuals, organisations, etc.) involved are pre-known or defined. However, the various components of an IoT ecosystem, including sensors, actuators, hubs, mobile devices, software tools, cloud services and so on, typically do not operate discretely or in isolation. Rather, they are employed as part of a *system-of-systems* [14]. That is, these systems involve interactions with others, forming an assemblage of socio-technical systems [15]. In this way, they are increasingly part of and reliant upon a data-driven supply chain of other (modular) systems, joined together to bring overarching functionality. We already see many such systems-of-systems that are composed of interconnected components; the popularity of cloud (*[anything]-as-a-service*), which provide underpinning and supporting functionality on demand, is a case in point [16].

To illustrate, a given ecosystem may involve a range of devices streaming data to cloud-based ML services to produce new data outputs (a classification), which drives an automated decision. The decision itself then forms an (data) input to another system, which, in turn, results in that system producing an output (actuation command) for a device that works to create a physical interaction with real-world objects or people. An example of such an arrangement, for instance, might be a smart home management system, which receives inputs from various systems (e.g. weather forecast, temperature sensor, traffic congestion), and works to control various aspects of the home (thermostat, windows, alarm clocks, etc.). In practice, an IoT deployment may involve several of these interconnected systems and their data supply chains, encapsulating sensor readings, manual user inputs, the contents of web forms, inputs to or outputs from machine-learned models, batch transfers of datasets, actuation commands, database queries, and more.

The potential complexity of these ecosystems (which may comprise several such supply chains) gives rise to significant accountability challenges, as it becomes increasingly difficult for those who build, deploy, use, audit, oversee or are otherwise affected by these systems to fully understand their workings. It may not always be clear (i) why certain actions occur, (ii) where the information driving particular decisions, actions or functionality originates and, in some cases, (iii) even which entities are involved. Things can and will go wrong, and we may find ourselves increasingly dependent on opaque, 'black box' systems of which we have little oversight. The potential for emergent properties and behaviours in these complex environments further reduces the ability to understand what happened and why.

This chapter explores how greater accountability might be facilitated in the increasingly complex IoT deployments that surround us, arguing that implementing technical and organisational measures to facilitate the holistic review of IoT ecosystems is an important way forward. We begin by elaborating on the challenges that complex systems-of-systems pose to accountability, before outlining the need for reviewability in such deployments. Next, we discuss how reviewability can assist with legal accountability, before setting out some potential benefits for developers and other parties.

We then set out some measures that may help implement reviewability, focusing particularly on *decision provenance*, which concerns recording information regarding decisions, actions and their flow on effects. Finally, we explore a 'smart city' case study that illustrates how reviewability can assist complex IoT ecosystems. In all, we aim to draw more attention to accountability concerns in complex systems-of-systems and argue that more needs to be done in order to facilitate transparency, reviewability and, therefore, accountability regarding the IoT.

5.2   The need for reviewability

The IoT operates as part of a broader socio-technical ecosystem. As IoT deployments become increasingly automated and consequential, it becomes ever more important that they are designed with accountability in mind. In the event of failure or harm, a natural first step is to look at what went wrong and why. In determining legal compliance, it is important to understand how systems are and have been operating. Yet the complexity, opacity, interconnectedness and modularity of these ecosystems pose particular challenges for accountability [17]. Complex data flows across legal, technical and organisational boundaries can produce emergent behaviours and can affect systems in unpredictable ways [10, 14]. An unexpected behaviour or failure in one system or device can propagate throughout the ecosystem, with potentially serious consequences.

There has been some consideration by the technical community of issues of accountability, though these tend to focus on particular technical methods, components or systems (see Section 5.5). Considering accountability by focusing only on particular technical aspects or components of the IoT misses the bigger picture of their context, contingencies, dependencies and of the organisational and human processes around their design, deployment and use. We therefore argue here for a more holistic view of transparency and accountability in these complex socio-technical ecosystems. We term this approach *reviewability*. This encompasses a targeted form of transparency involving technical and organisational logging and record-keeping mechanisms. The purpose is to expose the information necessary to review and assess the functioning and legal compliance of socio-technical systems in a meaningful way and to support accountability (and redress, where appropriate).

5.2.1   Challenges to accountability in socio-technical ecosystems

As we have discussed, an IoT ecosystem is driven by data flows and may involve data moving between any number of different components and entities. As data passes from one entity or component to another (which can involve crossing a technical or organisational boundary), the data flows that drive these interconnected systems will often become invisible or opaque [14, 16]. For example, it may not be clear to a developer how an external AI as a Service (AIaaS) model[a] actually works or how reliable its predictions are. Similarly, it may not always be apparent where data provided by online services come from, or how sensors are calculating and pre-processing data before feeding it to the next component. This loss of *contextual integrity* [19] risks the inadvertent misuse of that data, perhaps losing crucial information regarding how it should be used, information about biases or sampling errors, or other potential problems that could continue to propagate throughout the wider ecosystem.

Though there are methods for logging and ongoing research efforts on explaining technical components, their benefit may be limited in terms of improving accountability in an IoT context (Section 5.5). As we will discuss, there is a need for tracking data as it flows between systems and across boundaries, given the interconnected nature of the IoT [20]. Moreover, even where records of system behaviour

---

[a]This is where a machine learning model is offered as a service, and can be applied by customers to their data on demand, typically as a request-response interaction. Example services include those for detecting objects, faces, converting text-to-speech, etc. [18].

(including data flow) are collected, the usability and utility of this information remains a recognised challenge [21, 22].

Having multiple components involved in a given deployment also increases the number of points of possible failure, and the potential for unpredictable emergent properties and behaviours. This increases the difficulty of determining where issues are occurring. As data flows through an ecosystem, decisions and actions taken by one component might propagate widely, which makes it difficult to trace the source (organisational or technical) and all the consequential (flow-on) effects of an issue. For example, a reading from a faulty sensor could lead to cascading knock-on effects causing significant disruption throughout an IoT deployment, though the relationship of the fault to these consequential effects may not be readily evident given the gaps in time and space [14, 17]. Developers will often lack the means for seeing inside the various systems operated by others that comprise an IoT ecosystem. And although developers might have an understanding of the organisational processes in the development and deployment of their own systems, they are unlikely to have a similar understanding in relation to the components and systems on which their product will depend.

In all, the general opacity surrounding the interconnections between systems, of the technical and organisational processes within and around these systems, and with the general lack of technical means for tracking data flow at such a scale, poses a challenge for improving IoT accountability. Due to these factors, it can be difficult to discern the technical components involved in a given decision or action, why a failure has occurred, and who is responsible when failures do occur [20, 23]. While technical mechanisms for recording the flow of data between and across systems are necessary to identify where failures originated and which entities are responsible, there is a need to make this and other information, from right throughout the entire system lifecycle, meaningfully available across a broad range of stakeholders [24].

Importantly, providing technical transparency on its own is not necessarily sufficient to provide the information required to understand the functioning of complex socio-technical ecosystems. We therefore continue this chapter with a focus on the *reviewability* of IoT systems, components and organisational processes, i.e. providing targeted transparency and accountability mechanisms that allow for a holistic view to be taken of the socio-technical ecosystem as a whole. Auditors and others assessing systems can then hone in on specific systems, components, organisations and their practices where further investigation is required.

5.2.2   *Reviewability*

In view of these challenges to accountability in complex IoT ecosystems, we argue for *reviewability* as an approach for shedding light on socio-technical processes.

From a legal point of view, accountability is often tied to notions of responsibility, liability and transparency; indeed transparency is often a regulatory requirement for identifying responsibility or liability and thus facilitating accountability, as we will discuss in Section 5.3. However, from a legal perspective, transparency does not necessarily mean full transparency over the internal workings of a system, nor

Reviewability

Reviewability involves systematically implementing comprehensive technical and organisational transparency mechanisms that allow the design, deployment and functioning of socio-technical systems and processes to be reviewed as a whole [24]. Reviewable systems are those that are designed and operate in such a way as to record and expose (though means such as, for example, record-keeping and logging) the contextually appropriate information necessary to allow technical systems and organisational processes to be comprehensively interrogated and assessed for legal compliance, that they are operating appropriately and so on. This targeted, holistic form of transparency supports meaningful accountability of systems, processes and organisations to whomever is relevant in a given context (auditors, investigators, regulators, users, other developers and so on).

is it limited only to technical components and processes. Instead, the transparency required in law often involves information about the entities involved, high-level information about what is happening with data or about what systems are doing (rather than necessarily the specifics of how they function), and information about the risks of using those systems [17].

In other words, legal mechanisms for accountability depend upon the ability of stakeholders to meaningfully review technical and organisational systems and processes (partially or as a whole) in order to determine which person or organisation is responsible for a particular system, device or process, its effects, and from (and to) whom an explanation or redress is owed [17]. This may or may not involve exploring the inner workings of particular technologies or algorithms, as tends to be the focus of the technical research community. It could equally involve examining the broader socio-technical processes in and around a technical system itself. Indeed, there is debate about the degree to which exposing the details of code and algorithmic models actually helps with accountability [24, 25]. Therefore, instead of exposing the inner workings of technical systems and devices, achieving reviewability of IoT ecosystems requires (i) technical and organisational mechanisms for making transparent the connections and data flows across these entire ecosystems, as well as (ii) information relating to decisions made in design, deployment, operation and during investigations, so as to indicate the context in which they are operating, their effects, and the entities involved (of which there may be a number). To support meaningful accountability, the information recorded about these systems and processes should be *contextually appropriate* [24], that is: information which is *relevant* to the kinds of accountability involved; *accurate*, in that is correct, complete and representative; *proportionate* to the level of transparency required and *comprehensible* by those to whom an account will likely be owed.

In practice, the information provided by reviewable systems will include that indicating who is involved, the nature of their role, how data are being processed and how data flow between systems for each component in the IoT ecosystem. In an

IoT context, reviewability could mean device vendors and service providers keeping records of, for example, the systems they are connecting to and interacting with (in terms of input and output), what choices were made about which kinds of data to process and how it should be processed, information about assessments for security, data protection and other legal obligations, and information about the design, training and testing of models (where applicable). At its most basic, this kind of information may indicate that Organisation B used an online service (e.g. AIaaS) provided by Organisation C, and that the response from that prediction was then fed into a service provided by Organisation D. But an analysis of even this high-level information could also provide an indication of where the source (either technical or otherwise) of a particular issue may lie. In this sense, such information can make it easier to review what went wrong (particularly for non-experts), prompting more targeted investigations involving the inner workings of particular components within the IoT ecosystem once they have been identified, of which reviewability mechanisms that provide more detailed and granular information will facilitate.

Of course, implementing reviewability to support the transparency and accountability of socio-technical systems introduces challenges of its own, given that what is meaningful for one stakeholder, such as a technical auditor, may be very different to that of another, such as a user. There is a need to ensure that the information provided by various transparency mechanisms is contextually appropriate such that it is useful for and can be interpreted by the likely audience [24]. This might involve, for example, different ways of presenting or processing various kinds of information for a broad range of stakeholders, as we discuss below.

While transparency as a general principle is important, it cannot in and of itself solve problems. Organisations need to think more about targeted transparency to support accountability from the requirements stage, all the way up to deployment, operation and beyond. Regardless of the approach to enabling meaningful transparency, reviewability should be a core consideration for those involved in the development and operation of IoT ecosystems. In the following sections, we explore some legal and technical ways forward that could help towards this aim.

5.3   The legal dimension

The complex, interconnected and data-driven nature of the IoT ecosystem poses particular challenges for legal accountability [17, 26]. Broadly speaking, these challenges come from two sources: (1) the lack of visibility over data flows in interconnected environments, which makes it difficult to know where in a system and with whom a problem originates and (2) the lack of visibility over the technical and organisational systems and processes of various entities within that ecosystem, which makes it difficult to assess their compliance with legal requirements and obligations.

From a legal point of view, each entity in an IoT ecosystem could potentially be accountable for the functioning of their systems and devices: to customers and users; the vendors of other IoT devices and systems; to regulators and other oversight bodies; to law enforcement agencies; and to courts and dispute resolution bodies; among others. For each of these, transparency as a general concept is unlikely to provide much benefit, nor is opening up code or the internal workings of technical systems likely to assist in every case (although it will, of course, in some [27, 28]). Rather, the information necessary to meet accountability and disclosure requirements, and obligations established in law, is more likely to relate (i) to technical and organisational processes, (ii) to data flows given the nature of the IoT and (iii) to understanding what happened, when, why and with what effect [17].

For example, data protection law, such as the EU's General Data Protection Regulation (GDPR) [29], establishes accountability mechanisms and requirements for various actors involved in processing personal data (defined broadly in GDPR to include any data from which an individual can be identified, whether directly or indirectly, either from that data alone or when combined with other data).[b] IoT ecosystems will often involve a flow of personal data, and *processing* means any operation or set of operations performed on that data.[c] Under GDPR, certain information is required to be provided by data controllers (the entities that determine the purposes and means of processing[d]) to data subjects (the individuals to whom personal data relates[e]) about the processing of their personal data. Data processors (who process personal data on behalf and under the instruction of data controllers[f]) are obliged to facilitate auditing of their processing by the relevant data controller. Data controllers can be obliged to provide information about processing to and facilitate auditing by supervisory authorities (national data protection regulators). Controllers will also need to know where personal data has been obtained from, under what circumstances and on what conditions.

Beyond data protection law, accountability requirements could also arise from a variety of other sources [26]; product safety law, for instance, could require device vendors to supply customers and oversight bodies with information. The adjudication and enforcement of contractual disputes could require disclosure of information about technical and organisational processes to counterparties and to courts. Criminal investigations could require the provision of information to law enforcement agencies.

In each case, approaching transparency through the lens of reviewability could assist in meeting these obligations, and help communicate legally relevant, contextually appropriate information to customers, users and technical partners, as well as the appropriate legal, regulatory and other oversight authorities. Although reviewability could assist across various legal frameworks, we now explore three general ways in particular where a reviewability approach to accountability would be legally beneficial: compliance and obligation management; oversight and regulatory audit; and liability and legal investigation. It is worth noting that while we have delineated

---

[b]GDPR, Art. 4(1), recital 26
[c]GDPR, Art. 4(2)
[d]GDPR, Art. 4(7)
[e]GDPR, Art. 4(1)
[f]GDPR, Art. 4(8)

these benefits, they are interrelated. As much of the IoT ecosystem will involve personal data, we use the transparency and accountability requirements and obligations established in GDPR as examples throughout.

5.3.1   *Compliance and obligation management*

As alluded to above, a reviewability approach to accountability (such as by using record-keeping, logging or other information capture mechanisms for technical and organisational processes) can assist those responsible for socio-technical ecosystems (such as the IoT) to comply with their legal and regulatory (and other) obligations [20, 30].

Where IoT ecosystems process personal data (perhaps, for example, containing names, user profiles/accounts, photographs or video of people, voice recordings or any other information that can be linked to an individual), and therefore come within the remit of data protection law, GDPR would typically consider those involved in operating the various aspects of that ecosystem to be data controllers. This will therefore place upon them certain legal obligations, including making them responsible for meeting GDPR's requirements and obligations, and for demonstrating compliance.[g] In this context, reviewability would not necessarily involve recording the personal data itself (a potentially significant data protection issue and privacy violation), but would involve metadata about organisational processes and technical processing. Organisations found to be in breach of the GDPR can face significant penalties, including warnings, fines of up to the greater of €20m or 4% of annual global turnover, and bans on processing.[h]

In the first instance, data controllers are obliged to take technical and organisational measures to ensure and be able to demonstrate compliance with GDPR.[i] Record-keeping and logging would assist data controllers with implementing GDPR's data protection principles and with showing that they have taken steps to do so. For instance, the purpose limitation principle requires that personal data be collected for specific purposes and only processed in a way compatible with those purposes.[j] The keeping of records, logs and other relevant information would provide controllers with relevant information on the purposes for which personal data was collected, and helps ensure that the data are only processed accordingly. Implementing such measures would also assist with fulfilling data subject rights, such as those to obtain copies of the personal data being processed[k] and, in some circumstances, to require its deletion.[l] Moreover, maintaining records of technical and organisational processes around the design and deployment of systems would help controllers demonstrate to supervisory authorities that processing is in fact taking place in line with GDPR's requirements and that rights have been fulfilled.

[g]GDPR, Art. 5
[h]GDPR, Art. 83
[i]GDPR, Art. 24
[j]GDPR, Art. 5(1)(b)
[k]GDPR, Art. 15
[l]GDPR, Art. 17

In advance of processing, data controllers will, in many situations, need to undertake a Data Protection Impact Assessment (DPIA).[m] This consists of a broad assessment of the risks posed by the proposed processing to the rights and freedoms to data subjects and of the steps taken by the controller to mitigate those risks. Where the DPIA indicates a high risk, controllers are obliged to consult with the supervisory authority before proceeding and to provide them with the information contained in the DPIA.[n] Reviewability can greatly assist with undertaking the kind of holistic analysis of processing and its risks required for DPIAs, by demonstrating how and whether any mitigating measures have actually been implemented, and with assessing on an ongoing basis whether processing is in fact being undertaken in line with the DPIA.

It is worth noting that controllers and processors are also already obliged in many circumstances to keep records of processing.[o] Controllers should record, among other things, the purposes of processing, the categories of data subjects and of personal data, the categories of those to whom data will be disclosed and a general description of technical and organisational security measures. Processors should record, among other things, the name and contact details of processors, the categories of processing and a general description of their technical and organisational security measures. Through comprehensive logging and record-keeping of technical and organisational systems and processes, reviewability can help controllers and processors fulfil these obligations and others.

Reviewability may also be of use in assisting compliance with future regulations, for example, the proposed ePrivacy Regulation [31], which establishes requirements on the use of some non-personal data. They can similarly assist in managing a broader range of legal, regulatory and other obligations (soft law, codes of practice and so on). For instance, where contractual obligations exist between entities, knowledge of their respective technical and organisational processes (and of the nature of data flow between parties) could make it possible to ensure and demonstrate that data are being processed in a legally appropriate way. And information on the selection of datasets, and on the sources and lineage of data used for analytics and ML, might assist with issues of unfairness and discrimination [32].

5.3.2 Regulatory oversight and audit

Reviewability also has much potential to aid the auditing and oversight activities of regulators, given that reviewability entails generating detailed information for assisting oversight that may otherwise be unavailable. As noted previously, data controllers and processors are obliged to maintain extensive records of processing. Data controllers are also obliged to undertake various assessments (in relation to data protection by design, for example, or for implementing security measures, carrying out DPIAs and so on), to use only processors who can comply with GDPR

---

[m]GDPR, Art. 35
[n]GDPR, Art. 36
[o]GDPR, Art. 30

and to consult with supervisory authorities in certain circumstances. Supervisory authorities are themselves empowered to audit data controllers, to inspect their systems, to access to their records and to require from controllers any other information necessary to perform the supervisory authority's tasks, including to investigate controllers' compliance with GDPR.[p]

Engineering socio-technical systems to be reviewable through mechanisms for record-keeping, logging and otherwise capturing information about technical and organisational processes would thus facilitate audit and oversight by supervisory authorities. Indeed, many of the potential legal benefits of reviewability discussed previously would also apply to regulatory oversight more generally. Moreover, recording information about data flows would allow data protection regulators to assess whether IoT ecosystems are legally compliant, and match that which was described by controllers. More broadly, this information would help supervisory authorities to assess whether data controllers and processors are managing their relationship as required, have the appropriate data management (and other) practices in place, and have taken the appropriate actions in relation to any specific incidents such as data breaches.

5.3.3   Liability and legal investigation

IoT systems have real-world impacts, including direct physical-world consequences given that IoT systems are typically people-facing and actuators can feature throughout. This means that questions of civil liability or criminal responsibility could arise where harm or injury is caused [17, 26]. Reviewability could therefore be particularly helpful in assessing liability and undertaking legal or criminal investigations. Where harm is caused by a system failure, comprehensive records and logs would allow the circumstances, causal behaviours, factors and consequences of the failure to be reviewed, determined and liability established. In complex, interconnected environments, records and logs about data flows to, from and between devices and systems could also help identify which system caused that harm. This, thereby, helps to identify the component (and entity) responsible and potentially liable for that harm, and can assist in holding them to account. This kind of reviewability information may even help absolve systems designers, operators or those otherwise involved from responsibility, by providing evidence demonstrating that the right decisions were made and actions were taken. For example, controllers and processors are exempt from liability for damage caused by infringements of GDPR if they can prove that they were not responsible for the infringement (such as where a controller can demonstrate that their processor acted unlawfully, for instance).[q]

[p]GDPR, Arts. 57-58
[q]GDPR, Art. 82(3)

As such, the information provided by implementing reviewability is useful for multiple actors in interconnected IoT ecosystems to vendors, in helping them manage their liability exposure; to users, in taking action and obtaining redress where harm has been caused by a product; to courts, in adjudicating claims in tort or contract; as well as to regulators and law enforcement as they investigate potential regulatory or criminal violations. Vendors and others could contractually require this kind of record-keeping and logging (of technical and organisational processes and data flows, both within organisations and across boundaries). This could give them a mechanism for monitoring how data are used, potentially in real-time, and enable action where data are being used in a way that is inappropriate or prohibited by law or by contract.

5.4 The broader benefits of systems review

In an IoT context, there are clear benefits of reviewability, in addition to those legal as just discussed. In Section 5.2, we described how the complex, interconnected, data-driven and multi-stakeholder nature of the IoT can result in transparency challenges at the technical level, making it difficult to determine how systems are designed, deployed and functioning. The opacity of these complex systems-of-systems arrangements means that the information necessary to properly review their functioning may not be available, which can significantly hinder accountability processes.

Information about the organisations, components and data flows driving IoT ecosystems therefore has an important role to play in supporting review processes. That is, certain details and related information about IoT systems and components, and their design, deployment and operation (which includes workflows, business processes and other organisational practices), will often be necessary for enabling proper oversight, audit, interrogation and inspection. Moreover, the *ongoing* review of the socio-technical systems is important. This is because the complexity, interconnectedness and long-lived nature of IoT ecosystems make it more likely that they will exhibit emergent properties and behaviours, potentially giving rise to unforeseen or unforeseeable problems.

In short, information about the design, deployment and functioning of the socio-technical systems that comprise the IoT facilitates their review. This includes whether they are designed and behaving appropriately, and for issues to be unpacked and consequences dealt with when they arise. This brings additional benefits to the legal aspects described in Section 5.3 for a range of actors in an IoT ecosystem.

5.4.1 Building, operating and managing systems

Implementing technical and organisational measures for logging, record-keeping or otherwise capturing information of systems increases their reviewability. This brings a range of benefits for technologists, who have a clear interest in overseeing the systems they build and operate. This is because details on how systems are designed, deployed, function, behave, interact, operate and so forth provide information relevant for testing, monitoring, maintaining and improving the quality of those systems, while helping them to meet and manage their responsibilities and obligations.

Specifically, greater visibility over the technical and organisational aspects of systems, and their interconnections with others, assists technologists with investigations, enhancing their ability to review errors and systems failures when they (inevitably) occur. That is, such information helps support processes of repair and debugging. Moreover, information about run-time behaviour also enables more proactive steps to be taken, where details of system operation can allow the identification and mitigation of certain issues in advance of them becoming problematic (e.g. by enabling the identification of abnormal deviations in system behaviour, or through run-time reaction mechanisms, alerts or automatic countermeasures that are triggered where unexpected events or interactions occur). This is particularly important given that, as discussed previously, IoT systems can exhibit emergent properties and behaviours. Further, in the IoT, components have the potential to be used or reused in ways that were not envisaged by the original designers. For instance, a temperature sensor in a building designed for climate control could suddenly be used to influence health wearables. It follows that the ability for technologists to undertake ongoing review will be crucial for ensuring appropriate system behaviour, while providing insight into (any) emerging properties.

5.4.2   Facilitating oversight activities

As we have described, the lack of technical information in an IoT context has the propensity to hinder investigations. While reviewability promises benefits for legal and regulatory oversight bodies (see Section 5.3.2), information about technical and organisational systems can also assist the activities of other overseers, such as civil society organisations, trade-sector groups or those internal to a technology firm. This is by giving (i) information on the nature of systems and their behaviour and (ii) insight into the practices of their designers and operators.

In this way, information on systems helps accountability processes, by providing evidence or lines for investigation that can assist overseers in determining whether the technology-related actions and measures taken were appropriate (thereby building the foundations for recourse where they are not). This can include information about design and development, as well as run-time systems behaviour, and details of the reviews and audits undertaken. In addition to supporting (ex-post) investigation, technical processes that produce streams of data on system operation also pave the way for more active and responsive oversight regimes. This is where certain system behaviours or events could trigger alerts, warnings or otherwise bring certain information to an overseers attention, and with timely action, may serve to mitigate the potential severity of outcomes.

5.4.3   Better informing users

The information derived from IoT systems can potentially also assist end-users by helping them to make better-informed decisions about whether or how they interact with a given deployment. Although overloading users with information and options is not a desirable or useful outcome [33], there may be opportunities for a greater degree of user empowerment. If a user could meaningfully and reliably know in advance that engaging with (having their data flow into) a particular system could, for example, (i) result in certain decisions being made that may have particular undesired consequences or (ii) involve data flowing to an undesired entity (such as a certain advertisement network), then the user could take reasonable steps to avoid engaging with such a system [14]. Proactive measures are again possible, such as where user policies might work to constrain particular information flows [20], or to keep users informed of any change in circumstance, thereby enabling them (manually or perhaps automatically) to respond. One can imagine, for instance, users being automatically told of changes in policy or system operation, for example, where the records of data flows indicate an online service suddenly engaging a new advertising network.

5.5   Technical mechanisms for supporting reviewability

Technology has a key role to play in supporting reviewability, as it provides the means to capture or otherwise produce information or records about systems, both about their design and during operation. As we have argued, reviews are assisted through mechanisms that can enable more (relevant) transparency over systems.

Though the idea of capturing information about systems is nothing new, much of the focus so far has been on the design and engineering phases. Logging and debugging frameworks, for example, are generally aimed at a technical audience, particularly those developing or administering systems. These tend to focus narrowly on particular technical specifics. There has been less consideration of recording information (i) to support broader accountability regimes (of which, we argue, reviewability enables) and (ii) in a manner appropriate for the broad vision for IoT.

That said, accountability is an area of increasing attention by the technical research community (e.g. see [17, 21]). Accountability is a term that gained traction, particularly in the machine learning community where the focus has predominately been on the explainability of machine learning models and decisions. While such work is important, perhaps particularly so for machine learning (engineering/testing) processes [34], a model does not operate in isolation. Rather, it exists as part of a broader socio-technical system [24, 35]. This broader aspect requires consideration, and work in the community is beginning to expand and recognise this [24]. One example is *datasheets for datasets* [36], which involves capturing metadata that describes the nature of datasets, including how the data were collated, pre-processed, the legal basis for its processing (e.g. consent), etc. Similarly, *model cards* [37] record various details about trained models, such as how they perform across a variety of different conditions and/or demographic groups, alongside the context in which they are intended to be used. The idea is to provide more information, for instance, to enable a fuller interrogation of model design (e.g. how it was trained), help inform engineers and investigators, for example, as to whether the dataset or model is (or was) appropriate for a particular use, give information about usage restrictions (e.g. consent) and so on.

Considering the broader systems context is important in the IoT; IoT ecosystems are complex, interconnected, dynamic, multi-actor, socio-technical environments, which are long-lived and can potentially elicit emergent behaviours not designed for or previously envisaged. As we have discussed, greater visibility over the interconnections and assemblages of systems is important for increasing accountability. Therefore, a natural starting point for reviewability is technologies which assist in uncovering, or 'mapping out', the (ongoing) nature of IoT ecosystems. This requires mechanisms for capturing information about components, systems and their interactions (data flows) that comprise IoT systems.

Particularly important in an IoT context are the ongoing interactions (data exchanges) with other technical components, as these provide a foundation for both (i) describing system behaviour (the how and why) and (ii) the actors involved (the who). However, mapping this represents a particular challenge given that while the IoT is data-driven, the visibility over the movement of data currently tends to be limited to particular scopes; it is often difficult to trace what happens to data once it moves across a technical (e.g. between/across different software or devices) or administrative (to another organisation, department, etc.) boundary.

Towards such a mapping, provenance mechanisms show real potential [20, 23, 30, 38, 39]. *Provenance* concerns capturing information describing data: it can involve recording the data's lineage, including where it came from, where it moved to and the associated dependencies, contexts (e.g. those environmental and computational) and processing steps [40].[r]

To reiterate, the IoT is data-driven, where functionality is brought about through the interactions (exchanges of data) between systems components. As such, provenance methods can be useful for reviewability as they entail taking a 'follow-the-data' approach, whereby information regarding the data flows in the IoT deployment can indicate (i) how systems behave, (ii) what led (or leads) to particular occurrences or consequences, as well as (iii) the components (and therefore the actors) involved [20, 23]. Data regarding the information flows driving systems also provide the foundation, paving the way for new accountability-related tools, methods and analysis [17].

In line with this, we have developed the concept of *decision provenance* [14], which can help in mapping out complex ecosystems. We argue this has real potential in the IoT space, accounting for its interconnectedness, and the role of automation (including the use of ML) in such environments. It works by recording what (and how) data moves from one system (device, model, service, etc.) to another. We now present an overview of decision provenance to indicate the potential for technical methods which can assist review and support accountability regimes more generally.

---

[r] See [40, 41] for more details on data provenance.

5.5.1   *Decision provenance: Exposing the decision pipelines*

Provenance is an active area of research [41] and is commonly applied in research contexts to assist in reproducibility by recording the data, workflows and computation of scientific processes [41, 42]. The potential for provenance to assist with specific information management (compliance) obligations has previously been considered [20, 23, 30, 38, 39], though these often focus on a particular technical aspect, be it representation or capture. However, the use of data provenance methods for general systems-related accountability concerns represents an emerging area warranting further consideration.

Decision provenance is a response to (i) the concerns around accountability for automated, algorithmic and data-driven systems (which naturally comprise the IoT), (ii) the increasingly interconnected nature of technical deployments, where functionality is driven through data exchanges, (iii) the current lack of visibility over data as it moves across technical and administrative boundaries and (iv) the potential of provenance methods in this space.

Specifically, decision provenance concerns recording information about the data flowing throughout a system, as relevant for accountability concerns. It involves capturing details and metadata relating to data, and of the system components through which data moves. This can include how data was processed and used, who the data comes from or goes to (by virtue of the components involved), and other appropriate contextual information, such as system configurations, business processes, workflow state, etc.

Decision provenance is predicated on the idea that it is the flow of data and the interactions between components in a system that drives system functionality. Its name is in recognition that the actions or decisions taken in a systems context, be they manual (e.g. initiated by users) or automated (e.g. resulting from the application of an ML model), entail a series of steps leading up to a particular happening, as well as the cascading consequences. All of these steps entail data flow (at some level) about which information can be recorded. Indeed, this characterisation directly accords with the grand visions of the IoT.

The purpose of decision provenance is to expose *decision pipelines*, by providing records regarding the happenings leading up to a particular decision/action, and the cascading consequences. This can be at design time (e.g. by capturing information about a machine learning process, such as the data sources comprising a dataset for model training), at run-time (e.g. capturing information about the data flowing to particular entities, and the decisions being made by algorithmic components), or at review-time (e.g. capturing information about how systems are audited or investigated). In this way, it can operate to provide a broader view of system behaviour and the interactions between the actors involved.

Decision provenance can assist various reviewability aims in an IoT context. That is, decision pipelines can allow, for example, those building and deploying systems to improve their quality and to identify points of failure, while empowering others by offering more insight into the nature of the systems and data that is beyond their direct control [17, 20, 23].

Decision provenance

Decision provenance concerns the use and means for provenance mechanisms to assist accountability considerations in algorithmic systems. Specifically, decision provenance involves (i) providing information on the nature, contexts and processing of the data flows and interconnections leading up to a decision or action, and the flow-on effects and (ii) also how such information can be leveraged for better system design, inspection, validation and operational (run-time) behaviour. In this way, decision provenance helps expose the *decision pipelines* in order to make visible the nature of the inputs to and cascading consequences of any decision or action (at design or run-time), alongside the entities involved, systems-wide (see Figure 5.1).

The broad aim is to help increase levels of accountability, both by providing the information and evidence for investigation, questioning and recourse, and by providing information which can be used to proactively take steps towards reducing and mitigating risks and concerns, and facilitating legal compliance and user empowerment. For more details on decision provenance, see [14].

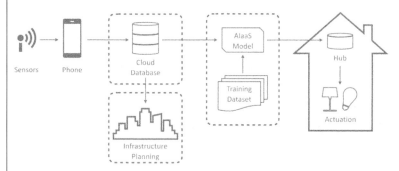

Figure 5.1   *An example IoT application, whereby sensor readings work to trigger an actuation in a smart home, with some data feeding to a city council's planning service. Even a simple scenario involves data flowing across a range of technical and organisational boundaries, as each arrow indicates. Decision provenance works to capture information about these data flows, thereby supporting review.*

Further, decision provenance, in providing information on data flow, also paves the way for more proactive accountability measures. This is because the provenance data captured regarding the nature of the data flowing into, within, and beyond a system provides the foundation for particular actions or behaviour to be taken in response. These responses may be human or organisational, or perhaps technical through pre-defined automated, event-based tooling [20]. Such mechanisms pave the way for proactive actions to assist compliance and obligation management [20]. For instance, information about data flows could be used to trigger particular compliance operations; such as to automatically report data breaches to the relevant authorities; to screen and filter out data based on compliance criteria (e.g. data past an expiry date or use); to not act on inputs that may have come from, or through, an unreliable entity [30]; or to automatically prevent data flows that are unexpected (in terms of a pre-defined management policy [20]). Such approaches may be particularly useful for IoT applications given their potential to exhibit emergent nature.

We present decision provenance to illustrate how provenance methods show promise in complex systems environments, such as the IoT. Provenance will, by no means itself, *solve* accountability challenges (nor will any technical measure). However, it does show potential in supporting review, by exposing and enabling the ongoing monitoring of the relations, interactions and dependencies of such systems where such visibility may not otherwise exist.

5.5.2   Technical challenges

We have outlined how information on the nature of systems is important for supporting review processes, with provenance representing but one way forward for capturing such information in an IoT context. Given accountability has received little attention by the technical community, there are a number of research challenges and opportunities for tools and methods that support accountability regimes [14, 17].

One key consideration is performance and scalability. Record keeping has the potential to be onerous, not least as there may be range of actors interested in reviewing such information. This means that a wealth of technical detail will often be required to satisfy the broad range of aims that they may have. It is therefore important to consider carefully what and how much information is likely to actually be needed to provide meaningful accounts of system behaviour (the relevant and proportionate dimensions of contextually appropriate information). Here, considerations include the overheads imposed on devices, especially given the heterogeneous nature of components and their capabilities in the IoT space. Also crucial for deployment are architectural considerations, including policy regimes that can flexibly determine what, when, where and how data are captured, stored and transmitted. Similarly, mechanisms are needed that are capable of working reliably and efficiently across both technical and administrative boundaries, and are able to aggregate or resolve data from across these.

Further, for a review to be meaningful, it must be based on complete and reliable information (the accurate dimension of contextually appropriate information). This can be a challenge in an IoT context, where components may be operated by different entities, with different aims. This means the information relevant for review might come from various sources, be they different technical components (potentially operating at different levels of technical abstraction), by different entities, and potentially requiring supplementation with non-technical (out-of-band) detail. Mechanisms for resolving and aligning captured information is an area requiring consideration. Similarly, the risks and incentives in an accountability context are complex, meaning that the records themselves can pose an organisational burden given that information might relate to their responsibilities, and has the potential to be used against them (as part of a recourse mechanism). Means for ensuring the integrity and validity of not only the technical information provided, but also the mechanisms that capture, manage and present that information are therefore important considerations.

Related is that capturing information of systems is essentially a form of surveillance. This bears consideration, as the information captured might be inherently sensitive, be it personal data, representing confidential business processes, or generally requiring a stringent management regime. Mechanisms that help ensure that only the appropriate parties are able to view the right information in the right circumstances is an important area for consideration and research.

Usability is another key consideration; as we have made clear for a review to be effective, the information of technical system *must be meaningful* for reviewers (the comprehensible dimension of contextually appropriate information). However, one challenge in this space is dealing with the complexity of the technical information (systems provenance information, for example, can quickly become extremely complex [42–45]), as well as how detailed technical information can be made accessible and understandable. Tools that facilitate the interrogation and representation of technical details will be crucial for facilitating meaningful review in an IoT context, though further work is required to explore the presentation of technical details for accountability purposes.

As such, there are real opportunities for human-computer interaction (HCI) research methods to be employed and extended to assist with the usability and interpretability of audit information. Through such means, the tools and techniques available can better support the aims and literacies of the various actors (technical experts, regulators, users, etc.) in conducting a review. Though there has been some consideration of this in certain contexts (e.g. in some specific provenance cases [22, 43, 44, 46–48]), there appears real scope for more general explorations into such concerns. The development of standards and ontologies could assist (e.g. [49] describes an ontology for the GDPR) with both the management and interpretation of information for review.

5.6   Reviewability in practice: A smart city

We now use an example of a smart city, a common IoT scenario, to illustrate at a high level how methods supporting reviewability relate to broader accountability concerns.

Smart cities aim to make better use of the public resources, increasing the quality of the services offered to the citizens [50], and the IoT is often seen as integral to achieving such functionality [51]. Some commonly considered examples include the automation of home security [2], traffic rerouting [4, 7, 8], vehicle control [3, 4] and disaster management [2, 5, 6]. Such deployments may involve data and interactions from a wide range of sensors (infrastructural and/or mobile), devices and actuators, online services (cloud storage, AIaaS), etc., which may be personally, privately or publicly operated. Naturally, a large number of actors may be involved, exchanging and processing data in order to achieve some overarching functionality.

Importantly, while the boundaries of an IoT application may appear clear and well-defined (at least to those that operate them), in practice they will often interact (communicate and exchange data) with other systems either to provide the expected functionality, or perhaps to be used and reused in ways beyond what may have been originally intended. For example, information may be collected independently by home, vehicle and mobile sensors, which might interact with deployments within public and private spaces (e.g. for automation, security, insurance, billing), which may in turn feed data into broader algorithmic systems and services (energy grid, emergency services, public transport, etc.), all of which may result in decisions and actions with real-world consequences.

In these complex systems arrangements, any number of things could potentially go wrong; a data breach could see the release of personal data, automated actions could be erroneously taken, inferences could be made on incorrect information and so on. Yet, given the ability for such issues to cascade throughout an IoT ecosystem, the true extent of the impact may not always be clear. As we have argued, the ability to review such systems (and their role at each step in the process) may be instrumental in identifying who was involved, how such incidents occurred, and any 'knock-on' effects. We now explore how such an investigation might take place, and how the ability to review IoT ecosystems can be leveraged to provide legal and operational benefits alike.

5.6.1   A traffic incident

Consider a traffic incident occurring in a smart city. While walking to a sporting event, a pedestrian crosses the road at a busy set of traffic lights and is struck and injured by a vehicle. A witness immediately calls an ambulance, which is dispatched to the scene of the incident, but takes a very long time to arrive. Given the nature of the smart city ecosystem, a regulator commissions an investigation to discover what parts of the IoT infrastructure may have contributed to the incident, what went wrong and who (if anyone) may be liable.

Speaking to those involved, the investigator gains three initial lines of inquiry: (i) the injured pedestrian claims that the driver ran a red light; (ii) one witness commented on how dark the streetlights were, despite it being a busy area with lots of vehicles and pedestrians, and questioned whether that might have affected visibility; (iii) the ambulance driver noted that they had been in that area earlier, but had been redirected away shortly before the incident occurred. In all cases, these three potential threads entail interactions with the smart city's infrastructure.

What role did the driver play?

The injured pedestrian had indicated that the driver ran a red light. However, the driver claims that they were not at fault, the argument being that their vehicle is one by CarNet, a highly popular manufacturer of networked 'smart cars', and could therefore not have breached the traffic rules. CarNet is known to use complex AI systems to detect and inform of hazards on the road, in collaboration with a mesh network of all nearby CarNet vehicles, and autonomously applies the brakes and other countermeasures to avoid accidents. Since the vehicle did not detect the hazard (the pedestrian), the driver believed that they couldn't have been at fault, and that the pedestrian must have suddenly and unexpectedly attempted to cross the road at a dangerous time.

Given that CarNet has built their systems to be reviewable, they retain extensive records about the design of their cars' systems, as well as ensuring each car produces logs of their operation. Log files containing certain information on how systems are functioning are sent to CarNet (including whether systems are operating correctly and sensors are reporting in line with expected parameters), however, some data (such as personal data, including information on vehicle movements and camera feeds) remain stored locally on each car. CarNet has also secured contractual obligations throughout their decision supply chain, ensuring that third-party suppliers (on which their vehicles depend) also have record keeping practices in place. The result is a high degree of oversight and reviewability over how CarNet's vehicles operate on the road.

The investigator reviews CarNet's records, which indicate that the car's systems and sensors were fully operational, and logs retrieved from the car in question indicate that there were four CarNet vehicles nearby at the time of the incident, which shared information about potential hazards at the particular area where the incident occurred. Looking more in-depth at the operational logs retrieved from the car (including camera footage fed into the car's AI system, and network communications sent from other vehicles), the investigator determines that the traffic light was indeed red; however, none of the vehicles detected any pedestrians or other hazards near to, or present on, the road.

Through reviewing the data from the car, the investigator also learns that CarNet vehicles work by using an object recognition model, which takes camera footage from their vehicles and determines the location of pedestrians and other vehicles on the road. This model is built and operated by CloudVision through their cloud-based AIaaS service, though the vehicle uses a locally stored version which is periodically updated from CloudVision's servers. The investigator notes that the model has not been updated in seven months and this was initiated by the mechanic, the last time the car was serviced. Decision provenance records from the car demonstrate that the object recognition model (as indicated by records of its outputs) had failed to detect either the red light or the pedestrian from the camera feeds sent to it. Speaking to CarNet, while they concede that the records show that their system had failed to detect the hazard prior to the incident, they argue that the driver should have been regularly updating their AI software in order to improve how it operates. They also argue that their interventions are meant as a last resort, that their systems are merely to support drivers and that the driver should have been paying more attention and taken action to avoid the incident.

The investigation then turns to CloudVision's role in the incident. Given their contractual obligations with CarNet to implement reviewability, CloudVision retains extensive documentation and logs over their service. This allows the investigator to perform an in-depth review of their object recognition model through using techniques discussed in the algorithmic accountability literature (e.g. [11]), including looking at the datasheets [36] of the datasets used to train the model, and the model card [37] for its performance benchmarks across different conditions. The investigator finds that the model was not adequately trained to handle low light scenarios, and its ability to accurately recognise objects decreased significantly when presented dark images. This indicates that their models would not be properly equipped for the low levels of street lighting that were observed at the time of the incident.

CloudVision were contacted, but claim that they were not responsible; they have their own conditions of use which specify that their models should be updated on a regular basis. CarNet's vehicles should therefore have been frequently updating to the latest version automatically, as opposed to relying on the driver manually looking for updates. Their change logs and model cards indicate that a recent update had improved the model's ability to classify objects in low light conditions, but their guidance for developers still recommends that other complementary or redundancy measures be employed where situations of low light may occur. CloudVision also produced records showing that these usage restrictions were reflected in the contract they have with CarNet, and that they previously discussed issues of low light with CarNet, but the distributed nature of the model (i.e. they run locally, on-vehicle) meant that CloudVision had limited oversight over when and how it was used once deployed.

Having holistically reviewed the records and logs made by CarNet and CloudVision about their processes and systems, the investigator concludes that while the driver may have been at fault, there was also a failure in CarNet's system, which did not employ automated braking or counter measures since the pedestrian and the red light were not detected. This was determined to be due to CarNet vehicles being able to function using an an outdated version of CloudVision's object recognition service, which did not operate appropriately in low light conditions, and identified failures in CarNet's processes that relied on drivers manually updating their vehicles software. However, the abnormally low levels of street lighting on the road at the time of the incident may have also contributed.

Why were the street lights dimmed?
The investigator learns that the management of the street lighting on the road of the incident was recently outsourced to SmartLight Inc., a supplier of automated street lighting solutions that vary the brightness of the lights according to the levels of activity (busyness) in the area. On reviewing the street lighting system, the investigator discovers that the service works by retrieving external information about the number of pedestrians and vehicles present on the street, which is obtained through CloudMap's popular mapping service. Through SmartLight's log files, the investigator determines that the mapping service had indicated that no vehicles or

pedestrians were present at the time of the incident, which led to SmartLight's system determining that the street lights should be dimmed in line with the Council's desire to conserve electricity. However, the camera footage from the vehicle clearly shows that the area was busy, and therefore CloudMap's information was incorrect. Asking SmartLight about the reliability of CloudMap, they explain that they have never had any past problems with the service, and that they had therefore not implemented any back up data sources or contingency plans for when the mapping service fails to supply accurate information.

In considering CloudMap's mapping service, the investigator can see that their pedestrian and vehicle density information is crowdsourced through the mobile devices and vehicles that have the mapping application installed. This data is aggregated to determine where congestion is high and where delays are likely. CloudMap is approached regarding the discrepancy, who (after checking their release schedule) inform the investigator that they had temporarily rolled out an update that appears to have negatively affected their cloud databases and mapping tool. This resulted in incorrect information relating the congestion of certain roads, including the one on which the incident occurred. On probing, CloudMap reveals that their access logs show that this incorrect information was also retrieved by EmergenSolutions Ltd., an organisation known to be responsible for coordinating and distributing emergency service vehicles across the city, and that they may have also been affected by the issue.

Why was the ambulance delayed?
The investigator turns to how this information was used by EmerSolutions. Records help reveal that the area where the traffic incident occurred had been classified as low risk for emergency services. This then led to an automated decision to redirect ambulances away from the area shortly before the incident took place. This low risk classification resulted from three data sources: (i) information from CityMap reporting that there was low congestion in the area; (ii) data provided by CarNet indicating that few pedestrians or vehicles were present on the street and (iii) historic information about emergency service call-outs showing that the street was not a hot spot for incidents.

On contacting EmerSolutions, the organisation emphasises that they have redundancy measures in place, and that their planning system distributes emergency response vehicles based on these disparate sources of information. Probing further, the investigator discovers that EmerSolutions had a process in place to adjust the impact of historic information when large-scale events are on, such as sporting and music events, however, this process had not been followed for several weeks, and no record had been made of the major sporting event that the pedestrian was walking to. This was not reflected in their models and, thereby, hindered the speed of response by the emergency services. Further review of the system indicates that had this process been followed, the diversion of emergency service vehicles from the area would not have occurred and an ambulance would have been closer to the incident when it occurred, as would have been appropriate and expected when a major event takes place.

Putting together what happened

This example indicates that even incidents that appear simple can be complex, and that deployments designed to facilitate review will not only be important, but necessary for supporting investigation. The ability to review the technical and organisational workings of complex IoT ecosystems can provide both legal and operational benefits to the various entities involved.

From a legal standpoint, effective record keeping and logging will assist investigators in mapping out what happened and where issues originated. For instance, the scenario shows that reviewability allowed the investigator to determine that (i) CarNet's ability to detect pedestrians was affected by the low street lighting and questionable software update procedures; (ii) CityMap's services had been temporarily affected by an update and (iii) EmerSolutions failed to follow their own operational procedures. As such, because systems and processes were designed to be reviewable, the investigator was able to identify multiple issues, with several entities contributing to the incident throughout the IoT ecosystem. This reflects that there may be several points of failure in any ecosystem, and further that apportioning blame will often be complex in reality. That said, mechanisms that shine light on the happenings of systems means that the appropriate legal consequences, in terms of assigning liability and pursuing redress, are able to follow from the information obtained through review.

Operationally, reviewability has also allowed the organisations involved in this example to obtain insights into weaknesses or potential misuses of their systems. As such, they are able to improve their operational processes and prevent problems from re-occurring in future. Such information may also feed into their processes for ensuring and demonstrating legal compliance, by showing that they are quick to identify and act upon failures. For example, based on the investigations that took place, CarNet may choose to change their processes around software updates to have their vehicles automatically look for updates every night. CloudMap may reassess their processes surrounding their deployment of updates, perhaps better staging releases or having a more rigorous testing process to prevent such issues from being deployed in production. Both CloudVision and CloudMap may also choose to more closely monitor what kinds of applications and clients are using their services, and work with those clients in more high-stakes scenarios to implement bespoke services or processes which ensure that a high level of functionality is maintained in critical situations. Similarly, SmartLight may review their role in the incident, and set up contingency plans for when the mapping service fails (perhaps using a second mapping service or other sources of information, such as historic data from past usage logs), to ensure that the lights are not dimmed on streets that are known to likely be busy. EmergenSolutions may learn from the incident that relying too heavily on CityMap's services may have implications for system resilience, and that their failure to follow internal procedures can lead to issues with potentially significant consequences.

In the cases above, reviewability plays an important role in identifying and addressing issues in socio-technical systems. Without access to the comprehensive records and logs needed to holistically review the operation and interaction of the various component parts of IoT ecosystems, it would be extremely challenging to reliably identify where problems arise and where failures occur. Without oversight of the various entities involved (as well as their roles in the incident and their organisational processes), it would be difficult, perhaps impossible, to act on the investigation and take next steps. As we have shown, implementing reviewability through comprehensive technical and organisational record keeping and logging mechanisms offers significant benefits in terms of the improving of accountability in these complex IoT ecosystems.

5.7 Concluding remarks

There is a push for stronger governance regimes as the IoT continues to become increasingly interconnected, algorithmic and consequential. However, the complexity of the socio-technical, systems-of-systems that comprise the IoT introduces opacity, which poses real challenges for accountability.

We have argued that a key way forward is approaching accountability through the concept of reviewability. This involves mechanisms such as logging and record-keeping, that provide the necessary information to allow technical systems and organisational processes to be comprehensively interrogated, assessed and audited. The aim is to provide for a targeted form of transparency that paves the way for meaningful accountability regimes.

There appears real potential for technical methods, such as those provenance-based, to capture information of the systems that form the IoT. Such information can work to facilitate processes of review; however, more research is required. Though here we have focused on some technical capture mechanisms, the wider concerns are socio-technical. This means that reviewability will therefore require a broader range of technical and non-technical record keeping measures alike; from the commission and design of the IoT infrastructure, all the way to its continued operation. In other words, implementing effective reviewability requires a holistic approach, encompassing a range of perspectives that expose the contextually appropriate information necessary to assess the wider contexts in which the system is deployed: there are legal, compliance and oversight considerations; issues around incentives and organisational processes; the usability and relevance of the information driving review; as well as technical aspects concerning system design, development and monitoring; to name but a few. Realising greater accountability involves considering the relationships and interplays between these concerns and more.

In discussing IoT reviewability, this chapter seeks not only to draw attention to issues regarding the complex, interconnected, data-driven and socio-technical nature of IoT systems but also aims to encourage more attention and collaborative actions towards improving IoT accountability regimes. These concerns will become all the more pressing as the IoT continues to pervade our world. And despite the challenges in bringing about reviewability at scale, there are real and immediate benefits in employing any mechanisms that support review *now*. Even mechanisms that only support internal review (i.e. within an organisation or development project) can help in the management of systems, processes and obligations, in addition to assisting compliance and providing evidence demonstrating good practice. In short, any reviewability undertakings can work to pave the way towards an IoT that is more understandable, transparent, legally compliant and therefore accountable.

5.8 Acknowledgements

We acknowledge the financial support of the Engineering & Physical Sciences Research Council (EP/P024394/1, EP/R033501/1), University of Cambridge and Microsoft via the Microsoft Cloud Computing Research Centre.

References

[1] Miorandi D., Sicari S., De Pellegrini F., *et al* . 'Internet of things: vision, applications and research challenges'. *Ad Hoc Networks*. 2012;**10**(7):1497–516.
[2] Dlodlo N., Gcaba O., Smith A. 'Internet of things technologies in smart cities'. *IST-Africa Week Conference*; New York, USA: IEEE; 2016. p. 17.
[3] McKee D.W., Clement S.J., Almutairi J. 'Massive-scale automation in cyber-physical systems: vision & chScale Automation in Cyber-Physical Systems: Vision & Challenges'. *13th International Symposium on Autonomous Decentralized System (ISADS)*; New York, USA: IEEE; 2017. p. 511.
[4] Xiong Z., Sheng H., Rong W., *et al*. 'Intelligent transportation systems for smart cities: a progress review'. *Science China Information Sciences*. 2012;**55**(12):2908–14.
[5] Asimakopoulou E., Bessis N. 'Buildings and crowds: forming smart cities for more effective disaster management'. *5th International Conference on Innovative Mobile and Internet Services in Ubiquitous Computing*; New York, USA: IEEE; 2011. pp. 229–34.
[6] Boukerche A., Coutinho R.W.L. 'Smart disaster detection and response system for smart cities'. *Symposium on Computers and Communications (ISCC)*; New York, USA: IEEE; 2018. pp. 1102–7.
[7] Misbahuddin S., Zubairi J.A., Saggaf A. 'IoT based dynamic road traffic management for smart cities'. *12th International Conference on High-capacity Optical Networks and Enabling/Emerging Technologies (HONET)*; New York, USA: IEEE; 2015. p. 15.
[8] Saha H.N., Auddy S., Chatterjee A. 'IoT solutions for smart cities'. *8th Annual Industrial Automation and Electromechanical Engineering Conference (IEMECON)*; New York, USA: IEEE; 2017. pp. 74–80.

[9]   Business Insider. *The Internet of Things 2020: heres what over 400 IoT decision-makers say about the future of enterprise connectivity and how IoT companies can use it to grow revenue [online]*. 2020. Available from https://www.businessinsider.com/internet-of-things-report?IR=T [Accessed 25 Jan 2021].

[10] Singh J., Pasquier T., Bacon J., *et al.* 'Twenty security considerations for cloud-supported Internet of things'. *IEEE Internet of Things Journal*. 2016;**3**(3):269–84.

[11] Diakopoulos N. 'Accountability in algorithmic decision making'. *Communications of the ACM*. 2016;**59**(2):56–62.

[12] Isaak J., Hanna M.J. 'User data privacy: Facebook, Cambridge Analytica, and privacy protection'. *Computer*. 2018;**51**(8):56–9.

[13] Bovens M. 'Analysing and assessing public accountability. A conceptual framework'. *European governance papers*. EUROGOV; 2006. p. No. C-06-01:137.

[14] Singh J., Cobbe J., Norval C. 'Decision provenance: harnessing data flow for accountable systems'. *IEEE Access*. 2019;**7**:6562–74.

[15] Kitchin R., Lauriault T. *Towards critical data studies: charting and unpacking data assemblages and their work. The Programmable City Working Paper 2 [online]*. 2014. Available from https://ssrn.com/abstract=2474112 [Accessed 25 Jan 2021].

[16] Cobbe J., Norval C., Singh J. 'What lies beneath: transparency in online service supply chains'. *Journal of Cyber Policy*. 2020;**5**(1):65–93.

[17] Singh J., Millard C., Reed C., *et al.* 'Accountability in the IoT: systems, law, and ways forward'. *Computer*. 2018;**51**(7):54–65.

[18] Javadi S.A., Cloete R., Cobbe J. 'Monitoring misuse for accountable artificial intelligence as a service'. *Proceedings of the AAAI/ACM Conference on AI, Ethics, and Society. AIES 20*; New York, USA: ACM; 2020. pp. 300–6.

[19] Nissenbaum H. 'Privacy as contextual integrity'. *Washington Law Review*. 2004;**79**:119158.

[20] Singh J., Pasquier T., Bacon J. 'Big ideas paper: Policy-driven middleware for a legally-compliant internet of things'. *Proceedings of the 17th International Middleware Conference. Middleware 16*; New York, USA: ACM; 2016. pp. 1–15.

[21] Crabtree A., Lodge T., Colley J., *et al.* 'Building accountability into the Internet of things: the IoT Databox model'. *Journal of Reliable Intelligent Environments*. 2018;**4**(1):39–55.

[22] Norval C., Singh J. 'Explaining automated environments: Interrogating scripts, logs, and provenance using voice-assistants'. *Adjunct Proceedings of the 2019 ACM International Joint Conference on Pervasive and Ubiquitous Computing and Proceedings of the 2019 ACM International Symposium on Wearable Computers. UbiComp/ISWC 19 Adjunct*; New York, USA: ACM; 2019. pp. 332–5.

[23] Pasquier T., Singh J., Powles J., Eyers D., Seltzer M., Bacon J. 'Data provenance to audit compliance with privacy policy in the Internet of things'. *Personal and Ubiquitous Computing.* 2018;**22**(2):333–44.

[24] Cobbe J., Lee MSA., Singh J. 'Reviewable automated decision-making: a framework for accountable algorithmic systems'. *Proceedings of the Conference on Fairness, Accountability, and Transparency. FAccT 21*; New York, USA: ACM; 2021. p. 112.

[25] Kroll J.A., Huey J., Barocas S., *et al.* 'Accountable algorithms'. *University of Pennsylvania Law Review.* 2017;**165**(3):633–705.

[26] Millard C., Hon W.K., Singh J. 'Internet of things ecosystems: unpacking legal relationships and liabilities'. *IEEE International Conference on Cloud Engineering (IC2E)*; New York, USA: IEEE; 2017. pp. 286–91.

[27] Mason S., Seng D. *Electronic Evidence.* London, UK: University of London Press; 2017.

[28] Cobbe J. 'Administrative law and the machines of government: judicial review of automated public-sector decision-making'. *Legal Studies.* 2019;**39**(4):636–55.

[29] European Union. 'Regulation (EU) 2016/679 of the European Parliament and of the Council of 27 April 2016 on the protection of natural persons with regard to the processing of personal data and on the free movement of such data, and repealing directive 95/46/EC (General data protection regulation'. *Official Journal of the European Union.* 2016;**L119**:1–88.

[30] Singh J., Powles J., Pasquier T., *et al.* 'Data flow management and compliance in cloud computing'. *IEEE Cloud Computing.* 2015;**2**(4):24–32.

[31] European Union. 'Proposal for a regulation of the European Parliament and of the Council concerning the respect for private life and the protection of personal data in electronic communications and repealing directive 2002/58/EC (regulation on privacy and electronic communications'. *Official Journal of the European Union.* 2017:1–35.

[32] World Economic Forum. *How to prevent discriminatory outcomes in machine learning [online].* 2018. Available from http://www3.weforum.org/docs/WEF_40065_White_Paper_How_to_Prevent_Discriminatory_Outcomes_in_Machine_Learning.pdf [Accessed 25 Jan 2021].

[33] Stohl C., Stohl M., Leonardi P.M. 'Managing opacity: information visibility and the paradox of transparency in the digital age'. *International Journal of Communication.* 2016;**10**:123–37.

[34] Bhatt U., Xiang A., Sharma S. 'Explainable machine learning in deployment'. *Proceedings of the 2020 Conference on Fairness, Accountability, and Transparency. FAT* 20*; New York, USA: ACM; 2020. pp. 648–57.

[35] Singh J., Walden I., Crowcroft J., *et al.* Responsibility & machine learning: part of a process. 2016. Available from https://ssrn.com/abstract=2860048 [Accessed 25 Jan 2021].

[36] Gebru T., Morgenstern J., Vecchione B. 'Datasheets for datasets'. Proceedings of the 5th Workshop on Fairness, Accountability, and Transparency in Machine Learning; 2018. pp. 1–24.

[37] Mitchell M., Wu S., Zaldivar A. 'Model cards for model reporting'. *Proceedings of the Conference on Fairness, Accountability, and Transparency. FAT* 19*; New York, USA: ACM; 2019. pp. 220–9.

[38] Aldeco-Prez R., Moreau L. 'A provenance-based compliance framework'. *Future Internet Symposium*; Berlin Heidelberg: Springer; 2010. pp. 128–37.

[39] Tan Y.S., RKL K., Holmes G. 'Security and data accountability in distributed systems: a provenance survey'. *IEEE 10th International Conference on High Performance Computing and Communications 2013 IEEE International Conference on Embedded and Ubiquitous Computing*; New York, USA: IEEE; 2013. pp. 1571–8.

[40] Carata L., Akoush S., Balakrishnan N., *et al.* 'A primer on provenance'. *Communications of the ACM*. 2014;**57**(5):52–60.

[41] Herschel M., Diestelkämper R., Ben Lahmar H. 'A survey on provenance: what for? what form? what from?' *The VLDB Journal*. 2017;**26**(6):881–906.

[42] Davidson S.B., Freire J. 'Provenance and scientific workflows: challenges and opportunities'. *Proceedings of the 2008 ACM SIGMOD International Conference on Management of Data. SIGMOD 08*; New York, USA: ACM; 2008. pp. 1345–50.

[43] Chen P., Plale B., Cheah Y. 'Visualization of network data provenance'. *19th International Conference on High Performance Computing*; New York, USA: IEEE; 2012. p. 19.

[44] Oliveira W., Ambrósio L.M., Braga R., Ströele V., David J.M., Campos F. 'A framework for Provenance analysis and visualization'. *Procedia Computer Science*. 2017;**108**(4):1592–601.

[45] Wang Q., Hassan W.U., Bates A. 'Fear and logging in the Internet of things'. Network and Distributed Systems Symposium; San Diego, CA, USA, 18-21 February 2018; 2018. pp. 1–15.

[46] Li F., Usability J.H. 'Databases, and HCI'. *Bulletin of the IEEE Computer Society Technical Committee on Data Engineering*. 2012;**35**(3):37–45.

[47] Bachour K., Wetzel R., Flintham M. 'Provenance for the people: an HCI perspective on the W3C PROV standard through an online game'. *Proceedings of the 33rd Annual ACM Conference on Human Factors in Computing Systems. CHI 15*; New York, USA: ACM; 2015. pp. 2437–46.

[48] Schreiber A., Struminski R. 'Visualizing provenance using comics'. *9th USENIX Workshop on the Theory and Practice of Provenance (TAPP 2017)*; Berkeley, CA, USA: USENIX association; 2017. pp. 1–6.

[49] Ujcich B., Bates A., Sanders W.H. 'A provenance model for the European Union General data protection regulation'. *Provenance and Annotation of Data and Processes*; Cham, Switzerland: Springer International Publishing; 2018. pp. 45–57.

[50] Zanella A., Bui N., Castellani A., *et al.* 'Internet of things for smart cities'. *IEEE Internet of Things Journal*. 2014;**1**(1):22–32.

[51] Liu Y., Yang C., Jiang L., *et al.* 'Intelligent edge computing for IoT-based energy management in smart cities'. *IEEE Network*. 2019;**33**(2):111–17.

Chapter 6

Building accountability into the Internet of Things

Andy Crabtree[1], Tom Lodge[1], Derek McAuley[1], Lachlan Urquhart[2], Hamed Haddadi[3], and Richard Mortier[4]

This chapter outlines the IoT Databox model as an in principle means of making the Internet of Things (IoT) accountable to individuals. Accountability is key to building consumer trust and is mandated by the European Union's General Data Protection Regulation (GDPR). We focus here on the *external data subject accountability requirement* specified by GDPR and how meeting this turns on surfacing the invisible actions and interactions of connected devices and the social arrangements in which they are embedded. The IoT Databox model articulates how this requirement might be met and individuals be provided with the mechanisms needed to build widespread consumer trust into the IoT.

6.1 Introduction

The European Union (EU) updated its data protection regulation, GDPR [1], in May 2018 in no small part due to the scale and ubiquity of personal data collection enabled by the emerging digital ecosystem.

> Rapid technological developments and globalisation have brought new challenges for the protection of personal data. The scale of the collection and sharing of personal data has increased significantly (GDPR, Recital 6). The proliferation of actors and the technological complexity of practice make it difficult for the data subject to know and understand whether, by whom and for what purpose personal data relating to him or her are being collected. (GDPR, Recital 58)

[1]School of Computer Science, University of Nottingham, UK
[2]Edinburgh Law School, University of Edinburgh, Edinburgh, UK
[3]Dyson School of Design Engineering, Imperial College London, UK
[4]Computer Laboratory, University of Cambridge, Cambridge, UK

A key driver of this rapid technological development and technological complexity is the Internet of Things (IoT), which embeds billions of sensors in everyday devices that are designed to communicate unobtrusively and exchange data in a seamless way. The Article 29 Data Protection Working Party (A29WP), which has become the powerful European Data Protection Board under GDPR, is of the opinion that the invisibility of data collection enabled by the IoT raises 'new and significant personal data protection and privacy challenges' [2]. GDPR seeks to tackle these challenges by putting measures in place to protect personal data and with it the rights and freedoms of the data subject. Key amongst these measures is the *accountability* requirement (GDPR, Article 5).

The notion or principle of accountability [3] mandates that any party that controls personal data processing, including the collection, use, retention, disclosure and/or disposal of personal data, by wholly or partly automated means, for professional or commercial purposes, and which otherwise provides persons with the means (e.g., cloud-based services) for processing personal data for their own household or domestic purposes, be able to *demonstrate compliance* with GDPR [1]. Failure to do so may result in administrative fines up to €20 000 000 or 4% of total annual worldwide turnover, whichever is greater (ibid.).

It might be argued that while the consequences of ignoring the accountability requirement may be severe, GDPR only applies in Europe. However, if we consider the territorial scope of the regulation (GDPR, Article 3) it is clear that any such argument is misplaced.

> In order to ensure that natural persons are not deprived of the protection to which they are entitled under this Regulation, the processing of personal data of data subjects who are in the Union by a controller or a processor not established in the Union should be subject to this Regulation where the processing activities are related to offering goods or services to such data subjects irrespective of whether connected to a payment. (GDPR, Recital 23)

The global relevance of the accountability requirement is further underscored by the US legislation. While new data protection law appears to be terminally 'bogged down' in the United States [4], the accountability requirement is enshrined in existing Fair Information Practices [5], and the Federal Trade Commission has been proactive in championing data subject accountability in the IoT [6]. Add to this the Japanese effort to harmonise its data protection regulation with international law and update the Act on the Protection of Personal Information [7] and it becomes clear that the accountability requirement exerts considerable force on the IoT, whether developers like it or not.

Were we to define the accountability requirement we would say that it (a) requires any party that controls data processing to put policies, procedures and systems in place to demonstrate to *itself* that its processing operations comply with the requirements of data protection regulation. This internal focus is emphasised by data protection guidance [8], including data protection impact assessments (DPIAs) [9, 10]. Less pronounced at first glance, though as equally important, is (b) the external dimension of accountability, which requires that a data controller demonstrate to *others*, particularly regulatory authorities and individual data subjects, that its data processing operations comply with regulation. Internal and external demonstrations are not isomorphic. Thus, accountability cannot be reduced to showing that a DPIA has been carried out. More is required, especially with respect to making data processing accountable to the data subject.

Below we unpack the external data subject accountability requirement and how it has been translated into practical recommendations for IoT developers by the A29WP [2]. These recommendations seek to enable individual control over the flow of personal data through the design of computational mechanisms that enable consent as an ongoing matter, make data processing transparent and permit fine-grained data flow management, online access and data portability. Satisfying the external data subject accountability requirement requires that we surface and articulate hidden aspects of the IoT ecosystem [11]: not only machine-to-machine actions and interactions but also, and importantly, the social arrangements connected devices are embedded in [12], for it is not only the data collected by Internet-enabled 'things' that must be made accountable but also *what* is done with the data and by *whom*.

We outline the IoT Databox model as a means of surfacing device actions and interactions, and the social arrangements they are embedded in, in order to enable accountability. The IoT Databox is an edge device that is intended to be situated within the home, a key sector for IoT development. It collates data from IoT devices, either directly or via APIs, and makes them available to apps that enable data processing and actuation. Data processing takes place on-the-box. Moving computation to the data at the edge of the network, rather than data to centralised processing, has a range of potential benefits that are particularly relevant to the IoT and drive the shift to fog and edge and computing [13, 14]. These include low latency (data do not have to be moved to and from remote data centres), resilience (actuation does not need to rely on continuous connectivity), efficiency (centralised data processing costs are significantly reduced) and data minimisation (only the results of processing queries are distributed). Making the IoT accountable may, then, have manifold advantages, which also includes opening up data that is currently distributed across manifold silos to on-the-box innovation.

6.2 The external accountability requirement

The external accountability requirement plays a key role in the processing of personal data, i.e., any data that relate to an identified or identifiable person, including data generated by connected devices. It requires, by definition, that data processing operations are demonstrably compliant with regulation. This includes, but is not limited to, the following.

- **Data minimisation**. Article 5 GDPR requires that the processing of personal data is limited to what is necessary to meet the purposes for which they are collected and is thus conducted under the auspices of the data minimisation principle.

- **Lawfulness of processing**. Article 6 GDPR specifies that data processing should also be lawful. The processing of personal data is considered lawful to the extent that at least one of the following applies. It is *necessary* for a data controller (i.e., the party who commissions data processing and determines its purpose) to process personal data (a) in exercising official authority or performing a task carried out in the public interest, (b) complying with a legal obligation, (c) protecting the vital interests of the data subject, (d) pursuing the legitimate interests of an organisation or (e) fulfilling a contract. Otherwise processing is only lawful if the data subject has given *consent* to the processing of his or her personal data for specific purposes.

- **Fairness of processing**. Given the manifold grounds upon which processing may be lawfully conducted it may sound on the face of it that just about anything goes, especially given the legitimate interests clause. However, Article 5 GDPR also specifies that data processing must be *fair*. This requires that the data controller be clear and open about how they will use an individual's data [15]. Consent thus becomes a key ingredient in the processing of personal data, especially where consumer-oriented IoT devices and services are concerned, insofar as it makes data processing *transparent* and thus allows individuals to make *informed* choices.

- **Information to be provided to the data subject**. The processing of personal data also requires that certain information be provided to the data subject. This includes the specific purposes of data processing, just what data are required and by whom. Article 13 GDPR also requires that data subjects be informed of any other recipients of their data and the legitimate interests those recipients pursue, including the transfer of data to an international organisation or third country for processing. If the data are to be transferred, then individuals must be informed of the safeguards that have been put in place to provide effective legal remedies for data subjects and/or an adequacy decision by the EU on the level of protection offered by a third country. Individuals must also be informed of any further processing of personal data, if those purposes are different to and incompatible with those for which they were originally collected [16]. GDPR thus renders the *international distribution* of data processing and *data reuse* accountable to the data subject.

- **Data subject rights**. Individuals should also be informed as to the period for which data will be stored and, in accordance with Article 15, be able to access data via a secure remote system that enables them to export their data in a structured commonly used machine-readable format as per the right to data portability (Article 20). Other *rights* that must be made accountable to the data subject include the right to lodge a complaint (Article 15), the right to rectification (Article 16) and the right to be forgotten and to erasure (Article 17). Where automated decision-making, including profiling, is applied then the logic, significance and envisaged consequences of data processing must be made accountable to the individual (Article 13). Furthermore, individuals have the right *not* to be subject to decisions based solely on automated data processing, which has significant effects (such as automatic refusal of an online credit application) without the implementation of measures that safeguard their rights, including the right to obtain human intervention and to contest decisions (Article 22).

Consent clearly plays a key role in meeting the accountability requirement in situations of consumer choice. However, it is not simply a matter of obtaining permission to process personal data but requires that data processing be made accountable to individuals in terms of specific (legally defensible) purposes that reveal any and all recipients of the data, data transfers (including EU authorisation or legal safeguards) and further processing. The individual's rights must also be made accountable, including the right to complaint, rectification, and erasure and the right to online access (wherever possible) and data portability. Automated processing producing legal effects or having significant consequences for the individual (e.g., refusal of credit) must also be made accountable to individuals and measures put in place that safeguard their rights, including the right to human intervention. These requirements must be articulated in an intelligible and easily accessible form, using clear and plain language (Article 12), at the time when personal data are obtained (Article 13) wherever and whenever *possible*.

Satisfying the external accountability requirement is challenging for the IoT, and not only due to the fact that data processing is routinely distributed across an unobtrusive and seamless infrastructure [2] in which connected devices typically lack user interfaces and the communication of data is invisible. Challenging too is the shifting status of the accountability requirement itself. Something which has traditionally been construed of in engineering terms as a non-functional requirement – a matter of providing information to people (e.g., via terms and conditions or privacy notices) – has shifted under GDPR into a *functional* requirement and something that must therefore be *built into* the IoT.

The emphasis GDPR puts on providing information to the data subject (Article 13) no doubt bolsters the non-functional view. However, rights to do with online access and data portability clearly signal the shifting status of the accountability requirement, and that it extends beyond the initial moment of consent. While information will have to be provided about a raft of processing issues from purpose to recipients, data transfer and automated processing, the demonstration of compliance with the external data subject accountability requirement can no longer be reduced to the provision of up-front information, any more than it can be reduced internally to a DPIA. Accountability needs to be engineered into the IoT, a point underscored by A29WP and the practical recommendations it proposes to manage the data protection risks that lie within the ecosystem of the IoT by implementing 'privacy and data protection *in* products and services' [2].

6.3   Implementing the external accountability requirement

One of the key risks that attaches to the IoT from a EU perspective is the potential for an opaque infrastructure of connected devices to dehumanise the world, alienate people and reduce human freedom [17]. This is particularly acute in a domestic context, which is seen to constitute a mini IoT environment in its own right, capable of revealing its inhabitants' lifestyles, habits and choices. Ensuring that end-users fully understand the role, functioning and impact IoT services can have on their lives thus becomes a critical challenge (ibid.), which the external accountability requirement seeks to address. More than that, however, it seeks to put end-users in control. Accountability is not simply about *explaining* data processing in the IoT to people, it is about giving them the tools to *exercise personal control*.

> User empowerment is essential in the context of IoT. Data subjects and users must be able to exercise their rights and thus be 'in control' of the data at any time according to the principle of self-determination. [2]

In addition to furnishing end-users or individuals with the information required by GDPR, A29WP recommends that control turn on the implementation of a range of awareness mechanisms. This recognises that, at the current moment in time at least, communication between devices in the IoT ecosystem often occurs without the individual being aware of it, which in turn makes it extraordinarily difficult to control the generated flow of data. The lack of awareness increases the risk of excessive self-exposure and functional creep as data flows invisibly around the ecosystem. It is further recognised that standard mechanisms for promoting awareness are difficult to apply in the IoT, given the seamless character of communications and the current inability for connected devices to make the data they generate reviewable by the data subject prior to publication. A29WP thus recommends that a number of practical measures be implemented to increase awareness and reflexively put users in control of the flow of data in the IoT. In addition to implementing adequate security measures, these include:

- **Providing granular choice over data capture**. Device manufacturers must provide users with granular choices over data capture. The granularity should not only concern the category of collected data, but also the time and frequency at which data are captured. As a feature of granular choice, it is also recommended that devices inform users when they are active, e.g., via a physical interface to a device or by broadcasting a signal on a wireless channel. Also, similar to the do not disturb feature on smartphones, IoT devices should offer a do not collect option to quickly disable data collection.
- **Limiting data distribution**. In keeping with the data minimisation principle and purpose limitation, IoT devices should limit the amount of data that leaves them by transforming raw data into aggregated data and deleting raw data as soon as the data required for processing has been extracted. As a principle, deletion should take place at the nearest point of data collection of raw data and where possible directly on the device.
- **Enforcing local control**. To enforce user control, IoT devices should enable local controlling and processing entities that allow users to have a clear and transparent picture of data collected by their devices and facilitate local storage and processing without having to transmit the data to the device manufacturer.

Furthermore, IoT devices should provide tools enabling users to locally read, edit and modify the data before they are transferred to any data controller.

It is also recommended, in keeping with GDPR (Article 7), that users should be able to revoke consent and that the tools provided to register this withdrawal should be 'accessible, visible and efficient' [2]. Such tools should allow users to continuously withdraw their consent 'without having to exit the service' provided by connected devices (ibid.). Furthermore, and where relevant (e.g., with respect to smart appliances), in withdrawing consent users should still be able to *use* a device.

The controls recommended by A29WP may sound severe but are not dissimilar to the recommendations of the Federal Trade Commission (FTC), the chief agency tasked with protecting personal data in the United States. Accordingly, the FTC proposes a number of practical measures to put the individual in control of personal data generated by IoT devices. These include the implementation of management portals or dashboards that enable users to configure IoT devices; privacy menus enabling the application of user-defined privacy levels across all of their IoT devices by default; the use of icons on IoT devices to quickly convey important settings and attributes, such as when a device is connected to the Internet, and to enable users to quickly toggle the connection on or off; and the use of out of band communications to relay important privacy and security settings to the user via other channels, e.g., via email or SMS.

Properly implemented, such dashboard approaches can allow consumers clear ways to determine what information they agree to share. [6]

Clearly there is some resonance between the FTC recommendations and the granular choice measures proposed by A29WP, insofar as both are concerned to put computational mechanisms in place that allow end-users to understand data collection and to control the flow of personal data in the IoT ecosystem. There is agreement too on the relevance and importance of minimising data collection and that greater transparency would help customers and businesses by promoting trust in the IoT marketplace (ibid.), though we note that there are no overarching principles of data minimisation or transparency in US data protection law.

Nonetheless, seen through the lens of key agencies tasked with implementing data protection in Europe and the United States, satisfying the external accountability requirement becomes a matter of enabling individual control over the flow of personal data through the design of computational mechanisms that provide for consent as an ongoing matter, make data processing transparent and permit fine-grained data flow management. In Europe that requirement also extends to computational mechanisms that enable online access and data portability, and more radically that *local processing entities* be implemented to enforce control.

One direct implication of the local control recommendation is that a great deal of the processing of IoT data that currently takes place in the cloud is moved to the edge of the network.

The edge of the Internet is a unique place located often just one wireless hop away from associated devices, it offers ideal placement for low-latency offload infrastructure to support emerging applications. It can be an optimal site for aggregating, analysing and distilling bandwidth-hungry sensor data. In the Internet of Things, it offers a natural vantage point for access control, privacy, administrative autonomy and responsive analytics (edited extract). [18]

Moving data processing to the edge will minimise the collection of personal data insofar as aggregates or the results of data processing need only be passed on, and in doing so will reduce the threat to privacy that accompanies widespread data distribution. It also holds out technical and economic benefits, reducing latency, making device actuation more resilient and enabling significant reductions in data processing costs. It may also be the case that in moving to the edge to meet the external accountability requirement, consumers may be more willing to open up their personal data to innovation in the knowledge that it will not be made available to others. Time will tell.

6.4   Accountability at the edge: The IoT Databox model

Under GDPR the external data subject accountability requirement locates the principle of self-determination in technical practice and requires that accountability be built into the IoT. For a vast range of consumer devices this means that *consent* can no longer be reduced to ticking a box on a remote website; that data processing be *transparent* and clearly articulates the specific purposes for which it is done, any recipients or transfers of the data, and the logic, significance and consequences of automated processing; that data collection is *minimal* and involves only that which is needed to meet the purposes of processing; and that individuals be able to *access* their data online and *export* it. Furthermore, it is recommended that external accountability be implemented through computational mechanisms that allow individuals to exercise *granular choice* over data collection; keep raw data as close to source as possible and *limit data distribution*; and exercise *local control* over data processing including be able to review the results of processing operations prior to distribution of results. Limiting data distribution and permitting local control inevitably nudges solutions enabling external accountability to the edge of the network.

6.4.1   Origin and evolution of the model

The IoT Databox model provides an in principle means of implementing the external accountability requirement. It builds on the Dataware model [19], which sought to develop a business-to-consumer service-oriented architecture enabling a new wave of personalised applications, and it extends the Databox concept [20] to incorporate the IoT. The IoT Databox model posits a physical device as a gateway to a distributed platform that is embedded in the physical environment, e.g., a dedicated mini-computer on the home network, under the direct control of the data subject.

The model also posits a *user* (by and/or about whom data are created), *data sources* (connected devices, which generate data about the user), *datastores* (which collate the data produced by data sources) and *apps* (code that performs processing locally on data). Data stores are containerised, application-specific processes [21] that reduce the security problems associated with general purpose operating systems. Apps are untrusted code and can only ever communicate with datastores (to read data or actuate a device) with explicit consent from a data subject. The IoT Databox model represents a distinctive approach to personal data processing, not only enabling user control but also data minimisation insofar as data distribution is limited to the *results* of data processing. The raw data remains on-the-box, under the user's control. The model thus takes a significant step towards implementing the local control recommendation.

6.4.2   Architecture of the model

Architecturally the IoT Databox model consists of three key components: (a) the Databox, (b) an app store, of which there may in principle be many and (c) third party processors (Figure 6.1). Data processing is done via apps that run on the Databox and are publicly distributed by developers via the app store. The Databox

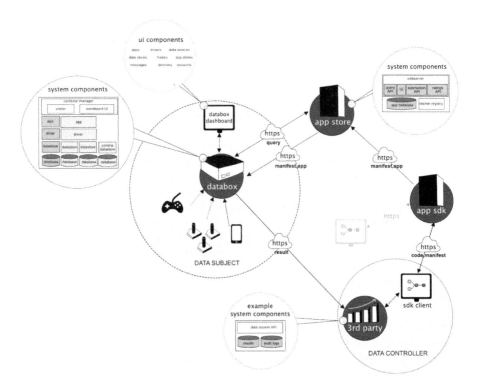

Figure 6.1   The IoT Databox model

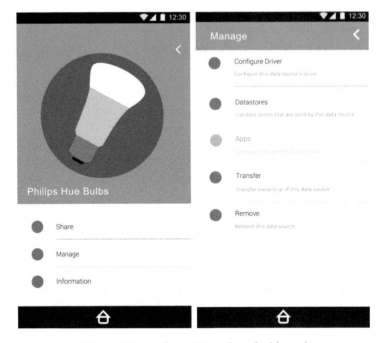

Figure 6.2   The IoT Databox dashboard

itself is a small form factor computer consisting of a collection of containerised system services, including the IoT Databox dashboard (Figure 6.2).

The dashboard seeks to make a range of management functions available to users, including:

- Creating *User Accounts* on the IoT Databox
- Adding *Data Sources*, including assigning ownership to data sources, naming data sources, and sharing data sources with local and remote users.
- Configuring *Drivers* to enable data sources to write to data stores.
- Managing *Data Stores*, including redacting, clearing or deleting stores and sharing stores with other users.
- Managing *Apps*, users can search for and download apps from app stores and update or delete apps from the box.
- Receiving *Notifications*, including the results of data processing prior to distribution, sharing requests, app updates, etc.
- *Auditing* data processing operations, including all accesses to data stores, and any data transactions.

An app store is a dashboard interface that reads sets of manifest files residing in a GitHub repository. The manifests themselves provide a reference to IoT Databox

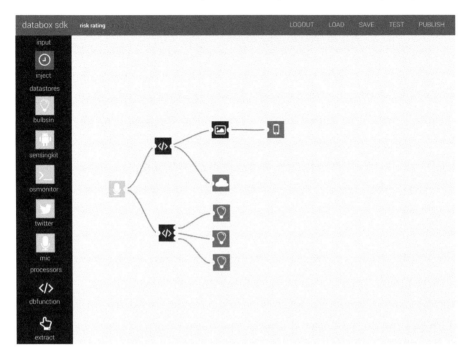

Figure 6.3   The IoT Databox IDE

apps, which are packaged as Docker containers and stored in Docker repositories.[a] Users are able to gain access to a variety of different app stores, by pointing their databox to alternative GitHub repositories via the IoT Databox dashboard.

6.4.3   App development

App developers are free to create their own containerised apps as they wish, but an integrated development environment (IDE) supporting the app building and publication process is also provided. The IDE is a cloud-hosted visual code editor based on IBM's open source Node-RED,[b] which utilises a flow-based programming paradigm in which black-box processes called *nodes* are connected together to form applications called *flows*.

There are three principle node types: data sources, processes and outputs. Process nodes are functions that operate on data; they typically have a single input connection and one or more output connections. Output nodes typically perform an action, such as actuation, visualisation or data export. Figure 6.3 depicts a flow taking the output from a microphone, performs some processing on the data and updates a visualisation, turns on one or more bulbs and exports the processed data to

[a]https://www.docker.com
[b]https://nodered.org

Figure 6.4   App manifest

the cloud. It is composed of a single data source (yellow node), three processes (blue nodes) and five outputs (orange nodes).

The app editor smooths and simplifies the development (build-test-deploy) workflow:

- It presents a high-level abstraction (e.g., an app developer can build an app without needing to be familiar with the interoperation between sources, stores and drivers).
- It provides the scaffolding needed to help build an app (e.g., developers can quickly inspect the structure and type of data entering and exiting a node).
- It provides a full testing environment, where flows are deployed (as containers) and connected to test data.
- It handles the app publication process by presenting tools for building an app manifest (see Figure 6.4), which enables end-user consent and granular choice.
- It containerises an app and uploads it to the app store when it is for release.

The IDE also takes care of source code management as all stages of the app development cycle are recorded in a developer's GitHub account.

6.4.4 Managing risk

The IDE also seeks to sensitise *app developers* to the potential risks that accompany personal data processing. We differentiate between three types of risk: (a) legal risks associated with GDPR, particularly those implicated in taking data off-the-box including data export within and out with the EU, transfer to other recipients, the provision of adequacy decisions or safeguards and access; (b) technological risks, including apps that use devices that have not been validated by the IDE, use unverified code or physically actuate essential infrastructure or potential dangerous devices in the home and (c) social risks, including apps that access sensitive information or produce results that may be deemed sensitive as articulated, for example, by the notion of 'special categories' of personal (Article 9 GDPR).

We appreciate that identifying risk is a challenging business, given that it can be introduced by any individual component of a system, both hardware, such as sensors/actuators, and software, such as drivers and apps, as well as arbitrary combinations of the two in particular operating contexts. However, we take the view that app developers should understand as best they can the nature and level of risk posed by an app and provide information about the risks to which users are potentially exposed. The IDE attempts to inform developers and users alike by generating a risk rating for apps based on the aggregate risk of the nodes from which it is composed. Each node in the development environment has a pre-defined spectrum of risk attached to it. The final risk rating assigned to the node (Figure 6.5) will sit within this spectrum and be determined by how nodes are configured, e.g., the hardware they work with, the proposed data rate, the particular actuation to be performed, etc.

An app's risk rating is also made available to users on the app store (Figure 6.6) to inform users of the potential hazards associated with an app and to encourage the development of low-risk and even no-risk apps that do not export data and otherwise provide users with granular choice over data sampling and reporting frequency, online access if apps do take data of the box, flag that they actuate essential infrastructure in the home (e.g., central heating or windows and doors) and use accredited hardware and trustworthy software. Low-risk apps are visibly indicated in the app store by shields and clearly display their IoT Databox accredited status. User ratings are also displayed by stars and written feedback can also be accessed via the app store.

The risk rating assigned by the IDE is written into an app manifest. An app cannot be posted on the app store or installed on the IoT Databox without an app manifest and data (i.e., the results of local processing) cannot be taken off-the-box without an app manifest being completed by the individual or data subject.

6.4.5 Enabling consent and granular choice

Manifests are *multi-layered notices* [22] that (a) provide a *short* description of the specific purpose of data processing, (b) a *condensed* description providing the information required by GDPR and (c) *full* legal terms and conditions. The IoT Databox also adds app information to the short description, including user ratings and an

Figure 6.5   Risk rating apps during development

app's risk profile, and enables control to be exercised over data collection at device level (Figure 6.4).

The IoT Databox transforms multi-layered notices into user-configurable consent mechanisms. They make visible who wants to access which connected devices and what they want to process their data for. They make socio-technical data processing arrangements, implicating specific connected devices, data controllers and their processors, accountable to the data subject and available to local control. Manifests provide an easy-to-read description in clear and plain language of the data sources an app will use and the risks that attach to using the app. They also allow users to exercise granular choice over data collection, selecting just which data sources may be used and, insofar as connected devices permit, at which sampling frequencies

Figure 6.6   The app store: displaying at-a-glance risk ratings

data can be gathered. Once a manifest has been configured by the individual and has been installed it assumes the status of a Service Level Agreement (SLA), which the IoT Databox transforms into a set of machine readable policies that enforce a data processor's access to the particular data sources agreed upon by the individual and regulates any subsequent data processing operations. Apps, like data stores, run within isolated containers and interact with data stores to perform a specified (i.e., purposeful) task defined in the SLA. Thus apps may query data stores, write to a communications data store that sends query results to external machines or write to a connected device's store to perform actuation. Data stores record all actions performed on them (queries, external transactions and actuation) in an audit log. Access to data stores is enforced by an arbiter component (Figure 6.1), which issues and regulates the use of access tokens.

6.5   Responding to the privacy challenge

GDPR requires that external data subject accountability be built-in to the emerging digital ecosystem in a bid to respond to the data protection challenges occasioned by the Internet of Things and related developments, notably automated decision-making enabled by advance in machine learning and artificial intelligence. The Article 29 Data Protection Working Party (A29WP) provides a number of practical recommendations as to how data protection can be implemented in the IoT. Together these legal requirements and recommendations suggest that meeting the external data subject accountability requirement is a matter of enabling individual control over the flow of personal data through the design of computational mechanisms that (a) provide for consent as an ongoing matter, (b) make data processing transparent, (c) permit fine-grained data flow management, (d) allow online access and data portability and (e) exploit local processing entities to enforce control. The IoT Databox model provides an in principle means of meeting the external accountability requirement insofar as it provides tangible computational mechanisms that address these concerns.

- **Consent**. The requirement here is not only that users be able to consent to data processing in the IoT, but they can do so as an ongoing matter and thus be able to revoke consent as and when they see fit. Consent is provided for by the IoT Databox through dynamic multi-layered notices, which do not sit at some remove from data processing (e.g., on a remote website) but are installed on-the-box where processing occurs. That means they can also be uninstalled at any time by the user and that data processing will thus be terminated. We cannot guarantee that a connected device will still work, as per A29WP recommendations, but that is a matter for device manufacturers to address.
- **Transparency**. The information required by GDPR to make data processing transparent – including purpose specification, recipients, transfers and salient details of automated processing – is also provided by multi-layered notices. Additionally, the IoT Databox provides additional transparency mechanisms

articulating the potential risks that attach to apps, dashboard notifications allow-ing users to review the result of data processing, and audit mechanisms that allow users to inspect the historical operations of apps on the box.

- **Fine-grained data flow management**. Multi-layered notices also enable users to exercise granular choice over data collection, insofar as connected devices provide a range of data sampling frequencies. It is also the case that well-designed apps might support granular choice in offering users a range of report-ing frequencies (e.g., continuous, hourly, daily, weekly, monthly) and that these may be built into multi-layered notices. The IoT Databox additionally supports fine-grained data flow management in limiting and minimising data distribution in only returning the results of a processing query to a controller. Raw data thus remains on-the-box subject to user control.

- **Access and portability**. Insofar as raw data remains on-the-box, and audit mechanisms log all processing operations, then data portability is non-issue in the IoT Databox model: the data are always available (subject to deletion policy), and the results of specific queries can always be recovered. Providing access to data that has been transferred off-the-box is more problematic. Minimally data controllers will have to provide a secure endpoint and an encrypted con-nection if they wish to take any data off-the-box, which the box will monitor. While access is a legal requirement under GDPR, we cannot enforce it. It can be encouraged, however, by attaching relatively high risk profiles to apps that take data off-the-box but do not provide online access and, where possible, recom-mending alternatives.

- **Local control**. Situated at the edge of the network, the IoT Databox enables local control, which is seen as key to user empowerment. Taking computing to the data, rather than data to the computing, provides individuals with strong data protection mechanisms. It also has potential computational advantages, decreasing latency, enhancing resilience insofar as devices only need to talk to a local box rather than a remote server, and decreasing network traffic insofar as this approach is adopted at scale [23].

In limiting and even eradicating the need to hand over data to others, edge solutions may foster the broad societal trust needed for consumers to open up their data to innovation. Solutions like the IoT Databox may give users the confidence to allow applications to access personal and even sensitive data with the assurance that it will not be distributed but stay on-the-box or otherwise be limited to the results of a query, which may itself be terminated before data are distributed. The possibility turns to some extent on it being possible to route IoT devices through such platforms as the IoT Databox. That is, on device manufacturer's enabling local control on their products. However, even if they do not, and instead provide users with APIs for apps to access their data, the data itself may still be collated on the IoT Databox and opened up to broader use and the delivery of personalised services that are accountable to users and add tangible value to their everyday lives.

6.6 Fit with the state-of-the art

A raft of technological platforms offering secure Personal Data Stores (PDS) has emerged over the recent years in a bid to protect consumer data and enhance privacy. The World Economic Forum reported that more than one PDS a week was launched between January 2013 and January 2014 [24]. Many provide users, like Mydex,[c] with online data stores that are encrypted and distributed to enhance security, against which a wide a variety of third-party applications can be run with user consent. Perhaps most notably Tim Berners-Lee launched his own PDS, Solid,[d] in 2016. Solid allows users to store their data in Pods, of which there may be many, all of which are under the user's control. With the user's permission, authenticated Solid Apps may request data from a Pod, which is organised in a common, machine-readable format called Linked Data, thereby enabling any Solid App to read and write data to any Solid Pod. The computational efficiencies of Linked Data are reasonably obvious. However, much less clear is the power such solutions actually give users over their data, when much of it is not under their direct control but the control of the services they interact with. Limited control begs the question of the ability of PDS solutions to preserve or enhance user privacy? Furthermore, as Bolychevsky [25] puts it,

> If Solid uptake is big enough to attract app developers, what stops the same data exploitation happening, albeit now with an extra step where the user is asked for 'permission' to access and use their data in exchange for a free or better service?

It is also the case that despite the phenomenal growth of PDS solutions in the marketplace, widespread public uptake has been less pronounced somewhat ironically research suggests [26] because of the *privacy and security risks* users attach to storing their personal data *online*.

HATDeX[e] seeks to provide a platform that furnishes a range of storage solutions that potentially include 'a box in your home' [27]. It also provides purpose-built Data Plugs to retrieve personal data from APIs provided by online services (e.g., Facebook, Spotify, Google) and deposit them into a user's Personal Data Account. Data Debits allow users to control app access to data in the PDA 'in a direct debit manner', including termination of data sharing agreements (ibid.). The primary purpose of HATDeX is to create a data marketplace that builds users into the value chain. The platform is commercialised by Dataswift, which uses HATDeX to manage real-time, on-demand data transfers in much the same way that Visa and MasterCard run the credit card payment infrastructure [28]. Data transfers are accepted by merchants and they pay HATDeX transaction fees who in turn pay the owner of the PDA that transacted the data. Data are shared on the basis of first-party

[c]https://mydex.org
[d]https://solid.mit.edu
[e]https://hatdex.dataswift.io

licensing, much as one might do with music, rather than consent. Apps are rated to provide an 'at a glance' indication of Data Debit requests made by merchants. However, app ratings are 'not verified by the HAT platform' [29]. Furthermore, data may be transferred anywhere in the world and used for other purposes, as recognized by the HATDeX rating system (ibid.). Despite the potential for local control and the ability to retrieve online data, HATDeX begs much the same questions as Solid with regards to data exploitation and does nothing to prevent abuses once data are *off-the-box*.

The MyData[f] initiative takes a different approach. It does not provide a PDS solution, but instead seeks to enable consent management. MyData provides a digital service that focuses on managing and visualising data use *authorisations*, rather than storing data itself. It seeks to encourage service providers to build MyData APIs, which enable their services to be connected with MyData accounts. MyData APIs enable interaction between distributed data sources and data processors, and the MyData account provides users with a single hub for granting processors the authority to access and use their personal data [30]. While the MyData account lets individuals activate or deactivate the sharing of specific data flows and lists currently active authorisations, it does not put further measures in place to *limit access* and *minimise data distribution*.

openPDS [31] is similar to the IoT Databox. The platform implements a secure space that can be installed on any server or virtual machine under the control of the individual or can be provided as a service by vendors or service providers. It provides a centralised location where the user's data are stored and allows users to view their data and manage fine-grained access. openPDS exploits the SafeAnswers approach [32] to compute third-party queries inside a software sandbox within the user's PDS returning, like the IoT Databox, only the results of processing not the raw data.

> When a third party, like an app, needs some information from a user, it sends a couple of lines of code to openPDS. If approved and validated, the personal data store runs this algorithm on their data accordingly and sends back a validated 'answer' containing only the indispensable information. Through this strict need-to-know basis, apps can't actually see the data and it never leaves the safety of your PDS. [33]

openPDS is also aligned with the European Commission's reform of data protection regulation [7]. However, it does not respond directly to the external accountability requirement. Furthermore, the IoT Databox recognises the need to move beyond the 'individual-centric' approach adopted by openPDS [32] and other PDS solutions. As we have previously commented [34], most personal data do not belong to a single individual but are *social* in nature, especially in the IoT where connected

[f]https://mydata.org

devices are embedded in the fabric, furniture and mobilia of buildings. The ability to share devices, data and applications within and between homes, and to collectively as well as individually manage data processing, is critical to the adoption of privacy-enhancing technologies [35]. Nevertheless, we are mindful as Helen Nissenbaum and her colleagues remind us that 'users rarely pick a product based on privacy alone [36]', utility is an essential determinant, and privacy-enhancing technologies *also* provide services that add value to users'everyday lives.

MyData, HATDeX and Solid seek to add value by placing data in secure environments and opening it up to innovation through platform accredited apps and APIs in a bid to build consumer confidence and trust. In doing so they expose raw data third-party processing and allow it to be distributed. Such developments thus fail to limit the potential 'function creep' [2] that currently characterises data processing in the IoT and results in personal data flowing unfettered around the digital ecosystem, which undermines consumer confidence and trust [24]. openPDS and the IoT Databox provide an alternate pathway, putting severe constraints on the flow of data by minimising data distribution to the *results* of local data processing. The IoT Databox also makes local data processing accountable to data subjects in terms required by data protection regulation, surfacing the invisible actions and interactions of connected devices and the social arrangements in which they are embedded in order to render data processing transparent, provide the information required for data subjects to make informed choices and the tools needed to permit fine-grained control over the flow of personal data in the digital economy.

6.7   Conclusion

The EU updated its data protection regulation, GDPR [1], in 2018 to put in place measures to protect the rights and freedoms of citizens in the twenty-first century. The update was motivated in no small part by the emergent effects of digital technology, which made it difficult for individuals or data subjects to know and understand whether, by whom and for what purpose personal data were being collected and processed. The EU's data protection Working Party (A29WP) viewed the IoT – an infrastructure expressly designed to communicate and exchange data unobtrusively and in a seamless way – as particularly problematic, raising new and significant privacy challenges. The updated regulation has global reach and applies regardless of whether or not data processing takes place in the EU insofar as it leverages personal data to monitor or deliver goods and service to individuals within the Union. It is also punitive, exacting heavy fines on parties that control data processing, and that otherwise provides individuals with the means to process personal data for household purposes, for non-compliance.

A key measure of compliance and pillar of the updated regulation is the *accountability* requirement (ibid.). The requirement has two distinct aspects to it. One is *internal* to a data processing operation and requires that the party or parties controlling data processing demonstrate to themselves that their operations comply with the regulation. The other is *external* and requires that the party or parties controlling data processing demonstrate to others, particularly supervisory authorities and data subjects, that their operations comply with the regulation. The demonstrations are not equivalent, and cannot be provided for in the same ways. The external data subject accountability requirement in particular requires a raft of measures be put in place to enable consent, to make data processing transparent, permit fine-grained data flow management, online access and data portability. Recommendations from A29WP for IoT developers also advocate providing granular choice, limiting data distribution and enabling local control to enforce user control over data processing [2].

These mandated measures and recommendations mark the shifting status of the external data subject accountability requirement from a non-functional requirement that may be satisfied through the provision of information (e.g., as contained in a privacy notice) to functional requirement that can only be satisfied through the implementation of computational mechanisms that build accountability into the IoT. This chapter has sought to address how this might be achieved. We have sketched out the external data subject requirement as laid down by the updated regulation, and salient recommendations provided by A29WP for making the IoT GDPR compliant, and how these might be built into the ecosystem via the IoT Databox model.

The IoT Databox is an edge solution that implements A29WP's local control recommendation (ibid.) to minimise data distribution and enable fine-grained user control. It meets the external accountability requirement by surfacing the interactions between connected devices and data processors, and articulating the social actors and activities in which machine-to-machine interactions are embedded, through a distinctive range of computational mechanisms. These mechanisms include:

- **The IoT Databox**. A physical networked device situated in the home that enables users to exercise direct control over IoT devices and to manage both internal (within the home) and external (third party) access to the data they generate. The IoT Databox puts the principle of data minimisation into effect, taking computing to the data, and limiting the potential for excessive self-exposure and function creep in executing processing locally and *only* returning the results of third party queries.
- **App store**. The app store provides a familiar environment that enables IoT Databox users to access data processing applications and services. It also provides resources to help them make informed choices about the services they wish to use, including app verification, risk ratings, and feedback from the user community. The app store puts the principle of self-determination into effect, and allows individuals to exercise direct control over the specific data processing operations that run on the IoT Databox.
- **Apps**. Apps provide a key interface for articulating the transparency requirements of GDPR in terms of manifests, which articulate who wants what data for what purposes along with recipients of the data, data transfers and the nature of any automated processing that may be applied. App manifests put the principle of informed consent into effect, and in being dynamic objects (not just text)

further allow users to exercise granular choice over data collection to enable fine-grained data flow management.

- **Dashboard**. The IoT Databox dashboard enables users to manage data processing operations on-the-box and data sharing between other users. It enables consent to be exercised in an ongoing manner, including revoking it at any time; provides transparency mechanisms, including review and audit functions; and allows individuals to terminate data processing should they wish. The dashboard thus enables individuals to exercise further fine-grained control over data processing and the flow of data.
- **IDE**. The IDE provides a development environment that supports app building and publication and sensitises app builders to potential legal, technical and social risks implicated in the processing of personal data. It assigns risk ratings to apps to encourage the development of apps that are low or no-risk and which provide access to any data taken off-the-box to enable compliance with GDPR. App ratings are displayed in the app store to inform IoT Databox users as to the potential hazards that accompany their use.

In adopting the local control recommendation and moving data processing to the edge of the network to ensure the individual can control the flow of personal data, the IoT Databox model may enhance the efficiency of data processing, make actuation more resilient, minimise the impact of IoT traffic on the network and negate the need for costly privacy regimes. Insofar as it is possible for data processing and data to demonstrably *stay on-the-box* then the IoT Databox model also holds the promise of opening up personal data, giving individuals the confidence to allow data processing across manifold sources of personal and even sensitive data rather than data from siloed devices.

Nonetheless, we are aware that the IoT Databox model is largely symbolic, a signal of what might be possible if the challenges occasioned by edge and fog computing can be overcome [13, 14]. The IoT Databox is not a theoretical model, however. It exists [37, 38], albeit in nascent form and its source code is freely available for widespread use.[g] The platform enables data controllers and app developers working on their behalf to demonstrate compliance with the external data subject accountability requirement. Its ability to support local computation minimises and even circumvents the widespread threat to privacy occasioned by the IoT. In circumventing the privacy threat, it opens up new possibilities for processing personal data in ways that build consumer confidence, and with it widespread trust, into the IoT.

Data protection must move from 'theory to practice'. Accountability based mechanisms have been suggested as a way [to] implement practical tools for effective data protection (edited extract). [3]

---

[g]https://www.databoxproject.uk

Acknowledgements

The research reported here was supported by the Engineering and Physical Sciences Research Council [grant numbers EP/M001636/1, EP/N028260/1, EP/N028260/2, EP/M02315X/1]. This chapter is based on the following original works:

- Crabtree, A. (2016) Enabling the New Economic Actor: Personal Data Regulation and the Digital Economy. *International Conference on Cloud Engineering Workshop*, Berlin, August 2016, pp. 124–9, IEEE. https://doi.org/ 10.1109/IC2EW.2016.18
- Crabtree A., Lodge T., Colley J., Greenhalgh C., Mortier R. and Haddadi, H. (2016) Enabling the New Economic Actor: Data Protection, the Digital Economy and the Databox. *Personal and Ubiquitous Computing*, vol. 20, pp. 947–7. https://doi.org/10.1007/s00779-016-0939-3
- Crabtree A., Lodge T., Colley J., Greenhalgh C. and Mortier R. (2017) Accountable Internet of Things? Outline of the IoT Databox Model. *Proceedings of the 18th International Symposium on a World of Wireless, Mobile and Multimedia Networks*, Macau, China, June 2017, pp. 1–6, IEEE. https://doi. org/10.1109/WoWMoM.2017.7974335
- Crabtree A., Lodge T., Colley J., Greenhalgh C., Glover K., Haddadi H., Amar Y., Mortier R., Moore J., Wang L., Yadav P., Zhao J., Brown A., Urquhart L. and McAuley D. (2018) Building Accountability into the Internet of Things: The IoT Databox Model. *Journal of Reliable Intelligent Environments*, vol. 4, pp. 39–55. https://doi.org/10.1007/s40860-018-0054-5

References

[1] 'Regulation 2016/679 General data protection regulation'. *Official Journal of the European Union*. 2016;**59**:1–149.

[2] Article 29 Data Protection Working Party. *Opinion 8/2014 on recent developments on the internet of things [online]*. 16 September 2014. Available from https://ec.europa.eu/justice/article-29/documentation/opinion-recommendation/files/2014/wp223_en.pdf [Accessed 30 Jun 2020].

[3] Article 29 Data Protection Working Party. *Opinion 3/2010 on the principle of accountability*. 13 July 2010. Available from https://ec.europa.eu/justice/article-29/documentation/opinion-recommendation/files/2010/wp173_en.pdf [Accessed 30 Jun 2020].

[4] Singer N. 'Why a push for online privacy is bogged down in Washington' [online] *New York Times*. 28 February 2016. Available from https://www.nytimes.com/2016/02/29/technology/obamas-effort-on-consumer-privacy-falls-short-critics-say.html [Accessed 30 Jun 2020].

[5] Gellman R. 'Fair information practices: a basic history'. *SSRN Electronic Journal*. 2014;**1**.

[6]   Federal Trade Commission. *Internet of Things: privacy and security in a connected world [online]*. January 2015. Available from https://www.ftc.gov/system/files/documents/reports/federal-trade-commission-staff-report-november-2013-workshop-entitled-internet-things-privacy/150127iotrpt.pdf [Accessed 30 Jun 2020].

[7]   Coos A. *'Data protection in Japan: all you need to know about APPI'*. Endpoint Protector. 1 February 2019. Available from https://www.endpointprotector.com/blog/data-protection-in-japan-appi [Accessed 30 Jun 2020].

[8]   Information Commissioner's Office. *Accountability and governance*. Available from https://ico.org.uk/for-organisations/guide-to-data-protection/guide-to-the-general-data-protection-regulation-gdpr/accountability-and-governance [Accessed 30 Jun 2020].

[9]   Information Commissioner's Office. *Data Protection Impact Assessments (DPIAs) [online]*. Available from https://ico.org.uk/for-organisations/guide-to-data-protection/guide-to-the-general-data-protection-regulation-gdpr/data-protection-impact-assessments-dpias [Accessed 30 Jun 2020].

[10]   Article 29 Data Protection Working Party. *Guidelines on data protection impact assessment [online]*. 4 April 2017. Available from http://ec.europa.eu/newsroom/document.cfm?doc_id=47711 [Accessed 30 Jun 2020].

[11]   Ziegeldorf J.H., Morchon O.G., Wehrle K. 'Privacy in the Internet of Things: threats and challenges'. *Security and Communication Networks*. 2014;**7**(12):2728–42.

[12]   Robertson T., Wagner I. 'CSCW and the Internet of Things'. Proceedings of the 14th European Conference on Computer Supported Cooperative Work; Oslo, Norway, September; 2015. pp. 285–94.

[13]   Mahmud R., Buyya R. 'Fog computing: a taxonomy, survey and future directions' in Di Martino B., K.C L., Yang L., Esposito A. (eds.). *Internet of Everything: Algorithms, Methodologies, Technologies and Perspectives*. Singapore: Springer; 2018. pp. 103–30.

[14]   Shi W., Cao J., Zhang Q., Li Y., Xu L. 'Edge computing: vision and challenges'. *IEEE Internet of Things Journal*. 2016;**3**(5):637–46.

[15]   Information Commissioner's Office. *Principle (a): lawfulness, fairness and transparency [online]*. Available from https://ico.org.uk/for-organisations/guide-to-data-protection/guide-to-the-general-data-protection-regulation-gdpr/principles/lawfulness-fairness-and-transparency [Accessed 30 Jun 2020].

[16]   Article 29 Data Protection Working Party. *Opinion 03/2013 on purpose limitation [online]*. 2 April 2013. Available from https://ec.europa.eu/justice/article-29/documentation/opinion-recommendation/files/2013/wp203_en.pdf [Accessed 30 Jun 2020].

[17]   European Commission. *Advancing the Internet of Things in Europe [online]*. 19 April 2016. Available from http://eur-lex.europa.eu/legal-content/EN/TXT/PDF/?uri=CELEX:52016SC0110&from=EN [Accessed 30 Jun 2020].

[18] Chiang M., Shi W. *NSF workshop report on grand challenges in edge computing [online]*. 26 October 2016. Available from http://iot.eng.wayne.edu/edge/NSF%20Edge%20Workshop%20Report.pdf [Accessed 30 Jun 2020].

[19] McAuley D., Mortier R., Goulding J. 'The dataware manifesto'. Proceedings of the 3rd International Conference on Communication Systems and Networks; Bangalore, India, Jan 2011; 2011. pp. 1–6.

[20] Chaudry A., Crowcroft J., Howard H., *et al*. 'Personal data: thinking inside the box'. *Proceedings of Critical Alternatives*; Aarhus, Denmark, August 2015. New York: ACM; 2015. pp. 29–32.

[21] Mudhavapeddy A., Scott D. 'Unikernels: the rise of the virtual library operating system'. *Communications of the ACM*. 2014;**57**(1):61–9.

[22] Article 29 Data Protection Working Party. *Opinion 02/2013 on apps and smart devices [online]*. 27 February 2013. Available from https://ec.europa.eu/justice/article-29/documentation/opinion-recommendation/files/2013/wp202_en.pdf [Accessed 30 Jun 2020].

[23] Harper J. 'The necessity of edge computing with the Internet of Things'. *AnalyticsWeek*, February 2016. Available from https://analyticsweek.com/content/the-necessity-of-edge-computing-with-the-internet-of-things [Accessed 30 June 2020].

[24] World Economic Forum. *Rethinking personal data: a new lens for strengthening trust [online]*. May 2014. Available from http://www3.weforum.org/docs/WEF_RethinkingPersonalData_ANewLens_Report_2014.pdf [Accessed 30 Jun 2020].

[25] Bolychevsky I. *'How solid is Tim's plan to redecentralize the web?' [online]*. *Medium*. 4 October 2018. Available from https://medium.com/@shevski/how-solid-is-tims-plan-to-redecentralize-the-web-b163ba78e835 [Accessed 30 Jun 2020].

[26] Larsen R., Brochot G., Lewis D., Eisma F., Brunini J. *Personal data stores'. European Commission [online]*. 7 August 2015. Available from https://ec.europa.eu/digital-single-market/en/news/study-personal-data-stores-conducted-cambridge-university-judge-business-school [Accessed 30 Jun 2020].

[27] Indiegogo. *Hub of all things [online]*. 26 October 2016. Available from https://www.indiegogo.com/projects/hat-claim-your-data-organise-visualise-control#/ [Accessed 30 Jun 2020].

[28] *HATDeX Platform [online]*. 2018. Available from https://hatdex.dataswift.io/the-platform [Accessed 30 Jun 2020].

[29] *HATDeX Platform Ratings [online]*. 2018. Available from https://www.hat-community.org/hat-dex-rating [Accessed 30 Jun 2020].

[30] Poikola A., Kuikkaniemi K., Honko H. 'MyData – a Nordic model for human-centered personal data management and processing'. *Open Knowledge Finland*, 2014. Available from http://urn.fi/URN:ISBN:978-952-243-455-5 [Accessed 30 Jun 2020].

[31] De Montjoye Y., Wang S., Pentland A. 'On the trusted use of large-scale personal data'. *Bulletin of the IEEE Technical Committee on Data Engineering*. 2012;**35**(4):5–8.

[32] De Montjoye Y.-A., Shmueli E., Wang S.S., Pentland A.S. 'openPDS: protecting the privacy of metadata through SafeAnswers'. *PLoS ONE*. 2014;**9**(7):e98790.

[33] OpenPDS. *Nesta [online]*. 2020. Available from https://www.nesta.org.uk/feature/me-my-data-and-i/open-pds/ [Accessed 30 Jun 2020].

[34] Crabtree A., Mortier R. Human data interaction: historical lessons from social studies and CSCW. *Proceedings of the 14th European Conference on Computer Supported Cooperative Work; Oslo, Norway, Sept 2015. Cham: Springer*; 2015. pp. 1–20.

[35] Kilic D., Crabtree A., McGarry G., Goulden G. 'The cardboard box study: understanding collaborative data management in the connected home.' Working paper, November 2020. Available from https://drive.google.com/file/d/1qrn n6bsUpvP5yDgG0mgehMGaYu8e0rd5/view?usp=sharing [Accessed 30 Nov 2020].

[36] Narayanan A., Barocas S., Toubiana V., Nissenbaum H. 'A critical look at decentralised personal data architectures'. *ArXiv*. 2012;**1202.450**.

[37] Amar Y., Haddadi H., Mortier R. 'Privacy-aware infrastructure for managing personal data'. Proceedings of SIGCOMM; Florianópolis; Brazil, August 2016; 2016. pp. 571–2.

[38] Mortier R., Zhao J., Crowcroft J., *et al*. 'Personal data management with the Databox: what's inside the box?'. Proceedings of the ACM Workshop on Cloud-Assisted Networking; Irvine, CA, USA, Dec 2016; 2016. pp. 49–54.

Chapter 7

Data protection by design and default: IoT app development

Tom Lodge[1] and Andy Crabtree[1]

Abstract

The European Union's General Data Protection Regulation (GDPR) requires that developers exercise due diligence and implement Data Protection by Design and Default (DPbD). Data Protection Impact Assessments (DPIAs) are recommended as a general heuristic. However, developers are not well equipped to deal with legal texts. Privacy engineering shifts the emphasis from interpreting texts and guidelines, or consulting legal experts, to embedding data protection within the development process itself. We present a privacy-oriented, flow-based integrated development environment (IDE) that enables due diligence in the construction of domestic IoT applications. The IDE (a) helps developers reason about personal data during the actual construction of IoT applications; (b) advises developers as to whether or not their design choices warrant a DPIA and (c) attach and make available to other relevant parties specific privacy-related information about an application.

7.1 Introduction

The European Union's General Data Protection Regulation (GDPR) [1] has recently come into effect. Core to compliance is the Data Protection by Design and Default (DPbD) requirement (Article 25). Recital 78 GDPR, which should be read in conjunction with Article 25, states that:

> Such measures could consist, inter alia, of minimising the processing of personal data, pseudonymising personal data as soon as possible, transparency with regard to the functions and processing of personal data, enabling the data subject to monitor the data processing, enabling the controller to create and improve security features.

[1]University of Nottingham, UK

Application developers who wish to process personal data are now obliged by regulation to take DPbD into account, unless they wish to be implicated in legal action that may result in fines of up €10 million or 2% of worldwide annual turnover, whichever is greater and which may be doubled if non-compliance is not rectified on the order of an EU member state. The DPbD requirement means that application developers can no longer treat data protection as someone else's problem, a disconnected process that sits solely within the province of legal specialists. On the contrary, GDPR (Article 5) renders 'data controllers', or the parties who commission data processing including the use of software applications, are accountable [2], which in turn places a due diligence requirement on developers.

A key heuristic mandated by GDPR is the Data Protection Impact Assessment (DPIA). DPIAs are a formal assessment of the privacy risks posed by a system. They are mandatory in cases where processing is likely to be 'high risk' and are otherwise recommended *wherever* personal data is processed. The assessment of whether or not a DPIA is necessary, and the act of conducting a DPIA, must necessarily draw upon implementation details, even if developers themselves are not personally accountable for performing a DPIA. This is underscored by the Article 29 Data Protection Working Party (now the European Data Protection Board): 'the processor should assist the controller in carrying out the DPIA and provide any necessary information' [3].

Software and application developers are not blind to the need to inform others of the risks as well as the benefits that accompany the use of their products [4]. However, developers generally lack the competence to deal effectively with privacy management [5–8] and the difficulties of complying with regulation are predicted to grow [9]. Traditionally, developers are faced with a couple of options. First, they may hand off due diligence to experts. This presupposes that (a) developers have access to experts, which is unlikely in the case of a lone developer or small business and (b) the privacy expert has the technical competence needed to understand the impact of development decisions upon privacy [10]. Guidelines exist to support the translation, yet these tend to be oriented towards a legal rather than technical domain. When they are aimed at the developer, either in the form of privacy patterns [11], checklists [12] or frameworks [13–15], they remain disconnected from the tools and environments developers use to build their applications. This can mean that they are employed in the later stages of the development workflow, rather than early on when changes to an application to improve privacy are most easily and effectively made.

The discipline of 'privacy engineering' [16] has recently emerged and aims to embed privacy practice more deeply in the actual development process. Privacy engineering practices are derived from privacy manifestoes such as privacy by design [17] and regulation (such as GDPR) and may include data flow modelling, risk assessment and privacy impact assessments. Good privacy engineering aims to embed privacy practice seamlessly into a developer's workflow, to allow it to be more easily assessed in relation to the specific artefacts being designed and implemented. By making privacy tools a core part of the development process, rather than something that sits alongside it, developers can be sensitised to the use of personal data (i.e., what it is and how it is being exploited) during the actual *in vivo* process of building applications. This, in turn, may encourage developers to reason about the implications of their applications and explore alternatives that minimise the risks of processing personal data. More concretely, by building notions of privacy into a development environment, the environment itself may provide guidance that relates specifically to the artefacts being built and can even feed into formal processes required by GDPR, such as the DPIA, to enable due diligence.

This chapter contributes to current efforts to engineer privacy through the design of an integrated development environment (IDE) enabling due diligence in the construction of domestic IoT applications. The IDE enables due diligence (a) in helping developers reason about personal data during the *in vivo* construction of IoT applications; (b) advising developers as to whether or not the design choices they are making occasion the need for a DPIA and (c) attaches and makes available to relevant other – including data processors, data controllers, data protection officers, data subjects and supervisory authorities – specific privacy-related information about an application. Our environment focuses on the development of domestic IoT applications as these present a highly salient privacy challenge operating as they do in traditionally private settings and processing data that is personal in nature but not, as we shall see, always immediately and obviously so.

7.2   Background

Various legal frameworks and regulatory guidelines impact application development that involves the processing of personal data. Of particular relevance to our work are (a) DPbD, a legally mandated successor to Privacy by Design that provides a set of best practice principles and emphasizes early engagement with data protection, and (b) DPIAs, a primary instrument and heuristic for assessing privacy and demonstrating compliance with the principles of DbPD. We outline support currently available to developers, covering frameworks and guidelines and work on codifying and translating legal concepts to technical domains. We conclude this section with a summary of various technical privacy tools and APIs available to developers.

7.2.1   Legal frameworks

7.2.1.1   Data protection by design and default
DPbD requires developers to engage in privacy-oriented reasoning early on in the design process, rather than late as a bolt-on stage to post hoc compliance. It has been embraced by Data Protection Authorities [18, 19], is supported by the European Commission [20, 21] and is legally required by GDPR [1]. DPbD promotes various data protection measures such as data minimisation, anonymisation, pseudonymisation and transparency as well as appropriate system security. Although the legal requirement for DPbD ought to provide sufficient incentive for developers to engage with its principles, there is no evidence that it has yet been widely adopted in the engineering process [22]. This may in part be due to the fact that its principles are largely disconnected from the actual practice of systems engineering; translating between the sometimes vague terminology in regulation to concrete engineering outcomes is non-trivial. Take, for example, the requirement for data minimisation. In practice this can include minimising data

collection, minimising disclosure, minimising linkability, minimising centralisation, minimising replication and minimising retention [23].

7.2.1.2   Data protection impact assessment

The DPIA is the recommended instrument for demonstrating compliance with regulation. However, DPIAs are not mandatory in all cases. This means that the decision as to whether or not a DPIA is required can only be made with reference to the detail of the design and implementation of code. DPIAs are legally required when a type of processing is 'likely to result in a high risk to the rights and freedoms of natural persons' [1]. While there is no definitive template for a DPIA, there is a list of when they are required [24] and GDPR states that there must be 'a level of rigour in proportion to the privacy risk arising'. This can be a nuanced distinction, especially when apps run on privacy enhancing technologies (PETs) designed to offer privacy protection. Even when personal data from IoT devices is processed, the requirement for a DPIA may be waived if the app presents a low privacy risk to a data subject. All of this and more draws into question how a developer is to assess the need for a DPIA? Any effort must draw heavily upon context and consider the particular environment an app will operate in and how it will process personal data.

7.2.2   Documentation

7.2.2.1   Frameworks

Several consortia promote the use of frameworks that adopt a common lexicon and standardised definitions for privacy practice. OASIS's Privacy Management Reference Model [13], for example, is a 11 000-word document that presents steps to identify risks and ways to address them. The NIST Privacy Risk Management Framework [14] is an ongoing effort at draft stage aimed at organisations to help 'better identify, assess, manage, and communicate privacy risks'. It takes a harm-based perspective on privacy, identifying a range of potential harms and developing a risk management approach including a set of specific privacy preserving activities to address them. There are also a variety of frameworks to help developers capture the development requirements necessary to mitigate likely privacy threats for a specific use case. Most notable is the LINDDUN methodology [15], which instructs developers as to the issues that should be investigated, and where in a design those issues could emerge. The methodology requires developers to construct use cases as Data Flow Diagrams (DFD) from a set of predefined elements, including (a) an external entity (an endpoint of the system), (b) a process (a computational unit), (c) a datastore (data at rest), (d) dataflow (data on the move) and (e) a trust boundary (the border between untrustworthy and trustworthy elements). The resulting use cases are translated into a set of high-level privacy engineering requirements, which are used as a basis for selecting from a set of privacy solutions to mitigate perceived threats (i.e. design patterns such as unlinkability, unobservability, etc.). The creation of the DFD is a key to the analysis. Naturally an incorrect DFD will lead to incorrect results.

7.2.2.2   Ideation cards

Luger *et al*. [25] consider an alternative approach towards enabling developers to respond to privacy risks. Their human-centered approach focuses on the early design stage of development, i.e., from the minute that 'pen hits paper'. They use an ideation card approach to sensitise and educate designers to regulation and its requirements. The cards foreground designers' reasoning about four core GDPR tenets: informed consent, data protection by design, data breach notifications and the right to be forgotten. Their work shows that 'a lack of awareness of the breadth of regulation' amongst developers limits the 'desire or ability to incorporate such considerations at an early stage'. In exploring ideation cards with a range of development practitioners (designers, programmers, human-computer interaction developers), Luger *et al*. make it visible that a threshold to knowledge needs to be bridged if developers are to understand and respond to regulation when designing and building applications that exploit personal data.

7.2.3   Bridging between tools and design

We turn now to consider technical tools that are currently available to developers, which offer a bridge between regulation and development practice.

7.2.3.1   Policies and ontologies

As with most legal texts, it is impossible to subsume GDPR in a purely technical system, though there have been attempts [26]. Policy and law frequently prescribe non-computational decisions that can only be affected by human judgement. In spite of the inherent difficulties of formalising regulation, work has been undertaken to create *translations* between the legal and technical domains. Typically, this has involved the codification of legal text to create formalisms that can be directly utilised by systems and code. The objectives vary from seeking to enforce legally binding policies [27, 28] to assessing a system's compliance or comparing the degree and scope to which systems comply with regulation. Pandit *et al.* [29], for example, provide an ontology for formalising relationships between regulations; Fatema *et al.* [27] present a method that uses Natural Language Processing to automate the translation between data protection rules and policy rules and Corrales *et al.* [30] elaborate an alternative approach that requires legal specialists to work more directly with code. The authors describe a system for building smart contracts that uses pseudo code in the form of a set of IF THEN clauses written by lawyers, which can be subsequently translated into a contract. However, the authors' goal is relatively modest to 'nudge' cloud providers to a greater level of compliance by aligning their data processing SLAs more closely with GDPR.

7.2.3.2   Design patterns

Privacy design patterns are repeatable solutions to recurring problems within a given context [11]. Patterns may be chosen and applied to satisfy a set of privacy goals, e.g. anonymity, unlinkability, unobservability, pseudonymity, minimisation, etc. In most cases, systems will require that a variety of patterns are composed together using a pattern language. In the context of privacy by design, few design patterns have been presented to date. Hafiz [31] presents a set of privacy mitigations in response to known attacks and has developed a pattern language [32] to help developers choose patterns that are relevant to a particular domain (the domestic IoT is not one). Pearson *et al*. [33, 34] seek to move beyond guides and checklists towards 'automated support for software developers in early phases of software development' given that they 'do not usually possess privacy expertise'. The authors utilise a decision support-based system where developers provide a set of requirements (in the form of a questionnaire), and these are then used to generate a candidate set of high-level privacy patterns (such as opt-in consent, or negotiation around privacy preferences) that must be implemented by the developer. Privacy patterns offer a useful reference for developers [35], though typically at a relatively late stage of design when a range of choices and decisions have been made. They also help document common practices and standardise terminology. Practically, however, the problem remains that developers must have the necessary competence to choose and implement patterns relevant to the artefacts that they are designing.

7.2.4   Privacy tools

The discipline of privacy engineering aims to improve support for developers by embedding privacy support more within everyday development tools. Various tools have emerged to help developers build applications and systems that are compliant with some aspect of GDPR. These tools concentrate on *technical compliance* with GDPR, for example, that their systems meet security standards, that they restrict the flow of personal data, or that they fulfil contractual obligations and meet auditing requirements.

7.2.4.1   Automated program analysis

Some progress has been made in considering how program analysis techniques might be used to help demonstrate privacy compliance. The approach has its roots in efforts to identify security vulnerabilities (e.g. data leakage, permission misuse, malware). Taint analysis, for example, examines program execution by tracking local variables and heap allocations. Sensitive data is labelled or 'tainted' so it can be tracked as it flows through a system and arrives at a 'sink' (the point where data is exposed, e.g. network access). Tainted data may move through multiple paths before arriving at a sink, so multiple flows may need to be analysed. An important consideration with taint analysis is identification of the sources of data that are deemed to be sensitive. In the mobile domain, the authors of Taintdroid [36] taint phone sensor data (e.g. microphone, accelerometer, GPS, camera), contacts and text messages, and device identifiers (IMEI, phone number, SIM card IDs). The authors of Flowdroid [37] extend taints to include data from user interface fields (e.g. user passwords). In IoT domains, SAINT [38] marks all sensor device states, device information, location data, user inputs and state variables as sensitive. To make analysis tractable, there is a trade-off between ensuring that all potentially sensitive data is tainted while minimising false positives that arise from tainting non-sensitive data. Ferrara [39, 40] applies taint analysis to demonstrate compliance with GDPR. The outputs from analysis take the form of privacy leak reports. However, further contextually dependent analysis is required to determine whether a 'leak' actually constitutes a violation of privacy. While program analysis techniques can be used to demonstrate that an application is free of certain security vulnerabilities and inform analysis of privacy vulnerabilities, higher-level analysis is needed to identify, for example, whether data exposure is a deliberate and legitimate design decision or data marked as 'sensitive' is or is not so within a specific context. The specific intentions of an application, the specific data being processed, the specific processing being undertaken and the context of disclosure all play a part in the analysis of taints.

7.2.4.2 APIs and services

Cloud-based data privacy services, or Data Privacy as a Service (DPaaS), are also beginning to emerge and sit between applications and data providers. The types of services on offer include disclosure notices, consent management, compliance software or solutions to more technically challenging privacy engineering tasks. Privatar, for example, provides Publisher [41], which offers policy-controlled data pipelines to de-identify data, and Lens [42] utilises differential privacy to provide insights over sensitive data. However, this class of solution is not aimed at the developer per se but instead seeks to enable businesses to *outsource* privacy management.

7.3   Designing for due diligence

Despite the best efforts of privacy engineering to date, we are unaware of any examples of privacy tools that are actually embedded *within* development environments and which allow developers to reason about the risks to privacy created by the specific artefacts that they are building *as* they are building them. In this section we consider how *in vivo* support for due diligence might be more strongly embedded within development environments. We begin by explicating DPIA before relating guidance to our own development environment.

GDPR promotes the use of a DPIA for two primary reasons: first, as a heuristic device enabling DPbD, and second as a tool for evidencing compliance. As Article 29 Data Protection Working Party (A29WP) guidance on the DPIA puts it 'in cases where it is not clear whether a DPIA is necessary [one should be] carried out nonetheless' [3]. Moreover, A29WP takes the view that 'carrying out a DPIA is a continual process, not a one-time exercise encourage[ing] the creation of solutions which promote compliance' (ibid.). From the developer perspective a more pressing concern might be to demonstrate to oneself and/or one's employer that reasonable steps have been taken to comply with the regulation. The primary practical consideration for a developer is, then, to *determine whether or not a DPIA is needed* in the first instance.

Article 35(1) of the GDPR states that a DPIA must be carried out:

Where a type of processing in particular using new technologies, and taking into account the nature, scope, context and purposes of the processing, is likely to result in a high risk to the rights and freedoms of natural persons.

Guidance on whether or not a DPIA is necessary is provided by each EU member state, though A29WP specifies nine 'common criteria' and that 'processing meeting *two criteria* would require a DPIA to be carried out'.

The criteria warranting the conduct of a DPIA include:

1. evaluation and scoring
2. automated decision-making with legal or similar significant effect
3. when the processing prevents data subjects from exercising a right or using a service or entering a contract
4. systematic monitoring
5. sensitive data or data of a highly personal nature
6. matching or combining datasets
7. innovative use or applying new technological or organisational solutions
8. data processed on a large scale
9. data concerning vulnerable subjects.

The first two criteria are concerned with the methods used to process personal data: evaluation and scoring relates to the use of personal data for the creation of models that might then be used as a basis for profiling or predicting; automated decision-making is concerned with outcomes generated without any human intervention with the principal risk being discriminatory algorithms that create legal or similarly significant effects. The third criterion applies to any and all cases of processing that can result in a denial of service, right or contract (e.g. insurance, government services, education, finance). Systematic monitoring is concerned with the observation, monitoring or control of data subjects, particularly when they are unaware and have not provided consent. The predominant scenario is monitoring in public spaces, where it may be impossible for individuals to avoid processing, but domestic settings are not exempt given that sensors often gather data without the explicit awareness of householders. In home environments it is tempting to treat all data from IoT devices as sensitive or of a highly personal nature as per criterion number 5, given that it relates to a private setting and may be attributable to an individual or household. However, this blanket approach may impede innovation and impact individual's ability to leverage their data for personal benefit. It would be more prudent to help developers explore the design implications of different types of personal data.

The risks involved in matching and combining datasets emerge from the potential for secondary inferences to be made without the explicit consent of a user. The guidance is primarily concerned here with cases where combined data derives from multiple sources rather than, for example, from within a single app, and thus stands outside the original remit for processing the data. With respect to criterion number 7, it has been suggested that the risks to privacy created by the IoT will render a DPIA mandatory for most IoT devices [20]. However, this is arguably a time limited viewpoint as the IoT will not remain innovative for long and is indeed already becoming commonplace. Furthermore, we imagine that any diligent developer will want to assess the privacy implications of any new solution they create if only to avoid the harsh financial penalties of GDPR. Criterion number 8 refers to processing that involves extensive numbers of users, volumes of data, geographic reach and/or duration of the processing activity. Criterion number 9, refers to data processing that relies on a power imbalance between data subjects and controllers and includes, for example, children, those with disabilities, workers, etc. Clearly, determining just what these common criteria amount to on any occasion of design requires a degree of *interpretive flexibility* [12], but A29WP nevertheless provides a framework around which we can consider embedding due diligence within the actual *in vivo* process of building IoT applications. In the following section, we consider how we can exploit knowledge about the way in which an app is constructed, and the method and type of data being processed, to enable due diligence in design.

7.4   Embedding support for due diligence in design

As underscored by AP29WP, the question of whether or not a DPIA is required lies at the heart of due diligence. It is a question that must be *continuously asked throughout development*. Accordingly, our aims in seeking to embed due diligence into an IoT application development environment are to:

1. Enable *in vivo* (i.e. during app construction) reflection on and reasoning about the impact of the developer's design choices on privacy and the risks they may occasion.
2. Provide advice to developers that responds to data protection regulation and which is specific to the application being built. This advice will relate to:
   (a) determining whether or not a DPIA is likely to be needed;
   (b) the details of design/implementation that most influence that decision.

Our starting point is to consider a paradigm that suits both the development of IoT applications and reasoning about privacy. GDPR is principally concerned with the *flow of personal data* and it is common, when assessing data privacy, to employ data flow diagrams, where data flows are represented as edges between nodes. Nodes may be locations (e.g. EU member states or third countries), systems, organisations or data subjects. Edges between nodes represent the flow of data. The building blocks of data flow modelling have also been successfully applied to programming paradigms. Data flow programming emphasises the movement of data between nodes (black boxes of functionality) along a series of edges (connections where data are transferred). It is particularly suited to the IoT, where it often makes sense to model systems and applications as sources of data, connected to processes *en route* to a final endpoint (i.e. actuation or external service).

We therefore use data flow programming as the basis of our development environment. We leverage it to simultaneously enable developers to build application functionality and support their reasoning about privacy. We distinguish between several top-level node types where there is a mapping between privacy and developer domains. The simplest application will be built from *sources of data*, *processors* that act upon the data and sinks or *outputs* that produce an event (which may or may not include external data transfer). We consider each in turn:

- *Sources of data.* When working with data, the first job of the developer is to determine which data are personal, and which are not. This is not straightforward. Take, for example, the UK Information Commissioner's Office which has published a 23-page document entitled 'What Is Personal Data?' [43]. Nevertheless, a developer must be able to reason about the fifth DPIA criterion (i.e., sensitive data or data of a highly personal nature) in order to judge whether a DPIA is necessary.
- *Processors.* When operating upon personal data, processors may: (a) reidentify a data subject; (b) generate new personal data (using, for example, data fusion, inference, profiling) or (c) remove personal data (e.g. through anonymisation/ pseudonymisation). To help map applications built in our IDE to regulation, we introduce two processor subtypes: a profiler and a privacy pattern. A profiler is a node that can infer *new personal information* (not already explicitly contained in its input data) about a data subject (for example, by employing machine learning). A privacy pattern is one of a set of 'off the shelf' privacy preserving techniques (e.g. pseudo/anonymisation, metadata stripping, encryption) that may be employed to resolve privacy issues. By making these distinctions, developers may more easily reason about the first, second and sixth DPIA criteria (evaluation and scoring, automated decision-making, matching or combining datasets).
- *Outputs.* These are the points in an app where data are consumed be it for sensor actuation, data visualisation or data export. It is here that careful reasoning about data usage must occur, and the remaining DPIA criteria must be considered.

Figure 7.1 provides an overview of the principle building blocks for constructing apps in our IDE. An application is simply a set of connections between combinations of nodes. The IDE furnishes a library of nodes that provide common operations, which can be specialised through configuration. We also provide a 'general' processing node that gives developers the ability to write raw code. The advantage of providing sets of library nodes, aside from simplifying development, is that we retain an understanding of how use of these nodes affects the data's characteristics as it flows through an app. We can present this information to developers to help them reason about the risks their app may pose to users.

7.4.1   Tracking personal data

The primary requirement is to be able to understand whether or not the data used by an app is personal and/or sensitive in nature. GDPR distinguishes between 'personal' and 'non-personal' (anonymous) data, with a further distinction around 'special categories' of data (Article 9) to which additional protections apply. Our aim

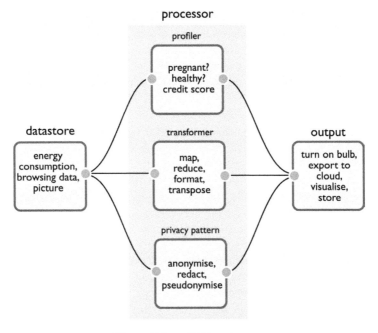

Figure 7.1   IDE node types

is to help developers reason about whether the often seemingly benign data that an app operates on has the potential to reveal personal and even sensitive insights. Furthermore, we want to flag cases where transformations – occasioned, for example, by the fusion of data with other sources, profiling or inference – change the personal information contained in the data. To tackle this challenge, we consider a minimum set of personal data features that will enable this reasoning:

- **Data categorisation.** This reflects the observation that all personal data is not equal. Article 17(1) and Recital 46, GDPR, confirm that the 'nature of the personal data' to be protected should be taken into account. Cradock *et al.* [44] note that categorising personal data is one way of contextualising it and understanding its nature. They note that categories can act as an anchor to which further information about processing can be attached, which can help with the creation of DPIAs. From the perspective of a developer, categorisation can act as an aid to reasoning around the nature and severity of risk for particular design decisions.
- **Derivable characteristics.** Personal data may be combined with other data to reveal further personal insights. To reflect this, we distinguish between *primary* and *secondary* sources of personal data. As with primary data, secondary data is fitted to category, but will also be attached to a set of conditions that must be met before the category is applied. Typically, these conditions might include the existence of particular combinations of personal data. For example, given

various physical characteristics, it may be possible to infer gender, but conditions could also include such things as sampling rate, e.g. of live energy data, which may make it possible to derive household occupancy patterns whereas daily readings will not. We distinguish between the possibility and actuality of an inference being made, to reflect, for example, cases where a set of conditions make inferences theoretically possible, even if they are not realised by an app.

- **Data accuracy.** Inaccurate data has as much potential to cause privacy harms as accurate data. There is a challenge in ensuring that applications do not lead to unfair, unrepresentative and even dangerous outcomes as a result of inaccurate data. Getting developers to reason about the accuracy of the data that their application process is therefore an important part of the mix.

With regard to data categorisation, various approaches have been proposed in the design literature [45], by data protection authorities [1] and technical consortia [46]. There is considerable divergence across approaches and weaknesses in each [44]. For our own purposes, none can be used to capture the types of IoT data that developers are working with, nor are any able to support the particular form of developer reasoning around personal data processing that we require to support due diligence. In developing our own categorisation, we are not presenting our work *fait accompli*, but as a vehicle for investigating how we might contextualise personal data to improve support for developer reasoning. With regard to *derivable characteristics,* we want to be able to calculate and present the creation or loss of personal data at each processing point within an app. Figure 7.2 provides a summary of each transformation we deal with. The blue squares represent a data processor that performs some kind of transformation on personal data inputs (Px). The conditions block (v) shows, in the first case, that when personal data is captured at a low

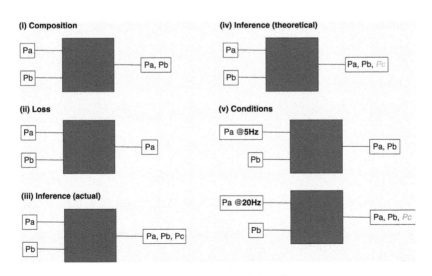

Figure 7.2   Personal data flows

frequency, it is not possible for an inference (Pc) to be made. In the second case, with a higher sampling frequency, the inference is made possible.

7.4.2   Developing a categorisation

We now present more detail on the schema we have developed to help developers exercise due diligence. Inspired by GDPR, our schema distinguishes between three top level classes of personal data: *identifier, sensitive, personal* each of which may be primary or secondary depending on whether or not they are inferred (Table 7.1).

As can be seen in Table 7.2, type and ordinal attributes establish the top-level type. The category, subtype and description attributes provide additional context to provide information to app developers. To illustrate with an example, a data subject's undergraduate degree is classified under type: personal; category: education; subtype: qualification. The schema has a required attribute to denote which attributes must be present for the particular categorisation to apply. For example, if an IoT camera provides a timestamp, bitmap and light reading, the bitmap is the only attribute that must be present for the data to be treated as personal.

We extend the schema for secondary (i.e., inferred) types to denote the conditions that must be satisfied to make an inference possible (see Table 7.3). We do not claim that our schema can classify all possible personal data types, but in the absence of a universal standard it is sufficient. We currently define two types of

Table 7.1   Personal data types

Label	Type	Ordinal	Description
i1	Identifier	Primary	Data that directly identifies a data subject
i2	Identifier	Secondary	Data that indirectly identifies a data subject
p1	Personal	Primary	Data that is evidently personal
p2	Personal	Secondary	Derived personal data
s1	Sensitive	Primary	GDPR special categories of data
s2	Sensitive	Secondary	Derived sensitive data

Table 7.2   Personal data attributes

Attribute	Description
Type	Identifier | sensitive | personal
Ordinal	Primary | secondary
Category	Physical | education | professional | state | contact | consumption | , etc.
Subtype	For example, physical includes hair colour, eye colour, tattoos, etc. education includes primary school, secondary school, university, etc.
Description	Details of this particular item of personal data (and method of inference if secondary)
Required	List of attributes of this data that must be present in order for it to constitute as personal

Table 7.3   Secondary data attributes

Attribute	Description
Confidence	An accuracy score for this particular inference, ranging from 0 to 1
Conditions	List of *granularity* | *attributes*
Evidence	Where possible, a set of links to any evidence that details a particular inference method
Status	*Inferred* | *inferable*

condition: *attributes* and *granularity*. Attributes are the additional set of personal data items that, if combined, make a further inference possible. Granularity relates to the threshold sampling frequency necessary for an inference to be possible. When multiple attribute and/or granularity conditions are combined, all must hold for an inference to be possible. Finally, our *status* attribute distinguishes between personal data where (a) an inference has been made and (b) the data are available for an inference to be possible. For example, web browsing data and gender may make pregnancy theoretically inferable but if a node uses this data to make an actual pregnancy prediction the data are inferred.

7.5   Implementation and overview of the IDE

We now provide implementation details of our web-based IDE, which utilises the concepts we have discussed thus far. It is important to note that this work presumes that the privacy constraints that are built into our IDE's applications can and will be respected at runtime, i.e. that there is a PET that can enforce the contracts entered into between a data subject and an application. In our particular case, the applications that are constructed in our IDE run on the Databox platform [47]. The Databox platform utilises an app store, from which privacy preserving apps can be downloaded to dedicated hardware, within the home. For the purposes of the work presented here, the critical features of the platform are that it:

1. **Supports local data processing**. Databox promotes, but does not mandate, local processing over data transfer and external processing. Thus, it is feasible and indeed preferable to run applications that either do *not* transfer data to an external service, or that ensure that the smallest amount of data are transferred for a specific purpose (i.e. data minimisation).
2. **Provides access to multiple silos of IoT data**. Databox has a growing set of drivers that communicate with and collect data from IoT devices and online services and make them available to apps.
3. **Enforces contracts between data subjects and applications**. Apps built in the IDE may be published to the Databox app store. When publishing an app, a developer must provide information to inform data subjects about the data that

will be accessed and the purpose, benefits and perceived risks that attach to its use. These contracts or SLAs are rigorously enforced by the Databox.

The IDE runs out of a web-browser; the frontend and backend are written in Javascript. We utilised Node-RED [48] as the starting point for the IDE, as this is a mature and popular community IoT development tool. We undertook a full rewrite of the Node-RED frontend and modified the backend to support our new features. The following lists the most significant differences between our IDE and Node-RED:

1. Datastore nodes and output nodes communicate with the Databox API to collect data.
2. Applications are bundled with a manifest that specifies the resources the app needs to access in order to function.
3. Nodes in the IDE provide a function that takes the node inputs as an argument and outputs a schema describing the output data (in Node-RED, nodes are oblivious to the details of the upstream nodes).

We also maintain two separate schemas for each node: (a) the *personal schema* contains the personal characteristics of each attribute of the data (i.e. a representation of the categorisation we described in Section 7.4.2) and (b) a *type schema* that is used to provide downstream nodes with the type of data that is output from node. The personal schema includes the rules that determine the conditions under which new personal data might emerge. For example, a part of a Bluetooth sensor's datastore schema has an entry as follows:

```
{
    type: "personal",
    subtype: "relationships",
    ordinal: "secondary",
    status: "inferable",
    description: "bluetooth  scan  information  can  be  used  to  infer
social relationships",
    required: ["payload.address"],
    conditions: [{
                type: "granularity",
            granularity: {threshold: 300, unit: "seconds between
        scans"}
            }],
    evidence: [
            "https://dl.acm.org/citation.cfm?id=2494176",
            "https://doi.org/10.1109/MPRV.2005.37"
    ],
}
```

This states that relationship data can be inferred if the Bluetooth sensor scans obtain the mac address (payload.address) with a frequency greater than or equal to once every 300 seconds. The personal schema also provides optional descriptive details on the details of the inference (e.g. how it is possible, any relevant details, papers, etc.); this information will be presented to developers when they construct applications that make use of the Bluetooth sensor.

The type schema is specified using JSON Schema.[a] Here is a snippet for the Bluetooth sensor:

```
{
    name: {
        type: 'string',
        description:    'the    name    of    the    node,    defaults    to
    \'sensingkit\''
    },
    id: {
        type: 'string',
        description: '<i>[id]</i>'
    },
    type: {
        type: 'string',
        description: '<i>sensingkit</i>'
    },
    subtype: {

        type: 'string',
        description: `<i>${subtype}</i>`
    },
    payload: {
        type: 'object',
        description: 'the message payload',
        properties: {
            ts: {
                type: 'number',
                description: 'a unix timestamp'
            },
            name: {
                type: 'string',
                description: 'user assigned name of the device'
            },
            address: {
                type: 'string',
                description:    'mac    address    in    the    form
aa:bb:cc:dd:ee:ff'
            },
            rssi: {
                type: 'number',
                description: 'received signal strength indicator'
            },
        }
    }
}
```

[a]https://json-schema.org/

Table 7.4   Accelerometer personal data schema

Attribute	Description
Type	Personal
Subtype	Gender
Ordinal	Secondary
Required	*[x,y,z]*

The 'description' field in the schema is used to provide more specific sensor type information to the developer. Every time a node's configuration changes, all downstream nodes will utilise the JSON Schema to re-calculate their own schemas.

The purpose of the schemas is to help the IDE to annotate the characteristics of personal data as it flows through an application. Each edge is marked with a summary of the personal data type (e.g. primary, secondary, sensitive). On the backend, all applications are saved as JSON node-RED compatible flow files, alongside a manifest file that describes the resources (sensors/storage) that the application will access as well as the purpose and benefits of the app. Some of these details are gathered from the developer at publication time. The application is bundled into a Docker container [49] and uploaded to a registry referenced in the manifest file.

7.5.1   Using the IDE

To illustrate a basic example consider Table 7.4, which outlines the relevant parts of the accelerometer schema for the flows in Figures 7.3 and 7.4.

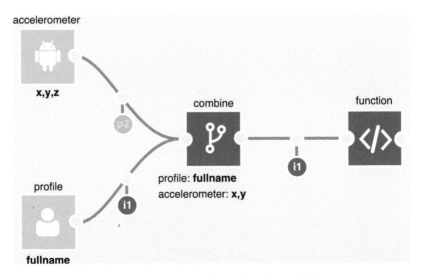

Figure 7.3   Applying the schema (a)

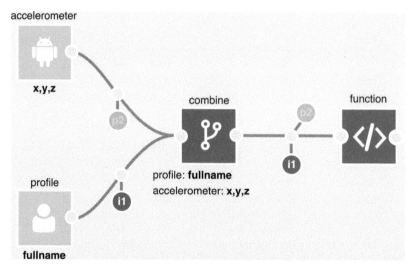

Figure 7.4   Applying the schema (b)

In Figure 7.3, *p2* is output from the accelerometer to show that personal data (i.e., a data subject's gender) is *inferable* from the *x,y,* and *z* components of its data (it is semi-transparent to denote it is *inferable* rather than *inferred*).

Similarly, with the profile node, *i1* is output to show *fullname*. When these are merged in the combine processor, the output schema will contain the accelerometer's *p2*, and the profile's *i1*.

In Figure 7.4, the combine node is now configured to only combine the *x* and *y* components of the accelerometer data with the profile data. Since *x, y* and *z* are all marked as required (Table 7.4) for a gender inference to be possible, the combine node's output schema will only contain *i1* (and not *p2*). The IDE automatically recalculates and re-represents the flow of personal data whenever a node or edge is removed, added or reconfigured. This becomes invaluable as flows get more complex as it provides the developer immediate feedback on how changes in configuration will affect the flow of personal data. The IDE also flags points in an app that may require further attention from the developer, e.g. when personal data is being exported off the box (i.e., connected to the *export* node).

7.5.2   *Providing DPIA recommendations*

In this section we illustrate, again with reference to an example, how the IDE can provide DPIA advice to a developer. We consider an app that provides a quote for medical cover, based principally on a user's personal data. The app will calculate a score by assimilating personal data about shopping habits, physical fitness and user profile information. It will export this score to an insurance broker to generate a personalised quote. Figure 7.5 shows three yellow data stores: smart watch electrocardiogram (ECG) data, user profile information (address and contact details) and grocery shopping data (from, for example, online orders or store card data).

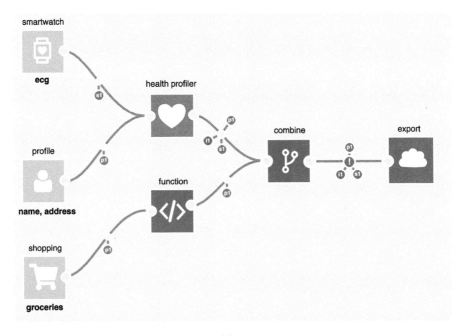

Figure 7.5   Health insurance app quote

The ECG and profile data are fed into a health profiler, which will calculate a score. Similarly, the shopping data is passed into a bespoke function which will generate a score. These two scores are passed into a 'combine' processor, which will generate the final score sent to the insurance broker. The badges on the output from the health profile node reflect the two classes of input data (the sensitive health data from the smart watch and the personal data from the profile) as well as the new inferred data (the health score). Note that there is a large red exclamation mark between the combine node and the export node that flags to the developer that personal and sensitive data is being exported off the box.

The exclamation mark represents a point within the app where a DPIA may be necessary, in this case because personal data is being exported. When selected, the IDE will present the developer with a DPIA screening form (Figure 7.6) which is tailored, in part, to the details of the app. The form is broken down into a set of questions with yes/no answers. These questions have been drawn from the nine criteria outlined by A29WP (see Section 7.3) and also provide the transparency required under Recital 78 GDPR. To provide as much guidance as possible to the developer, the IDE uses app-specific information to provide context for each of the questions. Take, for example, the use of sensitive and personal data: the DPIA screening form lists all of the personal data being processed (in this case, identity data from the profile node, personal data from the shopping node and sensitive data from the smart watch node).

DPIA

In some instances, in order to comply with **EU's General Data Protection Regulation**, you will need to undertake a Data Protection Impact Assessment (DPIA), prior to publishing your app. Please answer the questions below in order to get an indication whether a **DPIA may be required** in this instance.

status: DPIA recommended

3 of 9 criteria have been marked yes

Nature of your data

The type of data being collected will strongly influence the likelihood and severity of risk your app exposes a user to	
Sensitive or personal data use Your app uses **3** data sources which emit **identity data (name, address)**, **personal data (groceries)** and **sensitive data (ecg)**. Were this data exposed to third parties (either intentionally or accidentally), could it result in any serious impact on the app user's daily life or lead to any loss of rights or freedoms?	yes
Evaluation / scoring In the following part of your application, **ecg** and **name,address** data is input into the **health profiling node.** This means that your application **is** doing evaluation/scoring. ecg name, address → ❤ — combine Please indicate whether any of the parts of your app below are used to evaluate or score, profile or predict the nature or behaviour of a user. groceries — </> — combine	yes
Innovative technological solutions Your app is **not** making any use of new sensors or devices. Will you be applying any new organisational solutions to process personal data?	no

Data usage "off the databox"

Identity (name, address), Personal (groceries) and sensitive (ecg) data is is being exported off the databox, the app user will relinquish some or all control over its usage. There is an assumed elevated risk if it is used for any of the following:	
Automated decisions Will any decisions be made, without human intervention, that may significantly affect the user (for example, legal decisions or access to services or resources, credit checks, loan applications, use of machine learning?	yes
Systematic monitoring / tracking The **ecg** data could potentially be used to monitor or track a user's behaviour. Will this be the case with your app?	no
Restriction of rights or access to a service / contract Will the data be used to prevent or reduce access to a service or contract, or impinge upon a user's rights (e.g. freedom of speech, freedom of thought, freedom of movement, prohibition of discrimination, right to liberty, conscience and religion)?	no
Matching or combining datasets **Once exported**, will the data be combined with data from other data processing operations, performed for different purposes and/or by different data controllers in a way that would exceed the reasonable expectations of the data subject?	no
Processing on a large scale **Once exported**, will the data be combined with data from other data processing operations, performed for different purposes and/or by different data controllers in a way that would exceed the reasonable expectations of the data subject?	no

Envisaged user

Certain groups of user are deemed more vulnerable to risk, and will require an enhanced risk assessment	
Typical user Is your app aimed at children or vulnerable groups (e.g. the elderly, disabled, persecuted, health impaired)	no

Figure 7.6   IDE DPIA recommendation

In relation to the evaluation/scoring question, the DPIA screening form presents those parts of the application where it occurs (where data flows into the health profile node) as well as where it might occur (where shopping data is used by the function node). Because the IDE knows that the health profile node generates a score, the screening form sets the answer to the question as 'yes', and this cannot be toggled by the developer. The only way to set it to 'no' would be to remove the health profiler node. Five of the A29WP criteria are only relevant in cases where data are exported and may therefore be subject to further processing. In our example, because data are exported, the screening form asks an additional set of yes/no questions about follow-on processing. Finally of note, is the question of systematic monitoring. Again, the IDE is able to provide some context. In this case, the smartwatch data could, in theory, be used to systematically monitor a user, so this is flagged to the developer. Although a DPIA may not be recommended as a result of answering these questions, the answers provided will nevertheless be made available when the app is published to alert relevant parties to the fact that due diligence has been exercised.

7.6 Enabling due diligence

GDPR creates a practical imperative for developers to take reasonable steps to ensure the applications they build are compliant with regulation and that they implement DPbD. The DPIA provides a key heuristic enabling due diligence and the commensurate implementation of DPbD. We have sought to move beyond providing developers with external guidance and instead adopted a privacy engineering perspective to build due diligence into the development environment itself. Our goal in doing so has been (a) to help developers reason about personal data during the *in vivo* construction of IoT applications; (b) advise developers as to whether or not the design choices they are making occasion the need for a DPIA and (c) to make specific privacy-related information about an application available to relevant others implicated in application development and the processing of personal data, including data processors, data controllers, data protection officers, data subjects and ultimately, supervisory authorities.

We do not suggest that the IDE provides a silver bullet to the manifold challenges of compliance, nor that due diligence with respect to DPbD can be wholly automated. Of the nine criteria implicated in determining the need for a DPIA, five require that developers draw upon information external to app construction. Thus, criteria number 3 (where processing denies a right, service or contract), 6 (matching or combining datasets), 7 (innovative new solutions), 8 (data processed on a large scale) and 9 (data concerning vulnerable subjects) turn on a developer's knowledge of an app, its novelty, what it will be used for, its intended users and what might subsequently be done with their data. The IDE does not negate human skill and judgement, and in this respect there will still be need for education and learning (e.g. as to what constitutes 'vulnerable', or the 'rights and freedoms' that may be impacted through data processing). However, the IDE does sensitise developers to key DPbD concerns and make us aware of the issues we need to be able to address if we are to satisfy ourselves and those to whom we are professionally accountable that we have acted with due diligence.

The IDE demonstrates that it is not only possible to sensitise developers to core DPbD concerns to build due diligence into application development by surfacing salient information and advice within the *in vivo* process of app construction. While the IDE cannot directly address criteria six (matching or combining datasets) or eight (data processed on a large scale), it can *flag* to the developer that personal data is exported elsewhere (i.e., for processing outside an app) or when a function node (i.e., a node that permits arbitrary code) operates on personal data. Furthermore, by introducing different classes of processing node, and specifically profiling nodes, the IDE can flag concerns that directly relate to DPIA criteria number 1 (evaluation and scoring) and 2 (automated processing with legal or similar effect). Criterion four (systematic monitoring) is flagged by reference to the type and rate of flow of personal data, both of which the IDE can determine from an app's construction (i.e., when personal data flows to an output at a threshold rate). The IDE also has access to the personal data types and configurations of input nodes (i.e., sensors), and the characteristics of data flowing through an app also enable the IDE to assess whether criterion five (sensitive data or data of a highly personal nature) is a relevant concern and, if it is, to flag this to the developer.

Our IDE has been inspired by the program analysis community to some extent, particularly the use of taint tracking. However, unlike taint tracking, our goal is not to discover program vulnerabilities but to make the flow of personal data amenable to analysis by developers in order that they can make demonstrably diligent design decisions with respect to the DPbD requirement. Just as taint tracking has its limitations, so does the IDE: our schema will not cover all possible personal data types, we cannot encode an exhaustive set of rules for all possible inferences across all personal data and we cannot definitively state which DPIA criteria are met. We can only prompt the developer to assess potential conflicts. However, privacy assessments are unlikely ever to become fully automated, given the highly interpretable character of the law and the limits of mapping between technical and legal domains. Nonetheless, encouraging early reasoning that is directly relevant to the application in hand is in the spirit of regulation and manifestoes such as Privacy by Design. The IDE demonstrates that we can move DPbD beyond costly expert advice, disconnected documentation and after the fact considerations. Instead we might embed due diligence in the application development environment, and in the actual *in vivo* process of app construction, to assist developers in understanding the privacy risks that accompany their particular design choices and to help them arrive at an informed judgement as to whether or not a DPIA is needed to comply with the requirements of GDPR.

7.7 Conclusion

IoT application developers, like developers everywhere, find themselves confronted by the GDPR and the associated DPbD requirement. It is imperative that developers demonstrate due diligence and take reasonable steps to meet the DPbD requirement when building IoT applications. Yet developers largely lack the competence to understand legal requirements or to translate them into technical requirements, and legal experts are often similarly challenged in reverse. We have presented an IDE to demonstrate the possibility of building due diligence *into* IoT application development. The IDE is designed to help developers understand personal data and reason about its use, to identify potential DPbD conflicts and to make specific design choices available to others to whom the developer is professionally accountable. The IDE flags the privacy implications of the design choices a developer makes *as they make them* and provides them with the tools to reflect upon and alter a design decision when it is most easily accomplished. The IDE is not a silver bullet, but it does show that is possible to engineer privacy into the IoT at early stage in the design life cycle.

7.8   Acknowledgements

The research reported here was supported by the Engineering and Physical Sciences Research Council [grant numbers EP/M001636/1, EP/N028260/1, EP/N028260/2]. It is based on the following original works:

- Lodge T., Crabtree A. and Brown A. (2018) Developing GDPR Compliant Apps for the Edge. In *Data Privacy Management, Cryptocurrencies and Blockchain Technology* (eds. Garcia-Alfaro J., Herrera-Joancomartí J., Livraga G. and Rios R.). Cham: Springer, pp. 313-328. https://doi.org/10.1007/978-3-030-00305-0_22
- Lodge T., Crabtree A. and Brown A. (2018) IoT App Development: Supporting Data Protection by Design and Default. *Proceedings of the International Joint Conference on Pervasive and Ubiquitous Computing*, Singapore, October 2018. New York: ACM, pp. 901-910. https://doi.org/10.1145/3267305.3274151
- Lodge T. and Crabtree A. (2019) Privacy Engineering for Domestic IoT: Enabling Due Diligence. *Sensors*, vol. 19 (20), https://doi.org/10.3390/s19204380

References

[1] Crabtree A., Lodge T., Colley J., *et al.* 'Building accountability into the Internet of things: the IoT Databox model'. *Journal of Reliable Intelligent Environments*. 2018;4(1):39–55.

[2] General Data Protection Regulation. *Official Journal of the European Union.* 4 May 2016. Available from https://eur-lex.europa.eu/legal-content/EN/TXT/?uri=OJ%3AL%3A2016%3A119%3ATOC [Accessed 23 Feb 2021].

[3]   Urquhart L., Lodge T., Crabtree A. 'Demonstrably doing accountability in the Internet of things'. *International Journal of Law and Information Technology*. 2019;**27**(1):1–27.

[4]   Article 29 Working Party. *Guidelines on data protection impact assessment (DPIA)* [online]; European Commission: Brussels, WP248 rev.01. Available from   https://ec.europa.eu/newsroom/article29/item-detail.cfm?item_id= 611236 [Accessed 23 Feb 2021].

[5]   Roeser S. 'Emotional engineers: toward morally responsible design'. *Science and Engineering Ethics*. 2012;**18**(1):103–15.

[6]   Balebako R., Marsh A., Lin J., Hong J., Cranor L.F. 'The privacy and security behaviors of smartphone app developers'. *Proceedings of the Network and Distributed System Security Workshop on Useable Security*. San Diego CA, USA: Geneva Internet Society; 2014.

[7]   Balebako R., Cranor L. 'Improving APP privacy: nudging APP developers to protect user privacy'. *IEEE Security & Privacy*. 2014;**12**(4):55–8.

[8]   Jain S., Lindqvist J. 'Should i protect you? understanding developers' behavior to privacy-preserving APIs'. Proceedings of the Network and Distributed System Security Workshop on Useable Security; San Diego, CA USA, Feb 2014; 2014.

[9]   Van Der Sype Y.S., Maalej W. 'On lawful disclosure of personal user data: what should app developers do?'. Proceedings of the IEEE 7th International Workshop on Requirements Engineering and Law; Karlskrona, Sweden, Aug; 2014. pp. 25–34.

[10] Consumers International. *Connection and protection in the digital age: the internet of things and challenges for consumer protection [online]*. Available from   https://www.consumersinternational.org/media/1292/connection-and-protection-the-internet-of-things-and-challenges-for-consumer-protection. pdf [Accessed 23 Feb 2021].

[11] Norval C., Janssen H., Cobbe J., Singh J. 'Data protection and tech startups: the need for attention, support and scrutiny'. *Policy and Internet*. 2019:1–22.

[12] Graf C., Wolkerstorfer P., Geben A., Tscheligi M. 'A pattern collection for privacy enhancing technology'. Proceedings of the 2nd International Conference on Pervasive Patterns and Applications; Lisbon, Portugal, Nov; 2010.

[13] Data Protection Impact Assessments. 2018.Information Commissioner's Office. Available from   https://ico.org.uk/for-organisations/guide-to-data-protection/guide-to-the-general-data-protection-regulation-gdpr/accountability-and-governance/data-protection-impact-assessments/ [Accessed 23 Feb 2021].

[14] OASIS Privacy Management Reference Model. *Oasis open* [online]. Available   from   https://www.oasis-open.org/committees/tc_home.php?wg_abbrev=pmrm [Accessed 23 Feb 2021].

[15] NIST Privacy Framework. *NIST* [online]. Available from https://www.nist. gov/privacy-framework [Accessed 23 Feb 2021].

[16] LINDDUN Privacy Engineering [online].DistriNet Research Group. Available from https://linddun.org/ [Accessed 23 Feb 2021].

[17] Spiekermann S., Cranor L. 'Privacy engineering'. *IEEE Transactions on Software Engineering*. 2009;**35**(1):67–82.

[18] Cavoukian A. 'Privacy by design: the 7 foundational principles'. *Information and Privacy Commissioner of Ontario Canada*. 2009;**5**:12.

[19] Article 29 Working Party. The future of privacy [online]. European Commission: Brussels, WP168. Available from https://ec.europa.eu/justice/article-29/documentation/opinion-recommendation/files/2009/wp168_en.pdf [Accessed 23 Feb 2021].

[20] Resolution on Privacy by Design [online]. Available from https://edps.europa.eu/sites/edp/files/publication/10-10-27_jerusalem_resolutionon_privacybydesign_en.pdf [Accessed 23 Feb 2021].

[21] Towards a Thriving Data-Driven Economy [online]. European Economic and Social Committee. Available from https://www.eesc.europa.eu/en/our-work/opinions-information-reports/opinions/towards-thriving-data-driven-economy [Accessed 23 Feb 2021].

[22] Cybersecurity Strategy of the European Union: An Open, Safe and Secure Cyberspace [online]. Available from https://ec.europa.eu/home-affairs/sites/homeaffairs/files/e-library/documents/policies/organized-crime-and-human-trafficking/cybercrime/docs/join_2013_1_en.pdf [Accessed 23 Feb 2021].

[23] Hadar I., Hasson T., Ayalon O., *et al.* 'Privacy by designers: software developers' privacy mindset'. *Empirical Software Engineering*. 2018;**23**(1):259–89.

[24] Troncosco C. *Engineering privacy by design* [online]. Available from https://summerschool-croatia.cs.ru.nl/2017/slides/Engineering%20privacy%20by%20design.pdf [Accessed 23 Feb 2021].

[25] Opinion of the Board (art.64)*European data protection board* [online]. Available from https://edpb.europa.eu/sites/edpb/files/files/file1/2018-09-25-opinion_2018_art._64_uk_sas_dpia_list_en.pdf [Accessed 23 Feb 2021].

[26] Luger E., Urquhart L., Rodden T., Golembewski M. 'Playing the legal card: using ideation cards to raise data protection issues within the design process'. *Proceedings of the ACM SIGCHI Conference on Human Factors in Computing Systems*. Seoul, Korea, New York: ACM; 2015. pp. 457–66.

[27] Villata S., Harašta J., Křemen P. '*Legal knowledge and information systems*'. *IOS Press*. 2020.

[28] Fatema K., C D., D L., Morrison J.P., Mazed A.-A. 'A semi-automated methodology for extracting access control rules from the European data protection directive'. Proceedings of the IEEE Security and Privacy Workshops; San Jose CA, May 2016; 2016. pp. 25–32.

[29] Singh J., T P., J B., Powles J., Diaconu R., Eyers D. 'Policy-driven middleware for a legally-compliant internet of things'. Proceedings of the 17th International Middleware Conference; Trento, Italy, Dec 2016; 2016.

[30] Pandit H., K F., O'Sullivan D., Lewis D. 'GDPRtEXT – GDPR as a linked data resource'. Proceedings of the 15th European Semantic Web Conference; Heraklion, Greece, Jun; 2018. pp. 481–95.

[31]   Corrales M., Jurcys P., Kousiouris G. 'Smart contracts and smart disclosure: coding a GDPR compliance framework'. *Legal Tech, Smart Contracts and Blockchain.* 2019:189–220.

[32]   Hafiz M. 'A collection of privacy design patterns'. Proceedings of the 2006 Conference on Pattern Languages of Programs; Portland, OR USA, Dec; 2006.

[33]   Hafiz M. 'A pattern language for developing privacy enhancing technologies'. *Software: Practice and Experience.* 2011;**43**(7):769–87.

[34]   Pearson S., Benameur A. 'Decision support system for design for privacy'. Proceedings of Prime Life 2010; Helsingborg, Sweden, Aug 2010; 2010. p. 352.

[35]   Pearson S., Shen Y. 'Context-aware privacy design pattern selection'. Proceedings of the 7th International Conference on Trust, Privacy and Security in Digital Business; Bilbao, Spain, August 2010; 2010. pp. 69–80.

[36]   Privacypatters.org [online]. Available from https://privacypatterns.org [Accessed 23 Feb 2021].

[37]   Enck W., Gilber P., Chun B.-G., *et al.* 'TaintDroid: An information-flow tracking system for realtime privacy monitoring on smartphones'. Proceedings of the 9th USENIX Conference on Operating Systems and Implementation; Vancouver, Canada, Oct 2010; 2010. pp. 393–407.

[38]   Arzt S., Rasthofer S., Fritz C., *et al.* 'FlowDroid: Precise context, flow, field, object-sensitive and lifecycle-aware taint analysis for android apps'. Proceedings of the 35th Annual ACM SIGPLAN Conference on Programming Language Design and Implementation; Edinburgh, UK, June 2014; 2014. pp. 259–69.

[39]   Celik Z.B., Babum L., Sikder A., *et al.* 'Sensitive information tracking in commodity IoT'. Proceedings of the 17th USENIX Security Symposium; Baltimore MD USA, Aug 2018; 2018. pp. 1687–704.

[40]   Ferrara P., Spoto F. Static analysis for GDPR compliance. Proceedings of the 2nd Italian Conference on Cybersecurity; Milan, Feb 2018; 2018. p. 9.

[41]   Ferrara P., Olivieri L., Spoto F. 'Tailoring taint analysis to GDPR'. Proceedings of the Annual Privacy Forum; Barcelona, Spain; 2018.

[42]   Privatar Publisher. Privitar [online]. Available from https://www.privitar.com/publisher [Accessed 16 Jun 2020].

[43]   Privatar Lens. Privitar [online]. Available from https://www.privitar.com/lens [Accessed 16 Jun 2020].

[44]   Information Commissioners Office. *What is personal data?* [online] Available from https://ico.org.uk/media/for-organisations/guide-to-the-general-data-protection-regulation-gdpr/what-is-personal-data-1-0.pdf [Accessed 23 Feb 2021].

[45]   Cradock E., Stalla-Bourdillon S., Millard D. 'Nobody puts data in a corner? Why a new approach to categorising personal data is required for the obligation to inform'. *Computer Law & Security Review.* 2017;**33**(2):142–58.

[46]   Leon P., Ur B., Wang Y., *et al.* 'What matters to users? factors that affect users' willingness to share information with online advertisers'. *Proceedings*

of the 9th Symposium on Usable Privacy and Security; Newcastle, UK, Jul 2013; New York; 2013. p. 7.

[47] W3C. *The Platform for Privacy Preferences 1.0 (P3P1.0) Specification* [online]. Available from http://www.w3.org/TR/P3P/#Categories [Accessed 23 Feb 2021].

[48] Node-RED [online]. Available from https://nodered.org/ [Accessed 23 Feb 2021].

[49] Docker [online]. Available from https://www.docker.com/ [Accessed 23 Feb 2021].

Chapter 8

Distributed data analytics

Richard Mortier[1], Hamed Haddadi[2], Sandra Servia[1], and Liang Wang[1]

Machine learning (ML) techniques have begun to dominate data analytics applications and services. Recommendation systems are a key component of online service providers such as Amazon, Netflix and Spotify. The financial industry has adopted ML to harness large volumes of data in areas such as fraud detection, risk-management and compliance. Deep learning is the technology behind voice-based personal assistants [1], self-driving cars [2], automatic image processing [3], etc. Deployment of ML technologies onto cloud computing infrastructures has benefited numerous aspects of daily life.

The advertising and associated online industries in particular have fuelled a rapid rise in the deployment of personal data collection and analytics tools. Traditionally, behavioural analytics relies on collecting vast amounts of data in centralised cloud infrastructure before using it to train machine learning models that allow user behaviour and preferences to be inferred. A contrasting approach, *distributed data analytics*, where code and models for training and inference are distributed to the places where data is collected, has been boosted by two recent and ongoing developments: (i) increased processing power and memory capacity available in user devices at the edge of the network such as smartphones and home assistants and (ii) increased sensitivity to the highly intrusive nature of many of these devices and services and the attendant demands for improved privacy.

Indeed, the potential for increased privacy is not the only benefit of distributing data analytics to the edges of the network: reducing the movement of large volumes of data can also improve energy efficiency, helping to ameliorate the ever-increasing carbon footprint of our digital infrastructure, and enable much lower latency for service interactions than is possible when services are cloud-hosted. These approaches often introduce privacy, utility and efficiency trade-offs, while having to ensure fruitful user engagement. We begin by discussing the motivations for distributing analytics (Section 8.1) and outlining the different approaches that have been taken (Section 8.2). We then expand on ways in which analytics can be distributed to the

[1]Cambridge University, UK
[2]Imperial College London, UK

very edges of the network (Section 8.3), before presenting the Databox, a platform for supporting distributed analytics (Section 8.4). We continue by discussing personalising (Section 8.5) and scaling (Section 8.6) learning on such a platform, before concluding (Section 8.7).

8.1   Why distribute analytics?

Large-scale data collection from individuals is at the heart of many current Internet business models. Many current Internet services rely on inferences from models trained on user data. Data-driven solutions are now pervasive in areas such as advertising, smart cities and eHealth [4, 5]. Commonly, both the training and inference tasks are carried out using cloud resources fed by personal data collected at scale from users. Almost everything we do in our daily lives is tracked by some means or another. Although the careful analysis of these data can be highly beneficial for us as individuals and for the society in general, this approach usually entails invasion of privacy, a high price that progressively more people are not willing to pay [6]. Holding and using such large collections of personal data in the cloud creates privacy risks to the data subjects but is currently required for users to benefit from such services.

Access to these data allows companies to train models from which to infer user behaviour and preferences, typically leveraging the generous computation resources available in the public cloud. Most current approaches to processing big data rely on centralised, usually cloud-hosted, storage. This makes it easy to conduct analyses of datasets but has drawbacks: (i) the regulatory climate evolves, making centralised storage riskier and costlier; (ii) mashing up inherently distributed datasets (e.g. those originating from different partners in a supply chain) is awkward when the algorithms to do so are designed to operate on centrally stored data; (iii) even simple data sharing is challenging due to uncertain commercial risks, hence the comparative lack of traction of 'open data' efforts such as Google Fusion Tables [7] compared to 'open APIs'; (iv) such data collection is increasingly pervasive and invasive, notwithstanding regulatory frameworks such as the EU's General Data Protection Regulation (GDPR) that attempt to restrain it.

To date most personal data were sensed through consumers' computers, smartphones or wearable devices such as smart watches and smart wristbands. But nowadays smart technology is entering into our homes. We are heading towards an ecosystem where sooner or later, every device in our home will talk to an Amazon Echo, Google Home or Apple HomeKit. Apart from controlling smart home appliances such as light bulbs and thermostats with our voice, these smart controllers for the entire home will be required to perform more complex tasks such as detecting how many people are in the house and who they are, recognising the activity they are performing or even telling us what to wear, or understanding our emotions [8].

The result is that user privacy is compromised, an increasing concern due to reporting of the ongoing stream of security breaches that result in malicious parties accessing such personal data. But such large-scale data collection causes privacy to be compromised even without security being breached. For example, consider wearable devices that report data they collect from in-built sensors, e.g., accelerometer traces and heart rate data, to the device manufacturer. The device might anonymise such data for the manufacturer to use in improving their models for recognising the user's current activity, an entirely legitimate and non-invasive practice under the terms of the user's engagement with the device. However, the manufacturer might fail to effectively anonymise these data and instead use them for other purposes such as determining mood or even to sell to third-parties without the users' knowledge. It is not only data from wearables that create such risks: web queries, article views and searches, visits to shopping sites and browsing online catalogues are also indexed, analysed and traded by thousands of tracking services in order to build preference models [9].

In these new scenarios, users are becoming progressively more aware of the privacy risks of sharing their voice, video or any other data sensed in their homes with service providers, at the same time that these applications are demanding more accurate and personalised solutions. Sending personal data to the public cloud to perform these tasks seems no longer to be an acceptable solution, but solutions should take advantage of the resource capabilities of personal devices and bring the processing locally, where data reside.

Consider a home containing Internet of Things (IoT) devices, e.g., a smart energy meter. Occupants may be unwilling to release raw data to an external party for security, privacy or bandwidth reasons but might be willing to release certain summaries, especially if there is mutual benefit, e.g., from an external party sharing value generated by combining summaries from many users. The external party specifies which analyses each analytics engine should compute, and the occupants confirm they accept the exchange.

Larger organisations can also benefit from such a facility by holding their own datasets and providing for analyses based on requests from external parties. Examples might include data tracking provenance and reliability of components in a complex supply chain where the organisation would control the sorts of summaries that can be computed and shared, e.g., allowing a third party to discover which supplier's components are problematic without having to reveal to them details of all current suppliers. Similarly, the National Digital Twin being pursued by the UK government [10] can only feasibly be built by providing a federated infrastructure that enables many disparate sources of data owned by many organisations to contribute to a single whole. This saves the costs of transmitting and copying large datasets, reduces risks of bulk copying copyright or commercially sensitive datasets, and simplifies the contractual complexity of obtaining permissions from the various parties involved in data-mashup analyses. The same approach can even apply when privacy and regulatory issues are absent, e.g., decentralised processing is needed for live telemetry from remote vehicles with only a satellite uplink, or for ultra-high frequency monitoring of switches in a datacenter.

We are interested in alternative approaches where we reduce or remove the flow of user data to the cloud completely, instead moving computation to where the data already reside under the user's control [11]. This can mitigate risks of breach and misuse of data by simply avoiding it being collected at scale in the first place: attack incentives are reduced as the attacker must gain access to millions of devices to capture data for millions of users rather than accessing a single cloud service. However, it presents challenges for the sorts of model learning processes required: how can such models be learnt without access to the users' personal data?

These approaches require pervasive support for accountability [12], to make uses of data legible to data subjects, owners and controllers as well as to data processors, given that computations may be distributed to untrusted hosts. They also require development of novel underlying infrastructure in which computations can be efficiently distributed and results efficiently aggregated while exposing sufficient metadata about the operation of the system through interfaces designed for that purpose, so all users can be satisfied they have sufficient understanding of past, present and future activities involving their data and analytics.

8.2   Approaches to distribution

Some analytics are easy to distribute. In the smart energy metering example, suppose an energy company wants to know the mean and variance of daily energy usage per customer. Each customer's analytics engine would compute and share its individual mean and variance. The data analyst at the energy company would aggregate these summary statistics and compute the overall mean and variance. This could be an automatic weekly process, reporting the same statistics every week to underpin the energy company's dashboard. In this way, each customer limits how much data she shares, and the energy company limits how much data it collects and stores. Ad hoc queries will be needed as well as dashboards. For example, to answer the question 'How did energy consumption change in the recent cold snap?' the data scientist might ask each customer to summarise their data differently according to weather data by region.

More advanced data science queries use iterative computation. Building a predictive model for how a customer's energy consumption varies over time might start, for example, with a rough predictive model, then ask each customer to compute a summary statistic about the prediction quality of this model, aggregate summaries to improve the model and iterate. Such distributed computations are behind classic machine learning algorithms such as Google's PageRank. This pushes real-time distributed computation to its limits. Scaling this demands new techniques such as rapid iteration on small samples followed by slow iteration on large samples, using data from customers willing to share lots of their data to refine the questions to be asked of the rest of the population, making efficient use of summaries as they trickle in, settling for less accurate answers that can be computed from simpler summaries or using randomly re-sampled representative data from each customer rather than actual traces.

8.2.1 Distributed analytics

Distributed machine learning (DML) arose as a solution to effectively use large computer clusters and highly parallel computational architectures to speed up the training of big models over the large amounts of data available nowadays [13]. Systems dealing with very large datasets have already had to handle the case where no single node can contain and process the entire dataset, but the dataset and/or the model to learn are parallelised among different machines, models are sequentially trained on every single machine, and some sort of synchronisation mechanism is applied to aggregate the parameters of the model to learn [14–17]. DML may also be a potential solution when the volume of the data is not the main issue, but the distribution occurs when different entities own different datasets which, if aggregated, would provide useful knowledge. However, the sensitivity of such data often prevents these entities from sharing their datasets, restricting access to only a small set of selected people as in the case of patients' medical records [18].

Gradient descent is the workhorse for many machine learning algorithms. Distributing it to run on big data is theoretically straightforward if the dataset is sharded 'horizontally' so each worker holds a few rows. This style of algorithm has driven the development of big data platforms, e.g., Spark and GraphLab [17, 19]. Refinements address unevenly distributed data [20] and high communication overhead [21]. Related methods for iterative optimisation have also been studied [21, 22].

Big data allows us to explore heterogeneity using high-dimensional models. Topological models like PageRank and nearest-neighbour have one parameter per data point, and distributed computation requires that we shard the data according to topology [23]. Deep neural networks can be distributed by sharding the parameters [21]. While appropriate in a datacenter, wide-area distribution remains an open problem.

Much of modern statistics is based on MCMC algorithms for fitting large complex Bayesian models. These are computationally intensive and do not scale well to large datasets, which prompted work on distributed approaches using small random subsamples of data [24], along with studies of asymptotic correctness [25, 26]. Methods often rely on consensus techniques [27], expectation propagation [28] or stochastic optimization [29, 30]. But this is not settled science: even in simple real-valued parameter estimation there are issues of bias [31], and missing data (e.g., as users choose not to share their data, or because the statistical model involves hidden variables) increases the compute burden drastically [32].

8.2.2 Federated and hybrid learning

Recently, federated learning (FL, Figure 8.1) [33] has become a popular paradigm in machine learning. In FL, a global model is trained using continuous, async updates received from users' devices in a privacy-preserving and decentralised manner. This approach helps users train a large-scale model using their private data while minimising the privacy risks. FL addresses a number of challenges traditionally associated with large-scale models, including device availability, complexities with local

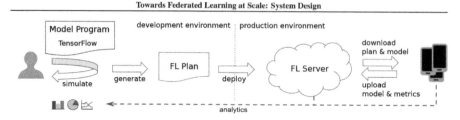

Figure 8.1   Google's federated learning framework [33]

data distribution (e.g., time zone or the number of users within a region), reliance on device connectivity, interrupted execution across devices with varying availability, and challenges with device storage and processing resources. One of the main design criteria is that the process should not interfere with a user's device usage experience and should be done when the device is idle.

Recently there has been a rise in hybrid models for distributed analytics, where parts of large deep neural network (DNN) models run locally on the device, providing local feature extraction on the raw data, then only sending these features to the cloud for further classification and analysis (see Figure 8.2) [34, 35]. These works often rely on the assumption that service providers can release publicly verifiable feature extractor modules based on an initial training set. The user's device then performs a minimalistic analysis and extracts private features from the data and sends it to the service provider (i.e., the cloud) for subsequent analysis. The private features are then analysed in the cloud and the result yielded back to the user. The fundamental challenge in using this framework is the design of the feature extractor modules that removes sensitive information accurately, without major impact on scalability by imposing heavy computational requirements on the user's device.

8.2.3   Personalised learning

Contrary to distributed or federated learning, personalised learning does not seek to learn a global model from sensitive data from multiple parties, but to learn a personalised model for each individual party by building on a model learnt from a

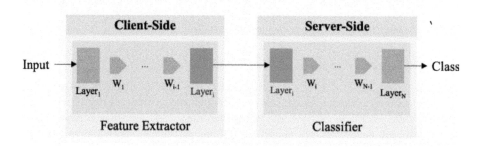

Figure 8.2   Hybrid deep learning frameworks [34, 35]

relatively small set of other parties but without requiring access to their raw data. Personal learning models [36] are similar to personal recommender systems [37] but generalise the solution to any learning algorithm. This approach takes advantage of transfer learning [38] to achieve better performance than algorithms trained using only local data, particularly in those common situations where local data is a scarce resource. This solution brings most of the data processing to where the data resides and not the other way around, exactly as the edge computing paradigm calls for [34, 39]. Recent popular machine learning frameworks provide libraries for running complex deep learning inferences on local devices such as smartphones [40–42]. While in these works models are previously trained in an offline manner, researchers have demonstrated that both the inference and the local retraining can be performed locally on low-power devices in a timely manner [36].

8.2.4   Securing data

Approaches such as homomorphic encryption allow user data to be encrypted, protecting against unintended release of such data, while still being amenable to data processing. This affords users better privacy – their data cannot be used arbitrarily – while allowing data processors to collect and use such data in cloud computing environments. However, current practical techniques limit the forms of computation that can be supported.

Lately, trusted executions environments (TEEs) such as Arm TrustZone or Intel Software Guard Extensions (SGX) have been used for providing attestation and trust in models and data being executed on the cloud and on user devices. Using these approaches, a secure area in memory can be used for securely storing sensitive data (e.g., a fingerprint scan or face features) or providing model privacy and defence against adversarial attacks such as membership inference attacks [43].

While numerous scalable distributed computation platforms exist, e.g. [19, 44], they do not target the wide-area deployment or multi-tenant hosting of computation we require, and neither are they designed and built to support accountability. Databox [11] supports accountability but presumes small-scale localised personal data.

Glimmers [45] explores using Intel SGX at the client to create a trusted party that can validate accuracy of client contributions before adding to an aggregate, without revealing the details of the contribution further. Distributed, federated provenance has been studied [46, 47]. Tango [48] provides a replicated, in-memory data structure backed by a shared log for recording such data.

8.3   Analytics at the edge

Increased ubiquity of sensing via mobile and IoT devices has caused a surge in personal data generation and use. Alongside this surge, concerns over privacy, trust and security are becoming increasingly important as different stakeholders attempt to take advantage of such rich data resources: occurrences of breaches of privacy are rising at alarming rates [49]. Tensions in the collection and use of personal data, between the benefits to various analytics applications, the privacy consequences and security risks, and the regulatory complexities of aggregating and processing data in the cloud are a significant barrier to innovation in this space. We have previously proposed that these topics, and the shortcomings of current approaches in this space, are the concern of a new – or at least, newly focused – discipline, human–data interaction (HDI) [50].

In our view, the core technical problem in this space is how to build networked services that enable individuals to manage their personal data so that they can permit other parties to make use of it while retaining personal control over such uses and understanding the implications of any data release. As digital data may be copied infinitely at negligible marginal cost and without loss of fidelity, the current common approach of centralising unencrypted personal data into a cloud-hosted service such as Google or Facebook is fundamentally flawed in this regard. Once data is given up to such a service, the data subject can only exercise control over it to the extent that the cloud provider allows them, and they have only social means (e.g., negative publicity campaigns, local per-jurisdiction regulation) to ensure such controls are provided.[a]

Personal data collection for profiling and mining data subjects' interests and relationships is the basis on which online platforms such as Facebook and Google and services such as Apple's Siri and Microsoft's Cortana operate. However, such data collection and profiling exposes the data subject to privacy leakage even when these communities are anonymous [51]. Simultaneously, these cloud-based services can have only a partial view of each data subject's digital footprint, resulting in inaccuracies and systemic biases in the data they hold and leading to ever more aggressive data collection strategies.

Ever since Edward Snowden revealed the secret large-scale government-level surveillance programmes, social awareness of privacy and personal data is quickly arising. The Internet Trends 2016 report [52] points out that, according to its survey, 45% of respondents feel more worried about their online privacy than 1 year ago, and 74% have limited their online activity because of privacy concerns.

Building privacy, trust and security into the evolving digital ecosystem is thus broadly recognized as a key societal challenge. Regulatory activities in the US [53], Europe [54] and Japan [55] are complemented by industry initiatives that seek to rebalance the 'crisis in trust' [12] occasioned by widespread personal data harvesting. All parties agree that increased accountability and control are key to this challenge. *Accountability* seeks not only to strengthen compliance but also to make the emerging ecosystem more transparent to consumers, while *control* seeks to empower consumers and provide them with the means of actively exercising choice.

Many online service providers who collect large-scale data from users are prone to data breaches. Users rely on the promises from big companies to keep their data private and safe [56]. However, these providers are not infallible. Yahoo, Tumblr

---

[a]We follow standard legal terminology and refer to individuals about whom data are collected from *sources* such as IoT sensors or online social network accounts as *data subjects* and organisations wishing to process data as *data processors*.

and Ashley Madison (an online dating service for married people) offer only a few high-profile examples of breaches in recent years [57].

There have been many responses to these challenges. Making databases private and secure is one of the solutions. Cloud Kotta [58] introduces a cloud-based framework that enables secure management and analysis of large, and potentially sensitive, datasets. It claims to ensure secure data storage that can only be accessed by authorised users. Joshi *et al.* [59] present an ontology so that big data analytics consumers can write data privacy policies using formal policy languages and build automated systems for compliance validation. Cuzzocrea *et al.* [60] present a short review of existing research efforts along this line.

Hiding data alone is not enough. The model itself can also reveal private information. For example, Fredrikson *et al.* [61] showed that access to the face recognition model enables recovery of recognisable images. Abadi *et al.* [62] developed a method that can prevent such model inversion attacks even by a strong adversary who has full knowledge of the training mechanism and access to the model parameters. Similarly, Papernot *et al.* [63] propose a 'teacher–student' approach based on knowledge aggregation and transfer so as to hide the models trained on sensitive data in a black box.

Several privacy-preserving analytical solutions have been proposed to guarantee the confidentiality of personal data while extracting useful information [18, 64–66]. Prominent among them are those that build on Dwork's *differential privacy* framework [62, 67–70], which formalises the idea that a *query* over a sensitive database should not reveal whether any one person is included in the dataset [71]. In the case of machine learning, the idea is that a differentially private model should not reveal whether data from any one person were used to train the model. Most of these techniques for differentially private machine learning are usually based on adding noise during the training, which leads to a challenging trade-off between accuracy and privacy.

Shokri and Shmatikov [72] and McMahan *et al.* [73] propose solutions where multiple parties jointly learn a neural network model for a given objective by sharing their learning parameters but without sharing their input datasets. A different approach is proposed by Hamm *et al.* [74] and Papernot *et al.* [63], where privacy-preserving models are learned locally from disjoint datasets and then combined in a privacy-preserving fashion. However, the privacy guarantees of some of these solutions have recently been called into question [75]. Data privacy when data is sharded 'vertically', so each worker holds a few columns, has been studied as a problem of secure communication using garbled circuits. Low-dimensional linear models can be fitted [76], but the extension to richer algorithms and high-dimensional modelling is an open problem.

Instead of hiding data or models, some suggest the user should choose which part of data to upload. Xu *et al.* [77] propose a mechanism to allow users to clean their data before uploading them to process. It allows for prediction of the desired information while hiding confidential information that client want to keep private. RAPPOR [78] enables collecting statistics data from end-user in privacy-preserving crowdsourcing.

Although numerous mechanisms supporting privacy preserving analytics, marketing and advertising have been proposed, e.g. recent studies on analysing network traces using differential privacy [79] and accessing databases while respecting privacy [80, 81], no operational system exists that also gives others visibility into statistics and trends [82–84]. Rieffel *et al.* [85] propose cryptographic, hierarchical access to data for processing aggregate statistics without decrypting personal data. However, this method still requires the collection of individual data items and complex yet critical management of many cryptographic keys. Privacy-aware centralised methods such as homomorphic encryption [86] are yet to be deployed in a commercial or consumer system. While these methods are likely to be important in the future, they are not enough alone: they cannot provide accountability and control in isolation.

However, all of the aforementioned work focus on the traditional cloud side solution. Users' data are still collected to the central server for processing, which are prone to issues such as increased service response latency, communication cost and single point failure. Numerous recent and current projects and startups have responded to specific problems of aggressive data collection by the online advertising industry[b] through more traditional means. These typically involve the production of services called variously *Personal Data Stores, Personal Information Management System, Vendor Relationship Management* and similar; examples include Mydex [87] and openPDS [88]. They allow the subject to retain ownership[c] of their data and provide it to third parties on demand [89], which offers some degree of accountability and control but only insofar as the service provider can be trusted.

One solution is to deploy ML services on edge devices. Moving services from cloud to users' edge devices can keep the data private and effectively reduce the communication cost and response latency. Some research has begun to emerge that aims to solve accompanied challenges. They recognise that mobile devices cannot afford to support most of today's intelligent systems because of the large amount of computation resources and memory required. As a result, many current end-side services only support simple ML models. These solutions mostly focus on reducing model size [90–92]. For example, Neurosurgeon [92] partitions a DNN into two parts, half on edge devices and the other half on cloud, reducing total latency and energy consumption. A key observation is that, in a DNN, output size of each node decreases from front-end to back-end, while the change of computation latency is the opposite.

Recently, computation on edge and mobile devices has gained rapid growth, such as personal data analytics in home [11], Intel's Movidius Neural Compute Stick [93] is a tiny deep learning device that one can use to accelerate AI programming and DNN inference application deployment at the edge. Edge computing is also boosting content distribution by supporting peering and caching [94]. Huawei

---

[b]http://www.technologyreview.com/view/530741/the-murky-world-of-third-party-web-tracking/
[c]Simple notions of ownership are problematic given the inherently social nature of even personal data and are dealt with elsewhere in this book but particularly Chapters 2 and 4.

has identified speed and responsiveness of native AI processing on mobile devices as the key to a new era in smartphone innovation [95].

Moving ML analytics from cloud to edge devices faces many challenges. One widely recognised challenge is that, compared with resource-rich computing clusters, edge and mobile devices only have quite limited computation power and working memory. To accommodate heavy ML computation on edge devices, one solution is to train suitable small models to do inference on mobile devices [96]. This method leads to unsatisfactory accuracy and user experience. Some techniques [90, 91, 97] are proposed to enhance this method.

To reduce the memory and disk usage of speech recognition application, Lei *et al.* [97] use a compressed n-gram language model to do on-the-fly model rescoring. Chen *et al.* [90] present HashNets, a network architecture that can reduce the redundancy of neural network models to decrease model sizes while keeping little impact on prediction accuracy. MobileNets [91] from Google reduces model size by a different technique: factorisation of the convolution operation.

8.4   Databox, a platform for edge analytics

Our response is to provide technical means to assist the data subject in managing access to their data by others. Perhaps the most extreme expression of this approach to date is the Databox, an open-source personal networked device augmented by cloud-hosted services that collates, curates and mediates access to our personal data, under the data subject's control [11]. It gathers data from local and remote sources, from online social networks to IoT sensors; it provides for data subjects to inspect data gathered from their data sources and to effect actuation via IoT devices and similar; it enables data processors to discover and request access to subjects with sources of interest; and it supports running applications to provide data processors with specific, limited and logged access to subjects' data.

Databox sits within an ecosystem of networked devices and associated services enabling individuals to manage their data and to provide other parties with controlled access to their data. Composed of a set of service instances, realised as Docker-managed containers in our current prototype, it supports placing these instances in different locations from a physical device in the subject's home to the public cloud and to future envisioned edge-network hosting resources such as smart lampposts and cell-towers.

Databox benefits data subjects by providing a regulated and privacy-enhanced communication mechanism between data subjects and data processors. Acting as an agent on behalf of the data subject, it can support queries over high-resolution personal data that would be difficult for a single company to obtain, permitting richer, more accurate data analytics. It also helps avoid the risks of data breach associated with collecting and curating large, personal datasets which malicious actors have significant incentives to attack and steal.

We envisage that all Databox applications will involve some software component running within the Databox. Specifically, applications provide derived stores to which external parties (whether data processing organisations or a browser operated by the data subject) can connect. These applications provide accountable entities through which the data subject can ascribe to a data processor behaviour involving use of their data. We envisage two main routes to the installation of these components, resulting from successful negotiation between the data subject and processor causing the processor to be given access to the subject's data: subject-driven and processor-driven.

8.4.1   Subject-driven

This model is strongly analogous to current app store models. Each app store is a service to which subjects can connect to discover applications they might wish to install. Apps advertise the data stores that they will consume, the frequency at which they will access those stores, and the computation they will carry out on data from those stores. Apps will be validated and verified by the app store operators and rated by the community. They will have only limited, approved external communications between their own store and an authenticated client.

8.4.2   Processor-driven

This model inverts the interaction, enabling data processors to discover cohorts of data subjects who have data available to meet the processor's needs.

Independent of the discovery model used, applications may either be limited to 1:1 interactions or may necessarily involve a larger cohort of subjects making data available. In the former case, the output of the computation is consumed in isolation, either by the data subject or the data processor. In the latter, there is an inherent need for the application to function as a distributed system, with communication taking place between instances as the computation makes progress. This latter case is considerably more complicated, so we discuss it briefly next.

Three key challenges of this sort of application present themselves: *scale*, *heterogeneity* and *dynamics*. These challenges arise due to the fundamental characteristics of the algorithms and deployment environments envisaged. Data processors might use machine learning and model generation algorithms that default to serial computation or, at best, execute in the controlled, high bandwidth, low latency environment of a datacenter. Scaling them across (potentially) millions of Databoxes moves most of these algorithms outside their normal operating regions. The computation resources on which they will be hosted will vary in capacity and connectivity, making scheduling and synchronisation of ongoing computations between instances considerably more complex, Finally, physical Databox instances are likely to have variable and unreliable connectivity which, when coupled with the envisaged scale, almost guarantees that the entire cohort will never be simultaneously available.

Approaches to addressing these challenges that we are exploring include the use of techniques such as delay-tolerant querying, introduced in the Seaweed database [98], where metadata statistics are incorporated into the decisions taken by the system as to when to wait for data to become available and when to give up and return (with appropriate indications of completeness) a potentially inaccurate answer and more flexible control over synchronisation barriers than permitted by Bulk Synchronous Parallel operation (e.g., Stale Synchronous Parallel Parameter Server [16]).

It is possible that other factors inherent in these data and the deployment of Databoxes may also mitigate against some of these problems. For example, the distributed computations may well be highly localised and so might be loosely coupled and require minimal coordination and exchange of data. Coupled with the use of aggregation in the computation graph, this might mitigate unreliability and scale, while also providing natural means to support privacy-preserving aggregation.

While it addresses concerns of privacy and ethics of these data, it does not try simply to *prevent* all such analysis and use by third parties as not all of this activity is harmful [99, 100]. Rather, it seeks to afford users the possibility to find personal equilibria with sharing and use of their data: simply preventing all access to personal data would fail to take advantage of the many potential benefits that sharing data can produce, whether immediate financial rewards, social benefits through, e.g., participation in friendship groups or broad societal benefits from the ability to participate in large-scale studies in, e.g., human mobility and activity for use in urban planning, or mental and physical health measures used to set healthcare norms.

8.5 Personalised learning at the edge

The approach of sending all users' personal data to the cloud for processing is one extreme of a spectrum whose other extreme would be to train a model for a specific user using only that user's data. For some applications, e.g., activity recognition, it has been shown that a model trained solely using data from the individual concerned provides more accurate predictions for that individual than a model trained using data from other individuals [101]. At the same time, this solution offers more privacy to the user as all computation, for both training and inference, can be done locally on the device [102]. However, this approach leads to substantial interactional overheads as training the model will likely require each user to label a significant amount of data by hand before they can obtain accurate inferences.

An alternative is an inversion of the hybrid approach described in (§8.1.2): split computation between the cloud and the users' personal devices by (i) training a *shared model* in the cloud using data from a small (relative to the population) set of users, (ii) distributing this shared model to users' personal devices, where (iii) it can be used locally to generate inferences and (iv) it can be retrained using locally stored personal data to become a *personal model*, specialised for the user in question [36].

In more detail, start by training a *shared* model, M_S, to recognise the activity that the user is performing using data sensed with his smartphone's built-in sensors. This *batch learning* is done on a remote server in the cloud using available public data, d_p. In the event of not having sufficient public data available for this task, data can be previously gathered from a set of users that have agreed to share their personal data perhaps by providing them with suitable incentives.

The user u then obtains the *shared* model from the remote server. With every new sample or group of samples gathered from the smartphone's sensors, the activity that the user is performing is locally inferred using this model. In order to allow for more accurate inferences, the user is prompted to 'validate' the results by reporting the activity they were performing. The new labelled data so gathered are then used for locally retraining the model, resulting in a new *personal* model, M_P.

This approach has been evaluated using (i) a neural network to recognise users' activity on the *WISDM* dataset [103] and (ii) the Latent Dirichlet Algorithm (LDA) [104] to identify topics in the Wikipedia and NIPS datasets [105, 106]. In both cases, the model resulting from local retraining of an initial model learnt from a small set of users performs with higher accuracy than either the initial model alone or a model trained using only data from the specific user of interest.

We have briefly presented the software architecture for the Databox, a hybrid locally and cloud-hosted system for personal data management (Section 8.4). We now sketch a system architecture that might be used to implement personalised learning using a device such as the Databox. This is divided into two parts: (i) residing in the cloud, the first part is responsible for constructing a *shared* model using batch learning, and (ii) residing on each individual user's device, the second part tunes the model from the first part using the locally available data, resulting in a *personal* model.

We identify five components in this architecture:

1. The **batch training module** resides in the cloud and is responsible for training a *shared* model as the starting point using public, or private but shared, datasets that it also maintains. As this component may need to support multiple applications, it will provide a collection of different machine learning algorithms to build various needed models. It may also need to perform more traditional, large-scale processing, but can easily be built using modern data processing frameworks designed for datacenters such as Mllib [107] or GraphLab [17].
2. The **distribution module** resides on users' devices and is responsible for obtaining the *shared* model and maintaining it locally. In the case of very large-scale deployments, standard content distribution or even peer-to-peer techniques could be used to alleviate load on the cloud service.
3. The **personalisation module** builds a *personal model* by refining the model parameters of the shared model using the personal data available on the user's device. This module will also require a repository of different learning algorithms, but the nature of personal computational devices means that there will be greater resource constraints applied to the performance and efficiency of the algorithm implementation.
4. The **communication module** handles all the communications between peers or those between an individual node and the server. Nodes can register themselves with the server, on top of which we can implement more sophisticated membership management.
5. The **inference module** provides a service at the client to respond to model queries, using the most refined model available.

In our implementation, we rely on several existing software libraries to provide the more mundane of these functions, e.g., ZeroMQ [108] satisfies most of the requirements of the communication and model distribution modules, and so we do not discuss these further here.

There are many toolkits, e.g., *theano* [109] and *scikit-learn* [110], that provide a rich set of machine learning algorithms for use in the batch training and personalisation modules. However, in the case of the latter, we must balance convenience with performance considerations due to the resource-constrained nature of these devices. In light of this, we use a more recent library, Owl [111, 112], to generate more compact and efficient native code on a range of platforms, and the source code can be obtained from its Github repository.[d]

We briefly summarise the workflow we envisage using activity recognition as an example.

1. When the user activates the device for the first time, the device contacts the server and registers itself in order to join the system. The device notices there is no local data for building the model and sends a request to the server to obtain the *shared* model.
2. After processing the registration, the server receives the download request. The *shared* model has been trained using an initial dataset collected in a suitably ethical and trustworthy way, e.g., with informed consent, appropriate compensation and properly anonymised. The server can either approve the download request or return a list of peers from whom the requesting user can retrieve the model.
3. Having obtained the *shared* model, the device can start processing inference requests. At the same time, the device continuously collects user's personal data, in this case, their accelerometer traces. Once enough local data is collected, the personalisation phase starts, refining the shared model to create a *personal* model.
4. After the personal model has been built, the system uses it to serve requests and continues to refine it as more personal data is collected.

The above system can suffer the attacks and consequences of malicious users. There are several potential attacks against any learning system [113, 114]. Here, we focus on how privacy and causative attacks might affect our system. On a privacy attack, the adversary obtains information from the learner, compromising the secrecy or privacy of the system's users. The aim of a causative attack is on altering the parameters of the target model by manipulating the training dataset. An example of this type of attacks are poisoning attacks, where an attacker may poison the training data by injecting carefully designed samples to eventually compromise the whole learning process. The target model then updates itself with the poisoned data and so is gradually compromised. Below we describe the potential effects of these attacks on our system.

8.5.1 Privacy attacks

Our solution guarantees the confidentiality of users' data (potential users) given that their devices are not compromised, since their personal data never leave their devices. Since both the data and the personal model reside on the user's device, attacks such as model inversion [70], where an attacker, given the model and some auxiliary information about the user, can determine some user's raw data, and membership query [115], where, given a data record and black-box access to a model, an adversary could determine if the record was in the model's training dataset, cannot affect our users. However, we cannot assure the confidentiality of the data, neither robustness against these attacks, for those users that have freely agreed to share their data in the same way as the big corporations are not doing so with their customers' data.

For many applications we envisage and describe in the introduction, such as those based on object recognition or those that work with textual data, there is already a large amount of data freely available on the Internet with which to build the shared model, and whose confidentiality does not need to be guaranteed. On the other hand, for applications such as face or speaker recognition, techniques based on differentially private training [63, 72–74] could be applied in order to, a priori, guarantee the confidentiality of the volunteers' data. On the contrary, the training of the personal model for the final users happens locally on their devices so that neither their data nor their personal model leaves their devices, and its confidentiality is guaranteed by the security offered by their device, security that is out of the scope of the methodology proposed here.

8.5.2 Poisoning attacks

We envisage two different points or steps in our system that adversaries might wish to attack: when building the shared model in a remote server in the public cloud using public data available or *shared* by a group of volunteers, and when personalising the model by local retraining in the user's device (*personalisation*). In the case of a poisoning attack to our proposed methodology, the shared model can be corrupted by malicious volunteers poisoning the data with fake samples. However, during the local retraining, if the adversary wishes to corrupt the personal model, he needs to gain access to the local device of the user to poison the data and fool the model. Poisoning the data to train the personal model needs the attacker to gain access to the local device of the user.

Some schemes have been proposed to conduct poisoning attacks against SVMs [116, 117], but we have barely seen any work about poisoning attacks against neural networks. Our goal is not on how to design the best poisoning attack to achieve a given output or to avoid being detected but on the effects of poisoning data into our model. Therefore, we consider a dumb adversary that randomly alters labels into our training set without any other goal than misclassifying samples. In the following, we

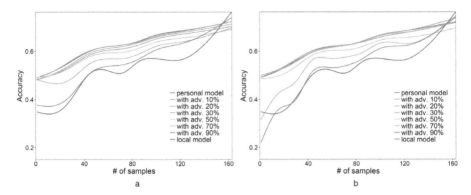

Figure 8.3   *Accuracy of the personal model in the face of dumb and not-so-dumb adversaries. (a) Accuracy of the personal model for different percentages of corrupted samples in the training set of the shared model ('dumb' adversary). (b) Accuracy of the personal model for different percentages of corrupted samples in the training set of shared model ('smarter' adversary).*

explore the effects of adding corrupted samples to the data used to train the shared model in the supervised learning task. Specifically, we simulate a scenario where part of the data used for training the *shared* model is corrupted. That is, a scenario where one or several volunteers intentionally alter the labels of their samples in the training set and explore the effect that different amounts of data corrupted in the training set of the *shared* model cause in the *personal* model of the user.

To this aim, we corrupted different samples of the training set (10%, 20%, 30%, 50%, 70% and 90%). In order to generate each corrupted sample, we consider the original features of the sample to be corrupted but assigning it a random activity. This random activity label was selected by a random generator with equal probability for each activity (walking, standing, etc.). Figure 8.3 represents the accuracy, on average, of the *personal* model for different percentages of corrupted samples in the training set of the *shared* model. We observe that the more corrupted samples used to build the *shared* model, the less improvement we get when starting to train the *personal* model. More interestingly, when less than 50% of the samples are corrupted, the accuracy obtained with the *personal* model is similar to the one when no samples are poisoned, especially when few samples are used to train the *local* model. Moreover, when the 90% of the samples are poisoned, the accuracy of the *personal* model is not worse than the *local* model.

Now we consider a 'smarter' adversary that has access to other volunteers' data and therefore can obtain the distribution of labels in the dataset. In order to minimise the chances of being discovered, this adversary corrupts its samples by adding random labels with the probability of each label being the same as the one in the original data. Figure 8.3b shows the results when the labels corrupted follow the same distribution than the original sample ('smarter' adversary). In this case, we observe similar results as when poisoning the samples completely random. One difference is that when few samples of the concerned user are used to train the *personal* model, the system behaves worse than the *local* model, especially when the percentage of corrupted samples is large. But, when using more samples, the system behaves better than the local one and similar to the system under the effects of the 'dumb' adversary. In conclusion, our system is quite robust against poisoning attacks against the *shared* model.

8.6   Extreme scaling at the edge

In contrast to a highly reliable and homogeneous datacenter context, the edge computing model espoused by systems such as Databox assumes a distributed system consisting of a large number (tens of thousands) of heterogeneous nodes distributed over a wide geographical area, e.g., different cities. Their network connections are unreliable compared to a datacenter network, and the bandwidth capacity is variable. The nodes are not static but rather join and leave the system over time giving rise to non-negligible churn.

Each node holds a local dataset and, even though nodes may query each other, we do not assume any specific information sharing between nodes or between a node and a centralised server. Exemplar data analytics algorithms that might run across the nodes include stochastic gradient descent (SGD) as it is one of the few core algorithms in many ML and DNN algorithms. Synchronisation of model updates is achieved using one of several synchronisation control mechanisms. Table 8.1 summarises the synchronisation control used in different machine learning systems: how the different nodes participating in the computation coordinate to ensure good progress while maintaining accuracy.

8.6.1   Bounded synchronous parallel

Bounded synchronous parallel (BSP) is a deterministic scheme where workers perform a computation phase followed by a synchronisation/communication phase where they exchange updates [123]. The method ensures that all workers are on the

Table 8.1   *Classification of the synchronisation methods used by different systems*

System	Synchronisation	Barrier method
MapReduce [44]	Map must complete before reducing	BSP
Spark [19]	Aggregate updates after task completion	BSP
Pregel [118]	Superstep model	BSP
Hogwild! [119]	ASP with system-level delay bounds	ASP, SSP
Parameter Servers [120]	Swappable synchronisation method	BSP, ASP, SSP
Cyclic Delay [121]	Updates delayed by up to N 1 steps	SSP
Yahoo! LDA [122]	Checkpoints	SSP, ASP
Owl+Actor [111]	Swappable synchronisation method	BSP, ASP, SSP, PSP

same iteration of a computation by preventing any worker from proceeding to the next step until all can. Furthermore, the effects of the current computation are not made visible to other workers until the barrier has been passed. Provided the data and model of a distributed algorithm have been suitably scheduled, BSP programs are often serializable — that is, they are equivalent to sequential computations. This means that the correctness guarantees of the serial program are often realisable making BSP the strongest barrier control method [16]. Unfortunately, BSP does have a disadvantage. As workers must wait for others to finish, the presence of *stragglers*, workers who require more time to complete a step due to random and unpredictable factors [123], limits the computation efficiency to that of the slowest machine. This leads to a dramatic reduction in performance. Overall, BSP tends to offer high computation accuracy but suffers from poor efficiency in unfavourable environments.

8.6.2   Asynchronous parallel

Asynchronous parallel (ASP) takes the opposite approach to BSP, allowing computations to execute as fast as possible by running workers completely asynchronously. In homogeneous environments (e.g., datacentres), wherein the workers have similar configurations, ASP enables fast convergence because it permits the highest iteration throughputs. Typically, P-fold speed-ups can be achieved [123] by adding more computation/storage/bandwidth resources. However, such asynchrony causes delayed updates: updates calculated on an old model state that should have been applied earlier but were not. Applying them introduces noise and error into the computation. Consequently, ASP suffers from decreased iteration quality and may even diverge in unfavourable environments. Overall, ASP offers excellent speed-ups in convergence but has a greater risk of diverging especially in a heterogeneous context.

8.6.3   Stale synchronous parallel

Stale synchronous parallel (SSP) is a bounded-asynchronous model that can be viewed as a relaxation of BSP. Rather than requiring all workers to be on the same iteration, the system decides if a worker may proceed based on how far behind the slowest worker is, i.e., a pre-defined bounded staleness. Specifically, a worker that is more than d_p iterations behind the fastest worker is considered too slow. If such a worker is present, the system pauses faster workers until the straggler catches up. This s is known as the staleness parameter. More formally, each machine keeps an iteration counter, P, which it updates whenever it completes an iteration. Each worker also maintains a local view of the model state. After each iteration, a worker commits updates, i.e., $c - s - 1$, which the system then sends to other workers, along with the worker's updated counter. The bounding of clock differences through the staleness parameter means that the local model cannot contain updates older than $c - s - 1$ iterations. This limits the potential error. Note that systems typically enforce a read-my-writes consistency model.

The staleness parameter allows SSP to provide deterministic convergence guarantees [16, 123, 124]. Note that SSP is a generalisation of BSP: setting $s = 0$ yields the BSP method, whilst setting $s = \infty$ produces ASP. Overall, SSP offers a good compromise between fully deterministic BSP and fully asynchronous ASP [16], despite the fact that the central server still needs to maintain the global state to guarantee its determinism nature.

8.6.4   Probabilistic synchronous parallel

Probabilistic synchronous parallel (PSP) is a new barrier control technique suitable for data analytic applications deployed in large and unreliable distributed system. When used to build, for example, an SGD implementation, it effectively improves both the convergence speed and scalability of the SGD algorithm compared to BSP, SSP and ASP. PSP introduces a new system primitive *sampling* that can be composed with existing barrier controls to derive fully distributed solutions. A full theoretical analysis of PSP is available [112] showing that it can provide probabilistic convergence guarantee as a function of sample size. PSP achieves a better trade-off than existing solutions, i.e., iterate faster than SSP and with a more accurate update. Both evaluation and theoretical results indicate that even quite small sample sizes achieve most of their benefits.

Practically, all iterative learning algorithms are stateful. Both model and nodes' states need to be stored somewhere in order to coordinate nodes to make progress in a training process. Regarding the storage location of the model and nodes' states, there are four possible combinations as below (*states* in the list refer to the nodes' states specifically):

1. **[Centralised model, centralised states]**: The central server is responsible for both synchronising the barrier and updating the model parameters, e.g., MapReduce [44] and Parameter Server [120] fall into this category.
2. **[Centralised model, distributed states]**: The central server is responsible for updating the model only. The nodes coordinate among themselves to synchronise on barriers in a distributed way. P2P engine falls into this category.
3. **[Distributed model, centralised states]**: This combination in practice is rare because it is hard to justify its benefits. We do not consider it further.
4. **[Distributed model, distributed states]**: Both model updates and barrier synchronisation are performed in a distributed fashion. A model can be divided into multiple chunks and distributed among different nodes.

Any of BSP, ASP, SSP and PSP can be used in case 1 but only ASP and PSP can be used for cases 2 and 4. With PSP, the sever for maintaining the model can become 'stateless' since it does not have to possess the global knowledge of the network. In case 2 particularly, the server takes the role of a stream server, continuously receiving and dispatching model updates, significantly simplifying the design of various system components.

Most previous designs tightly couple model update and barrier synchronisation but, by decoupling these two components using the *sampling* primitive, we can improve scalability without significant degradation of convergence. We present some simple simulation results here; for more detail see Wang *et al.* [112]. For simplicity we assume every node holds the same amount of independent identically distributed data. This evaluation covers both centralised and distributed scenarios. In the former, the central server applies the *sampling* primitive and the PSP implementation is as trivial as counting at the central server as it has global knowledge of the states of all nodes. In the distributed scenario, each individual node performs *sampling* locally whenever they need to make the decision to cross a synchronisation barrier, e.g., to apply an update. We use the Owl library for all the numerical functions needed in the evaluation [111].

Figure 8.4 shows the results of evaluating PSP by simulating five different barrier control strategies for 40 s on a network of 1 000 nodes running SGD algorithm. We use the parameter server engine to learn a linear model of 1 000 parameters and each node uses a sample of 1% of the total number of nodes in the system unless otherwise specified.

Figure 8.4a plots the progress in steps of all nodes after the 40 simulated seconds. As expected, the most strict BSP leads to the slowest but most tightly clustered step distribution, while ASP is the fastest but most spread due to no synchronisation at all. SSP allows certain staleness (four in our experiment) and sits between BSP and ASP. pBSP and pSSP are the probabilistic versions of BSP and SSP, respectively, and further improve the iteration efficiency while limiting dispersion.

For the same experiment, Figure 8.4b plots the CDF of nodes as a function of their progress in steps. ASP has the widest spread due to its unsynchronised nature. Figure 8.4c focuses on pBSP synchronisation control with various parameterisations. In the experiment, we vary the sample size from 0 to 64. As we increase the sample size step by step, the curves start shifting from right to the left with tighter and tighter spread, indicating less variance in nodes' progress. With sample size 0, pBSP exhibits exactly the same behaviour as that of ASP; with increased sample size, pBSP starts becoming more similar to SSP and BSP with tighter requirements on synchronisation. pBSP of sample size 16 behaves very close to SSP regarding its progress rate.

Finally, we note that with a very small sample size, even just one or two, pBSP can already effectively synchronise most of the nodes compared to ASP but with dramatically smaller communication overheads. The tail caused by stragglers can be further trimmed by using a larger sample size.

8.7   Conclusion

In this chapter we have covered the basic requirements and examples of distributed and decentralised analytics. A large number of these applications focus on optimisations between data utility and granularity, resources on the edge (memory, processing and battery) and privacy/security tradeoffs. Research in this space is providing novel methods for efficient and privacy-preserving methods for data collection, with the ability to provide instantaneous feedback and interaction with the user.

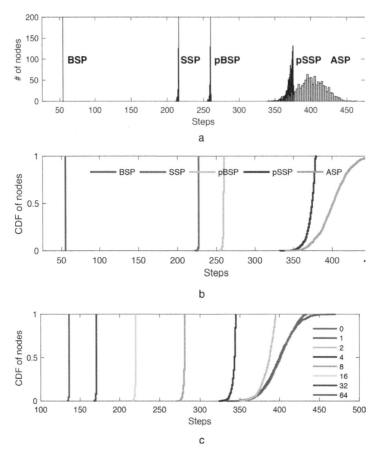

Figure 8.4 *SGD (stochastic gradient descendent) using five different barrier control strategies. Probabilistic synchronous parallel achieves a good trade-off between efficiency and accuracy. (a) Progress distribution in steps. (b) CDF of nodes as a function of progress. No node maintains global state. (c) pBSP parameterised by different sample sizes from 0 to 64. Increasing the sample size decreases spread, shifting the curves to the left replicating behaviour from the most lenient (ASP) to the most strict (BSP).*

8.8 Acknowledgements

This work was supported by the Engineering and Physical Sciences Research Council [grant numbers EP/N028260/1 and EP/N028260/2; EP/N028422/1; EP/G065802/1; EP/M02315X/1; EP/M001636/1; EP/R045178/1], and by the European Union Framework Programme 7 2007–2013 grant number 611001 and is is based on the following original articles:

- Servia-Rodríguez S., Wang L., Zhao J., Mortier, R. and Haddadi, H. (2018) 'Privacy-preserving personal model training'. IEEE/ACM Third International Conference on Internet-of-Things Design and Implementation (IoTDI), p. 153–64.
- Mortier R., Zhao J., Crowcroft J., *et al.* (2016) 'Personal data management with the databox: what's inside the box?' Proceedings of the ACM Workshop on Cloud-Assisted Networking (CAN). Irvine, California, USA, p. 49–54. http://doi.acm.org/10.1145/3010079.3010082.
- Wang, L., Catterall, B., and Mortier, R. (2017) Probabilistic Synchronous Parallel in arXiv:1709.07772 [cs.DC], https://arxiv.org/abs/1709.07772.

References

[1] Schuster M. 'Speech recognition for mobile devices at google'. *Pacific Rim International Conference on Artificial Intelligence*; Daegu, Korea; 2010. pp. 8–10.

[2] Bojarski M *et al.* 'End to end learning for self-driving cars'. *arXiv:1604.07316*. 2016.

[3] Google. *Google cloud vision API [online]*. 2017. Available from https://cloud.google.com/vision [Accessed 23 June 2021].

[4] Philip Chen C.L., Zhang C.-Y. 'Data-intensive applications, challenges, techniques and technologies: a survey on big data'. *Information Sciences*. 2014;**275**(4):314–47.

[5] Wu X., Zhu X., Wu G.Q., Ding W. 'Data mining with big data'. *IEEE Transactions on Knowledge and Data Engineering*. 2014;**26**(1):97–107.

[6] Brandimarte L., Acquisti A., Loewenstein G. 'Misplaced confidences'. *Social Psychological and Personality Science*. 2013;**4**(3):340–7.

[7] Shen W., Shapley R., Madhavan J., *et al.* 'Google fusion tables: Web-centered data management and collaboration'. Proceedings of the ACM SIGMOD Conference; IN, Indiana, USA; 2010. pp. 1061–6.

[8] Aloufi R., Haddadi H., Boyle D. 'Emotion filtering at the edge'. Proceedings of the 1st Workshop on Machine Learning on Edge in Sensor Systems; New York, NY, USA; 2019. pp. 1–6.

[9] Falahrastegar M., Haddadi H., Uhlig S., Mortier R. 'Tracking personal identifiers across the web'. International Conference on Passive and Active Network Measurement, PAM; Heraklion, Crete, Greece; 2016. pp. 30–41.

[10] National Infrastructure Commission. *Data for the public good [online]*. 2017. Available from https://nic.org.uk/data-for-the-public-good-nic-report/.

[11] Mortier R., Crowcroft J., Wang L., *et al.* 'Personal data management with the Databox: What's inside the box?'. Proceedings of the ACM Workshop on Cloud-assisted Networking (CAN); 2016. pp. 49–54.

[12]   World Economic Forum. *Rethinking personal data: A new lens for strengthening trust [online]*. 2014. Available from http://reports.weforum.org/rethinking-personal-data/.

[13]   Li M., Andersen D.G., Smola A.J., Yu K. 'Communication efficient distributed machine learning with the parameter server'. *Advances in Neural Information Processing Systems*. 2014:19–27.

[14]   Cormen T.H., Goodrich M.T. 'A bridging model for parallel computation, communication, and i/o'. *ACM Computing Surveys*. 1996;**28**(4es):208.

[15]   Agarwal A., Duchi J.C. 'Distributed delayed stochastic optimization'. *Advances in Neural Information Processing Systems*. 2011:873–81.

[16]   Ho Q., Cipar J., Cui H. 'More effective distributed ML via a stale synchronous parallel parameter server'. *Proceedings of the 26th International Conference on Neural Information Processing Systems – Volume 1*; Sydney, Australia; 2013. pp. 1223–31.

[17]   Low Y., Bickson D., Gonzalez J., Guestrin C., Kyrola A., Hellerstein J.M. 'Distributed GraphLab: a framework for machine learning and data mining in the cloud'. *Proceedings of the VLDB Endowment*. 2012;**5**(8):716–27.

[18]   Bellala G., Huberman B. 'Securing private data sharing in multi-party analytics'. *First Monday*. 2016;**21**(9).

[19]   Zaharia M. 'Resilient distributed datasets: a fault-tolerant abstraction for in-memory cluster computing'. *Proc. USENIX NSDI*; 2012. pp. 15–28.

[20]   Konecný J., McMahan B., Ramage D. 'Federated optimization: distributed optimization beyond the datacenter'. *CoRR*. 2015.

[21]   Dean J., Corrado G., Monga R., *et al.* 'Large Scale Distributed Deep Networks'. *Proceedings of the 25th International Conference on Neural Information Processing Systems*. 1. Lake Tahoe, Nevada: Curran Associates Inc.; 2012. pp. 1223–31.

[22]   Chu C.-T., Kim S., Lin Y.-an., *et al.* 'Map-reduce for machine learning on multicore'. *Proceedings NIPS*; 2006. pp. 281–8.

[23]   Malkov Y., Ponomarenko A., Logvinov A., Krylov V. 'Scalable distributed algorithm for approximate nearest neighbor search problem in high dimensional general metric spaces'. International Conference on Similarity Search and Applications; Toronto, Canada; 2012. pp. 132–47.

[24]   Neiswanger W., Wang C., Xing E. 'Asymptotically exact, embarrassingly parallel MCMC'. *arXiv:1311.4780*. 2013.

[25]   Teh Y.W., Thiery A.H., Vollmer S.J. 'Consistency and fluctuations for stochastic gradient Langevin dynamics'. *Journal of Machine Learning Research*. 2016;**17**(7):1–33.

[26]   Vollmer S.J., Zygalakis K.C., Teh Y.W. 'Exploration of the (non-) asymptotic bias and variance of stochastic gradient Langevin dynamics'. *Journal of Machine Learning Research*. 2016;**17**(159):1–48.

[27]   Scott S.L., Blocker A.W., Bonassi F.V., Chipman H.A., George E.I., McCulloch R.E. 'Bayes and big data: the consensus Monte Carlo algorithm'. *International Journal of Management Science and Engineering Management*. 2016;**11**(2):78–88.

[28] Hasenclever L., Webb S., Lienart T., *et al*. 'Distributed Bayesian learning with stochastic natural-gradient expectation propagation and the posterior server'. *arXiv:1512.09327*. 2017.

[29] Y.-A. Ma., Chen T., Fox E. 'A complete recipe for stochastic gradient MCMC'. Advances in Neural Information Processing Systems; 2015. pp. 2917–25.

[30] Hoffman M.D., Blei D.M., Wang C., Paisley J. 'Stochastic variational inference'. *The Journal of Machine Learning Research*. 2013;**14**(1):1303–47.

[31] Jacob P.E., Thiery A.H. 'On nonnegative unbiased estimators'. *The Annals of Statistics*. 2015;**43**(2):769–84.

[32] Fan J., Han F., Liu H. 'Challenges of big data analysis'. *National Science Review*. 2014;**1**(2):293–314.

[33] Bonawitz K.A., Eichner H., Grieskamp W., *et al. Towards federated learning at scale: system design [online]*. 2019. Available from https://mlsys.org/Conferences/2019/doc/2019/193.pdf.

[34] Osia S.A., Shamsabadi A.S., Taheri A., Rabiee H.R., Haddadi H. 'Private and scalable personal data analytics using hybrid Edge-to-Cloud deep learning'. *Computer*. 2018;**51**(5):42–9.

[35] Osia S.A., Shahin Shamsabadi A., Sajadmanesh S., *et al*. 'A hybrid deep learning architecture for privacy-preserving mobile analytics'. *IEEE Internet of Things Journal*. 2020;**7**(5):4505–18.

[36] Rodríguez S.S., Wang L., Zhao J.R., Mortier R., Haddadi H. 'Privacy-preserving personal model training'. Internet-of-Things Design and Implementation (IoTDI), The 3rd ACM/IEEE International Conference; Orlando, FL; 2018.

[37] Jain S., Tiwari V., Balasubramanian A., Balasubramanian N., Chakraborty S. 'PrIA: A private intelligent assistant'. Proceedings of the 18th International Workshop on Mobile Computing Systems and Applications; Sonoma, CA USA; 2017. pp. 91–6.

[38] Pan S.J., Yang Q. 'A survey on transfer learning'. *IEEE Transactions on Knowledge and Data Engineering*. 2010;**22**(10):1345–59.

[39] Shi W., Cao J., Zhang Q., Li Y., Xu L. 'Edge computing: vision and challenges'. *IEEE Internet of Things Journal*. 2016;**3**(5):637–46.

[40] Georgiev P., Lane N.D., Rachuri K.K., Mascolo C. 'Dsp. Ear: leveraging co-processor support for continuous audio sensing on smartphones'. *Proceedings of the 12th ACM Conference on Embedded Network Sensor Systems*; Memphis Tennessee, USA; 2014. pp. 295–309.

[41] Georgiev P., Lane N.D., Rachuri K.K., Mascolo C. 'LEO: scheduling sensor inference algorithms across heterogeneous mobile processors and network resources'. *Proceedings of the Annual International Conference on Mobile Computing and Networking*; New York, NY, USA; 2016. pp. 320–33.

[42] TensorFlow Lite. *TensorFlow lite [online]*. 2021. Available from www.tensorflow.org/lite.

[43] Mo F., Shamsabadi A.S., Katevas K., *et al*. 'Darkne T.Z: Towards model privacy at the edge using trusted execution environments'. Proceedings of

the 18th International Conference on Mobile Systems, Applications, and Services; Toronto, Canada; 2020. pp. 161–74.

[44] Dean J., Ghemawat S. 'MapReduce: simplified data processing on large clusters'. *Proceedings of the 6th Conference on Symposium on Operating Systems Design & Implementation*; San Francisco, CA, USA; 2004. p. 10.

[45] Lie D., Maniatis P. Glimmers: Resolving the privacy/trust quagmire, *CoRR*, vol. abs/1702.07436. 2017. Available from http://arxiv.org/abs/1702.07436.

[46] Missier P., Woodman S., Hiden H., Watson P. 'Provenance and data differencing for workflow reproducibility analysis'. *Concurrency and Computation: Practice and Experience*. 2016;**28**(4):995–1015.

[47] Watson P. 'A multi-level security model for partitioning workflows over federated clouds'. *Journal of Cloud Computing: Advances, Systems and Applications*. 2012;**1**(1):15.

[48] Balakrishnan M., Malkhi D., Wobber T. 'Tango: distributed data structures over a shared log'. *Proceedings of ACM SOSP*; 2013. pp. 325–40.

[49] Identity Theft Resource Center. *ITRC breach statistics 2005–2015 [online]*. 2016. Available from www.idtheftcenter.org/images/breach/2005to2015multiyear.pdf [Accessed 09 Mar 2016].

[50] Mortier R., Haddadi H., Henderson T., McAuley D., Crowcroft J., Crabtree A. *Human–data Interaction*. 2nd edn. The Encyclopedia of Human–Computer Interaction, Interaction Design Foundation; 2016.

[51] Diaz C., Troncoso C., Serjantov A. 'On the impact of social network profiling on anonymity'. *Privacy Enhancing Technologies*. 2008:44–62.

[52] Meeker M. *Internet trends 2016 report [online]*. 2016. Available from http://www.kpcb.com/internet-trends.

[53] US Consumer Privacy Bill of Rights. *Consumer data privacy in a networked world: A framework for protecting privacy and promoting innovation in the global digital economy [online]*. 2012. Available from www.whitehouse.gov/sites/default/files/privacy-final.pdf.

[54] EU General Data Protection Regulation. *Proposal for a regulation of the european parliament and of the council on the protection of individuals with regard to the processing of personal data and on the free movement of such data [online]*. 2012. Available from http://eur-lex.europa.eu/LexUriServ/LexUriServ.do?uri=COM:2012:0011:FIN:en:PDF.

[55] Strategic Headquarters for the Promotion of an Advanced Information and Telecommunications Network Society. *Policy outline of the institutional revision for utilization of personal data [online]*. 2014. Available from http://japan.kantei.go.jp/policy/it/20140715_2.pdf.

[56] Google. *Google privacy [online]*. 2017. Available from https://privacy.google.com.

[57] Cheng L., Liu F., Yao D.D. 'Enterprise data breach: causes, challenges, prevention, and future directions'. *Wiley Interdisciplinary Reviews: Data Mining and Knowledge Discovery*. 2017;**7**(5):e1211.

[58] Babuji Y.N., Chard K., Gerow A., Duede E. 'Cloud kotta: Enabling secure and scalable data analytics in the cloud'. Big Data (Big Data), 2016 IEEE International Conference on; 2016. pp. 302–10.

[59] Joshi K.P., Gupta A., Mittal S., Pearce C., Joshi A., Finin T. 'Semantic approach to automating management of big data privacy policies'. Big Data (Big Data), 2016 IEEE International Conference on; *Washington D.C., USA*; 2016. pp. 482–91.

[60] Cuzzocrea A., Mastroianni C., Grasso G.M. 'Private databases on the cloud: Models, issues and research perspectives'. Big Data (Big Data), 2016 IEEE International Conference; *Washington D.C., USA*; 2016. pp. 3656–61.

[61] Fredrikson M., Jha S., Ristenpart T. 'Model inversion attacks that exploit confidence information and basic countermeasures'. Proceedings of the 22nd ACM SIGSAC Conference on Computer and Communications Security; Denver, CO, USA; 2015. pp. 1322–33.

[62] Abadi M., Chu A., Goodfellow I., *et al.* 'Deep learning with differential privacy'. Proceedings of the 2016 ACM SIGSAC Conference on Computer and Communications Security; Vienna, Austria; 2016. pp. 308–18.

[63] Papernot N., Abadi M., Erlingsson Ú., Goodfellow I., Talwar K. 'Semi-supervised knowledge transfer for deep learning from private training data'. 2017.

[64] Agrawal R., Srikant R. 'Privacy-preserving data mining'. Proceedings of the 2000 ACM SIGMOD International Conference on Management of Data; Dallas, TX, USA; 2000. pp. 439–50.

[65] Aggarwal C.C., Philip S.Y. *A general survey of privacy-preserving data mining models and algorithms, Privacy-Preserving Data Mining*. Springer; 2008. pp. 11–52.

[66] Erkin Z., Troncoso-pastoriza J.R., Lagendijk R.L., Perez-Gonzalez F. 'Privacy-preserving data aggregation in smart metering systems: an overview'. *IEEE Signal Processing Magazine*. 2013;30(2):75–86.

[67] Sarwate A.D., Chaudhuri K. 'Signal processing and machine learning with differential privacy: algorithms and challenges for continuous data'. *IEEE Signal Processing Magazine*. 2013;30(5):86–94.

[68] Song S., Chaudhuri K., Sarwate A.D. 'Stochastic gradient descent with differentially private updates'. *Global Conference on Signal and Information Processing (GlobalSIP)*; EEE; 2013. pp. 245–8.

[69] Chaudhuri K., Monteleoni C., Sarwate A.D. 'Differentially private empirical risk minimization'. *Journal of Machine Learning Research: JMLR*. 2011;12:1069–109.

[70] Fredrikson M., Lantz E., Jha S., Lin S., Page D., Ristenpart T. *Privacy in Pharmacogenetics: AnEend-to-end Case Study of Personalized Warfarin Dosing*. USENIX Security; 2014. pp. 17–32.

[71] Dwork C. 'Differential privacy: a survey of results'. International Conference on Theory and Applications of Models of Computation; *Xi'an, China*; 2008. pp. 1–19.

[72] Shokri R., Shmatikov V. 'Privacy-preserving deep learning'. Proceedings of the 22nd ACM SIGSAC Conference on Computer and Communications Security; 2015. pp. 1310–21.

[73] McMahan H.B., Moore E., Ramage, S D. 'Communication-efficient learning of deep networks from decentralized data'. *arXiv preprint arXiv:1602.05629.* 2016.

[74] Hamm J., Cao P., Belkin M. 'Learning privately from multiparty data'. Proceedings of the 33rd International Conference on Machine Learning; New York City, NY, USA; 2016. pp. 555–63.

[75] Hitaj B., Ateniese G., Pérez-Cruz F. Deep models under the GAN: information leakage from collaborative deep learning, *CoRR*, vol. abs/1702.07464, 2017. Available from http://arxiv.org/abs/1702.07464.

[76] Gascón A*et al.* Privacy-preserving distributed linear regression on high-dimensional data. Cryptology ePrint Archive, Report 2016/892. 2016. Available from http://eprint.iacr.org/2016/892.

[77] Xu K., Cao T., Shah S., Maung C., Schweitzer H. 'Cleaning the null space: A privacy mechanism for predictors'. *AAAI.* 2017:2789–95.

[78] Erlingsson Ú., Pihur V., Korolova A. 'Rappor: randomized aggregatable privacy-preserving ordinal response'. *Proceedings of the 2014 ACM SIGSAC Conference on Computer and Communications Security*; Scottsdale, Arizona, USA; 2014. pp. 1054–67.

[79] Dwork C., Wegener I. 'Differential privacy' in Bugliesi M., Preneel B., Sassone V., Wegener I. (eds.). *Automata, Languages and Programming.* Germany, Berlin: Springer, Heidelberg; 2006. pp. 1–12.

[80] Johnson C.M., Grandison T.W.A. 'Compliance with data protection laws using hippocratic database active enforcement and auditing'. *IBM Systems Journal.* 2007;**46**(2):255–64.

[81] Popa R.A., Redfield C.M.S., Zeldovich N., Balakrishnan H. 'CryptDB'. *Communications of the ACM.* 2012;**55**(9):103–11.

[82] Haddadi H., Mortier R., Hand S., *et al.* 'Privacy analytics'. *ACM SIGCOMM Computer Communication Review.* 2012;**42**(2):94–8.

[83] Guha S., Reznichenko A., Tang K., Haddadi H., Francis P. 'Serving ads from localhost for performance, privacy, and profit'. *Proceedings of Hot Topics in Networking (HotNets)*; 2009.

[84] Haddadi H., Hui P., Brown I. 'MobiAd: private and scalable mobile advertising'. Proceedings 5th ACM MobiArch; 2010. pp. 33–8.

[85] Rieffel E.G., Biehl J.T., van Melle W., Lee A.J. 'Secured histories: computing group statistics on encrypted data while preserving individual privacy'. *CoRR.* 2010.

[86] Naehrig M., Lauter K., Vaikuntanathan V. 'Can homomorphic encryption be practical?' Proceedings of ACM Cloud Computing Security Workshop; 2011. pp. 113–24.

[87] Mydex. 2012. Available from https://data.gov.uk/library/mydex [Accessed 09 Mar 2016].

[88] de Montjoye Y.-A., Shmueli E., Wang S.S., Pentland A.S. 'openPDS: protecting the privacy of metadata through SafeAnswers'. *PLoS ONE*. 2014;**9**(7):e98790.

[89] Papadopoulou E., Stobart A., Taylor N.K., Williams M.H. *Enabling data subjects to remain data owners, in Agent and Multi-agent Systems: Technologies and Applications*. Springer; 2015. pp. 239–48.

[90] Chen W., Wilson J., Tyree S., Weinberger K., Chen Y. 'Compressing neural networks with the hashing trick'. International Conference on Machine Learning; Lille, France; 2015. pp. 2285–94.

[91] Howard A.G. MobileNets: Efficient convolutional neural networks for mobile vision applications, *CoRR*, vol. abs/1704.04861. 2017. Available from http://arxiv.org/abs/1704.04861.

[92] Kang Y., Hauswald J., Gao C., *et al.* 'Neurosurgeon: collaborative intelligence between the cloud and mobile edge'. Proceedings of the Twenty-second International Conference on Architectural Support for Programming Languages and Operating Systems; 2017. pp. 615–29.

[93] Movidius. *Movidius neural compute stick [online]*. 2017. Available from https://developer.movidius.com/.

[94] Yap K.-K. 'Taking the edge off with espresso: scale, reliability and programmability for global Internet peering'. Proceedings of the Conference of the ACM Special Interest Group on Data Communication; 2017. pp. 432–45.

[95] Huawei-News. *Huawei Reveals the Future of Mobile AI at IFA 2017 [online]*. 2017. Available from http://consumer.huawei.com/en/press/news/2017/ifa2017-kirin970/.

[96] Chun B.-G., Maniatis P. 'Augmented smartphone applications through clone cloud execution'. *HotOS*. 2009;**9**:8–11.

[97] Lei X., Senior A.W., Gruenstein A., Sorensen J. 'Accurate and compact large vocabulary speech recognition on mobile devices'. *Interspeech*. 2013;**1**.

[98] Narayanan D., Donnelly A., Mortier R., Rowstron A. 'Delay aware querying with seaweed'. *The VLDB Journal*. 2008;**17**(2):315–31.

[99] Boyd Danah., Crawford K. 'Critical questions for big data'. *Information, Communication & Society*. 2012;**15**(5):662–79.

[100] Ioannidis J.P.A. 'Informed consent, big data, and the oxymoron of research that is not research'. *The American Journal of Bioethics*. 2013;**13**(4):40–2.

[101] Weiss G.M., Lockhart J.W. *The Impact of Personalization on Smartphone-based Activity Recognition*; 2012.

[102] Haddadi H*et al.* 'Personal data: Thinking inside the box'. *Proceedings of the Fifth Decennial Aarhus Conference on Critical Alternatives*; Aarhus, Denmark: Aarhus University Press; 2015. pp. 29–32.

[103] Kwapisz J.R., Weiss G.M., Moore S.A. 'Activity recognition using cell phone accelerometers'. *ACM SIGKDD Explorations Newsletter*. 2011;**12**(2):74–82.

[104] Blei D.M., Ng A.Y., Jordan M.I. 'Latent Dirichlet allocation'. *Journal of Machine Learning Research : JMLR*. 2003;**3**:993–1022.

[105] NIPS. *Bag of words data set [online]*. 2017. Available from https://archive. ics.uci.edu/ml/machine-learning-databases/bag-of-words/.

[106] Wikipedia Dataset. 2017. Available from https://dumps.wikimedia.org/en-wiki/latest/.

[107] Meng X., Bradley J., Yavuz B., *et al.* 'Mllib: machine learning in APACHE spark'. *Journal of Machine Learning Research*. 2016;**17**:1235–41.

[108] ZeroMQ. *Distributed messaging [online]*. Available from http://zeromq.org.

[109] Theano Deep Learning. 2017. Available from https://pypi.org/project/Theano/.

[110] *Scikit Learn [online]*. 2020. Available from https://scikit-learn.org/stable/.

[111] Wang L. 'Owl: a general-purpose numerical library in OCaml', *CoRR*, vol. abs/1707.09616. 2017. Available from http://arxiv.org/abs/1707.09616.

[112] Wang L., Catterall B., Mortier R. 'Probabilistic synchronous parallel'. *ArXiv e-prints*. 2017.

[113] Barreno M., Nelson B., Joseph A.D., Tygar J.D. 'The security of machine learning'. *Machine Learning*. 2010;**81**(2):121–48.

[114] Huang L., Joseph A.D., Nelson B., Rubinstein B.I., Tygar J. 'Adversarial machine learning'. *Proceedings of the 4th ACM Workshop on Security and Artificial Intelligence*; Chicago, IL, USA; 2011. pp. 43–58.

[115] Shokri R., Stronati M., Shmatikov V. *Membership Inference Attacks Against Machine Learning Models*; 2017.

[116] Biggio B., Nelson B., Laskov P. 'Poisoning attacks against support vector machines'. *arXiv preprint*. 2012. arXiv:1206.6389.

[117] Xiao H., Xiao H., Eckert C. 'Adversarial label flips attack on support vector machines'. Proceedings of the 20th European Conference on Artificial Intelligence; Montpellier, France; 2012. pp. 870–5.

[118] Malewicz G., Austern M.H., Bik A.J.C., *et al.* 'Pregel: A system for large-scale graph processing'. Proceedings of the 2010 International Conference on Management of Data; Sydney, Australia: Association for Computing Machinery; 2010. pp. 135–46.

[119] Niu F., Recht B., Re C., Wright S.J. 'Hogwild!: a lock-free approach to parallelizing stochastic gradient descent'. NIPS'11 Proceedings of the 24th International Conference on Neural Information Processing Systems; Granada, Spain; 2011.

[120] Li M. *Parameter Server for Distributed Machine Learning*; 2013.

[121] Smola A.J., Zinkevich M. 'Slow learners are fast'. *Advances in Neural Information Processing Systems*. 2009:2331–9.

[122] Ahmed A., Aly M., Gonzalez J., Narayananmuthy S., Smola A. 'Scalable inference in latent variable models'. *WSDM*. 2012:123–32.

[123] Xing E.P., Ho Q., Xie P., Dai W. 'Strategies and principles of distributed machine learning on big data'. *CoRR*. 2016.

[124] Dai W., Kumar A., Wei J., Ho Q., GIbson G., Xing E.P. 'High-performance distributed ML at scale through parameter server consistency models'. *CoRR*. 2014.

Chapter 9
Human-centred home network security

Derek McAuley[1], Jiahong Chen[1], Tom Lodge[1], Richard Mortier[2], Stanislaw Piasecki[1], Diana Andreea Popescu[2], and Lachlan Urquhart[3]

This chapter draws from across the foregoing chapters discussing many core Human Data Interaction (HDI) approaches and disciplinary perspectives to consider the specific application of HDI in home network security. While much work has considered the challenges of securing in-home Internet of Things (IoT) devices and their communications, especially for those with limited power or computational capacity, scant attention has been paid by the research community to home network security, and its acceptability and usability, from the viewpoint of ordinary citizens.

It will be clear that we need a radical transformation in our approach to designing domestic networking infrastructure to guard against widespread cyber-attacks that threaten to counter the benefits of the IoT. Our aim has to be to *defend against enemies inside the walls*, to protect critical functionality in the home against rogue devices and to prevent the proliferation of disruptive wide-scale IoT Distributed Denial of Service (DDOS) attacks that are already occurring [1].

9.1 Introduction

The IoT represents a convergence of ubiquitous computing and communication technologies, with emerging uses that actuate in the real world. No longer do ubiquitous computing systems simply sense and respond digitally, now they physically interact with the world, ultimately becoming embodied and autonomous. Hence on top of the legal issues concerned with privacy (see Chapter 2), where it is often (contestably) cited that 'users don't care', to one of user safety, where users (along with regulators, governments and other stakeholders) certainly do care. Likewise, industry needs to become aware that this shift also changes the legal basis under

[1]School of Computer Science, University of Nottingham, UK
[2]Department of Computer Science and Technology, University of Cambridge, UK
[3]Law School, University of Edinburgh, UK

which companies need to operate, from one of disparate and often weakly enforced privacy laws to one of product liability.

The current widely adopted approach in which cloud services underpin IoT devices has already raised major privacy issues. Importantly in an actuated future, untrammelled communications implicating a plethora of heterogeneous online services in their normal operation also bring with it resilience challenges. We must ensure the integrity of actuating systems, which will require greater local autonomy, and hence localised security, alongside increased situated accountability to users.

This problem not only applies in many areas such as industrial control, autonomous vehicles, smart cities and buildings but also includes the intimate and commonly shared context of the home. Importantly, within the foregoing contexts there exist professional IT network support staff employed to ensure the systems are securely designed, configured and operated, and hence the underlying technology and its management are targeted at professional users with technical background and training. Likewise, such systems often limit device procurement, enforce device registration for network access, and mandate updates and patches be applied before allowing a device to communicate on the relevant network.

It is a very different situation in the home, where the majority of the deployments will not benefit from any specific technical knowledge or training of the users, while currently most home installations place any devices plugged in or having gained the WiFi password access immediately onto the same single network, providing no isolation between attached devices and the traffic they generate.

With this in mind, we created the DADA project (Defence Against the Dark Artefacts) to investigate how we could effectively provide usable network security for the now nearly ubiquitous local area network in peoples' homes. We have adopted an approach deeply rooted in pragmatism that recognises the 'real world, real time' conditions that attach to the IoT in the home:

- that the cyber security solutions currently being defined for IoT systems will not deal with legacy issues and will never achieve 100% adoption;
- that extant businesses limit the period of time for which they will provide software and security updates (even if they don't go out of business);
- that the cyber security is the arms race and threats will continue to emerge in future and
- that the public will never become network security experts.

Isolating and protecting IoT devices require that we develop and apply edge learning technologies (as covered in Chapter 8) to generate and evolve *models that profile device and inter-device behaviour*. These models will, in turn, implicate the capabilities of the switching and routing fabric that tightly constrains network communications in the home.

Key to the network design transformation is a *human-centric view of infrastructure* to ensure that secure systems providing the greatest degree of isolation between devices do not become burdensome to users, but rather are *accountable* and *socially relevant* [2], and thus provide the legibility, agency and negotiability required [3] to

Assisted Living

The scenario of assisted living helps to illustrate the goals of this research. Imagine a domestic future in which people are mixing devices with substantially different reliability requirements. First, there are critical devices that support the delivery of healthcare services where interference in their normal operation could be life threatening. Then, there are some devices that support building management and domestic security where interference could be extremely disruptive and costly. The integrity of these devices and their communications must be ensured. Add to this connected domestic appliances that support a wide range of mundane activities where interference amounts to little more than an annoyance – people will not die, or even be seriously affected by such interference, merely inconvenienced – even so, users still want to know what is happening in their network when things go wrong.

enable people to exercise control over IoT device behaviours and communications in their everyday lives.

Our focus then is on the evolution of the sociotechnical home network context into which domestic IoT is being deployed. This approach builds upon work from both the Databox home server infrastructure [2] and Homework user experience design methodologies [4] while looking at the new challenges of intelligent home cyber-defence.

9.2 Networking background

The fundamental network security concepts we adopt in DADA are already widely deployed in enterprise class networks: separation of functionality and isolation of devices by the use of Virtual Local Area Networks (VLANs), separate IP subnet address spaces and enforcement of 'Guest' status in networks so that devices are only able to send packets to the default router, and not even talk to other devices on the same layer 2 network. Likewise, traffic enforcement of both destination addresses is the standard issue firewalling technology, while traffic shaping to limit bandwidth use is widely deployed in the integrated communications infrastructure that mixes both data and voice traffic.

Within the DADA project, the challenges are then the specific requirements of domestic IoT, e.g. understanding the varied communication patterns of clusters of devices – like peer-to-peer or device-to-hub, in addition to the use of broadcast discovery mechanisms. These requirements then need to be mapped to specific switching, routing and firewalling mechanisms that can provide segregated subnetworks. Importantly, where shared resources are used (e.g. upstream Internet links and in-home links carrying multiple subnetworks), traffic shaping and rate control will enforce traffic profiles, with specific attention to rate limiting actuation events, which may involve compound network interactions, that could lead physical devices to be particularly susceptible to denial of service by excessive use [5] or operation outside of design envelope [6]. Traffic shaping will also be available on a per device basis, applying shared profiles created by the ubiquitous monitoring and made available through the profiling service, providing both traffic management and attack detection.

These enforcement mechanisms also need to be complemented by device profiling, where we seek to learn and share behavioural and communications patterns of IoT devices – such systems need to be lightweight and accurate, and being based on edge-based sampling techniques and modelling, engage in pseudonymous profile.

General characterisation of Internet-connected devices is known to be complex [7, 8]. However, domestic IoT devices have much simpler networking properties than general Internet-connected general-purpose computers, and the scale and degree of multiplexing is thus much smaller and amenable to enumeration and computation. While manufacturers could, in principle, supply device behaviour profiles (e.g. via a Hypercat endpoint) to provide a priori information to management systems, devices deployed in these environments are likely to have long lifetimes, and will undergo many firmware/software upgrades resulting in evolving behaviours, as will the natural evolution of the cloud services used to support such devices. Continual monitoring and re-profiling will thus be necessary. Furthermore, specific attention will be given to identifying physical actuation interactions, potentially involving compound network interactions with multiple devices. In addition, homes will often contain only a small number of instances of many devices (e.g. smart TVs, fridges and electricity meters) rendering it necessary to *share* information across a statistically representative number of monitored networks to build an evolving dynamic model of behaviour while being sure to preserve the privacy of individuals and avoid revealing personal information through sharing device behaviours [8].

Building new technical capabilities into home network infrastructure inevitably leads to questions of how do users interact with such systems and how are they made accountable to end-users in socially relevant ways that enable end-users to exercise control over their network.

9.2.1   Network mechanisms

In order to provide the basis for traffic interventions, we must first monitor traffic on the local network and provide a means to identify anomalies. Here we present eBPF-IoT, a customized system for securing IoT smart homes – in a future smart home, this would be running continuously within the home router or in more complex domestic networks within all active networking elements. Our specific implementation here is based on Linux.

The eBPF-IoT comprises two components: (i) eBPF-Mon, which computes traffic statistics and extracts machine learning features needed to train machine learning algorithms for IoT device identification and anomaly detection and (ii) eBPF-IoT-MUD – a traffic management module based on eBPF that implements traffic policies derived from Manufacturer Usage Description (MUD) files provided by the IoT manufacturer.

The extended Berkeley Packet Filter (eBPF) provides a very general way to hook code into network data paths within the Linux kernel without modifying the kernel source code. To ensure system stability, the eBPF framework ensures that the code loaded is both safe to execute and loop free (and so will terminate). Our eBPF-Mon component then uses these hooks to gather statistics about flows in real-time.

The eBPF program can hook into the eXpress Data Path (XDP) to efficiently implement packet dropping, for example, to block a Denial-of-Service (DoS) attack – in our scenario, we are specifically interested in blocking such traffic originating from devices within the home, whether a DoS on another device in the home or as part of a Distributed DoS targeting a service on the Internet. More complex controls are also possible, such as rate-limiting flows or blocking/forwarding packets at a fine grain, for example, specific ports on specific servers. In contrast to general-purpose computers, the Internet services that an IoT device would connect to in normal operation are fixed and known by the manufacturer, and the MUD specification (RFC8520) defines how these services can be listed and, in an extension, the expected traffic rates to each service when in operation. So, our eBPF-IoT-MUD component uses the MUD profiles of devices to configure the XDP to only permit certain communications from the IoT device (and block all others) and in combination with the eBPF-Mon enforce rate limits on the network flows.

Performance measurements show that we can sustain over 1 Gbps in most scenarios, with only modest added delay to processing the packets in the router.

9.3   Shaping user interaction

To what degree do users *need* to interact with home security systems? As we have seen in the previous discussion, monitoring and mitigation of network security threats can be handled transparently by the underlying system; developments in device profiling, pattern recognition and the network control plane can increase the ability of a system to effectively respond to, for example, misconfigured, malicious and poorly designed IoT devices. There is a strong argument for involving the user as little as possible, if at all, in the resolution of these problems to allow security experts and system designers to make the security choices for end-users; indeed [9] have argued that the network should be an unremarkable and mundane part of a household, and that foregrounding it to users may run the risk of making networks 'constantly remarkable and thus problematic'. Two factors, however, argue against fully cocooning a user from the concerns of their network security:

1.   Home network security pervades and is deeply entangled within the social fabric of a household. Privacy, for example, may be equally violated within the home as without. Similarly, the management of access to resources (devices, filesystems, printers and so forth) is subject to routine matters in the home, such as working or socialising.
2.   Security management may often be subordinate to the here and now of a household occupant's activities. Where remedial actions taken by a network are

disruptive (e.g. consuming bandwidth, rebooting devices or restricting or even disabling connectivity), automated fixes may be at odds with the immediate concerns of members of the household.

Our challenge, therefore, is to design interactions that support users in the management of the security practices mentioned in (1) whilst ensuring that the home network remains 'unremarkable'. Security-based interactions must defer those out-of-band priorities that arise from day-to-day living. Put another way, we must design with an awareness of the typical philosophy that 'some kind of working is good enough for now' [9].

Rules and policies are a key feature of network systems, and one approach to folding in social concerns to the management of home network security is to have the system capture and recognise those events (temporal, system and household) that form the basis of a householder's reasoning about how their system should behave. Temporal events might be 'between 10 and 11 in the morning', system events might be 'using social media or device uploading 10% more data than normal', whereas household events might be 'when Mum gets home' or even 'Jamie is watching TV'. Ideally, events might be composed to reflect the nuanced needs of the household, then used to trigger appropriate system behaviours. Though a beguiling notion, in practice there are a set of (perhaps intractable) issues that limit its use, not least the thorny technical challenges of capturing and codifying higher-level constructs (such as ownership and activities such as 'shopping' or 'doing homework') into sane system primitives. Moreover, given that 'different people are allowed to do different things with different devices at different times of the day and in different places' [4], it is simply too difficult for users to anticipate and express rules to cover even a subset of scenarios; studies have shown that, in reality, rules are established retrospectively in response to experience (ibid.).

Edwards *et al.* [10] argue more expansively against relying on fully automated systems security, suggesting that there are inherent limitations to how well automation can succeed in practice *even if the technology behind it is faultless*. They suggest that these limitations can lead to not only 'failures' of automation that are not only technical (i.e. when the automation system simply stops working) but also failures of meeting the actual needs of the users. Moreover, as the authors of [11] suggest, we 'only need to make the wrong decision once to discourage future use'.

Given that fully automated approaches to system security are unlikely to provide a complete solution, we continue to require mechanisms to help users interact with their network security; these will include manually responding to issues, restricting or elevating resource access, updating firmware or software, and monitoring behaviours and usage. The prevalent support provided today is by graphical user interfaces; these vary in complexity and functionality but will typically provide a degree of *monitoring* and *control*. As the range of security vulnerabilities increases alongside the number of devices in our homes, there may need to be a corresponding increase in the complexity of the interfaces we use to monitor and control them. These interfaces may even come to resemble enterprise systems, though these are often simply 'too complex for home users' [12]. In response, alternative approaches have been developed and studied. Yang *et al.* [12], for example, provide spatial and logical views of a user's home that can be directly manipulated. Others mimic already understood home devices such as alarm or heating panels [13], and we've even seen standalone physical, single-purpose devices built to simplify traditionally problematic tasks [14, 15].

Outside technical tools for controlling the network, there is some evidence that householders use non-technical approaches to assume control; access control, for example, may be managed by negotiation, though where enforcement is required, more imaginative approaches have been observed, such as locking devices away, or the deliberate creation of 'dead zones' in the house where broadband is unavailable due to an access point being out of range [9].

9.3.1   Designing for control

To address the observations and challenges we have discussed, and to walk the line between on one hand keeping the network 'unremarkable' and on the other providing adequate interaction support when required, we have built a mobile and physical interface to facilitate a further examination of a householder interactions with their devices and networks. In the first instance, we have designed mechanisms for users to *control* rather than *monitor* network security. We have limited the scope of 'control' to a range of simple actions: rebooting devices, restricting access to resources, device monitoring, and switching between privileged and unprivileged networks. We are explicitly assuming that *all* householders may wish to perform network control actions on one or more sets of devices, but that social constructs, such as ownership and household hierarchy (rather than, e.g. technical competence) can be respected when determining the set of control mechanisms that are available. We have built a physical component for several reasons: first, it is *situated*, meaning that we can explicitly require that a householder is present to perform some tasks and that the act of performing a task can be made visible to other occupants. Second, it enables us to simplify the interactions and corresponding effort of performing control tasks (so, use is predicated upon little to no technical competence). Third, it extends the opportunity for householders to elevate or remove control mechanisms, using non-technical and familiar means (e.g. moving out of reach, hiding, locking away and loaning); something that we are especially interested in studying.

We use physical tokens as proxies for home devices (Figure 9.1); an approach reminiscent of the interactive 'tokens and constraints' work first proposed by [16]. The tokens use MiFare[a]1K RFID tags to communicate with an Android smartphone and a reader. The reader consists of a microprocessor (Adafruit Feather M0 Wifi)[b] that is connected (over I^2C) to a (MFRC522[c]RFID) reader, which is capable of reading multiple tags simultaneously. The microprocessor has a WIFI chip and communicates with an MQTT broker running on our home access point.

[a]https://www.mifare.net/en/
[b]https://www.adafruit.com/product/3010
[c]https://www.nxp.com/docs/en/data-sheet/MFRC522.pdf

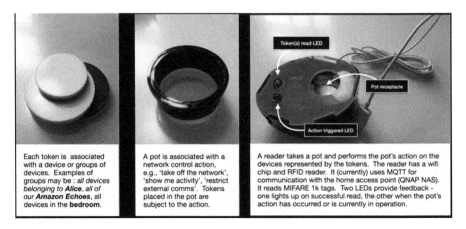

The three panels contain the following descriptions:

Each token is associated with a device or groups of devices. Examples of groups may be : *all devices belonging to Alice, all of our Amazon Echoes*, all devices in the **bedroom**.

A pot is associated with a network control action, e.g., 'take off the network', 'show me activity', 'restrict external comms'. Tokens placed in the pot are subject to the action.

A reader takes a pot and performs the pot's action on the devices represented by the tokens. The reader has a wifi chip and RFID reader. It (currently) uses MQTT for communication with the home access point (QNAP NAS). It reads MIFARE 1k tags. Two LEDs provide feedback - one lights up on successful read, the other when the pot's action has occurred or is currently in operation.

Figure 9.1   Tokens, pot and reader

Those that are in receipt of tokens will have control of the corresponding device(s) that the token represents. Crucially, tokens can be associated with a single device or arbitrary device groups that make sense to a particular household (e.g. all of Ellie's devices, all televisions and the thermostats in the top bedroom). Tokens can be replicated so that users can share control, and they can be modified to add or remove devices as required.

To perform a security-related task, tokens are placed into a 'pot'; a pot is associated with an action, such as 'remove from the network' or 'provide access to printer' or 'log all traffic'. The pot also has an RFID tag but is encoded to distinguish it from tokens. When a pot is placed into a reader, all of the tokens that are in the pot will be subject to the associated action. The reader will light up an LED to show that the action has been triggered. Actions may be *continuous* or *discrete*. That is, in some cases, removing tokens from the pot or reader will undo the action (e.g. revoke permissions and stop traffic logging); in other cases, the action will remain until superseded by placing the token in another pot; this allows a user to compose sets of actions whilst keeping hold of the token. Note that, once in receipt of user study data, we may eventually choose to exclusively support only one of these two modalities.

Our mobile app is used to bootstrap and configure our tokens and pots. The app presents a list of devices on the home network and, using Google's quick draw API[d], provides a simple interface for sketching the device (to help users distinguish between all of their devices) (Figure 9.2).

To associate tokens with devices, a user holds a token against the mobile phone. If the token is not already associated with any devices, the user is invited to select a set of devices to associate it with (Figure 9.3). The mac addresses of the devices are

[d]https://quickdraw.readthedocs.io/en/latest/api.html

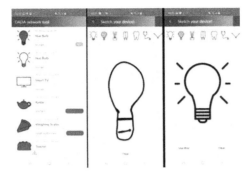

Figure 9.2   App device introduction

then written to the token's tag. If the token already has devices associated with it, the user will be shown the devices and can remove them and re-associate if required.

The process of configuring pots is similar. To configure a pot, a user holds it against the phone, and they will then be presented with a set of system activities that they can have the pot perform (Figure 9.4). Again, if the pot already has an action associated with it, the user can remove them and add alternatives.

To begin with, we will only support a small set of actions, though this can be expanded in the future. Where it makes sense, the system will allow actions to be composed and associated with a single pot. By designing our system in this way, with programmable pots and configurable tokens, our intention is to enable users foreground and simplify problematic or frequently needed functionality (e.g. rebooting a router, dealing with visitors and revoking access to social media) whilst ignoring (or leaving the system to deal with) any features or devices that are or little

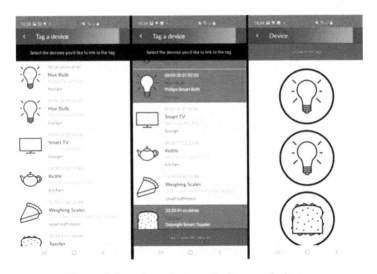

Figure 9.3   Association of tokens with devices

Figure 9.4   Association of pots with actions

or no interest. Though the system is principally designed to be reactive, the actions associated with pots can themselves be made contingent upon events if required.

9.4   Compliance by design

One of the challenges facing smart home technologies is the uncertainties within the regulatory environment where multiple forms of normative enablers and constraints may come into play, such as design codes, technical standards and law. At the same time, being a concept for a future domestic IoT security solution, DADA is by definition a smart home technology itself and will thus be subject to a similar set of challenges as well. To ensure smart technologies – including security solutions, such as DADA – are designed to be truly usable by non-expert users in their everyday life, it is crucial to understand how compliance requirements have affected design, and how design can support compliance.

We take the view that 'secure by design' [17] is not just about bringing the development of smart technologies in line with the security requirements but also about creating the right conditions for law and technologies to co-evolve in such a way that all involved parties are incentivised to be on board – what one might call the 'legal design' [18]. In this regard, reaching out to different sectors throughout the entire project lifecycle, so as to understand the regulatory landscape as well as the stakeholder expectations, forms an important part of our work at DADA. Through working with the academic, industrial and policymaking communities, we have envisaged, discovered, verified and pre-empted some of the design and compliance challenges facing the industry as well as DADA.

9.4.1 Outlining the regulatory framework with academic research

In the scholarly literature, while there has been a growing body of discussions in improving privacy and security in the IoT environments, such efforts have largely focused on the technical aspects of the IoT artefacts or the interactions between such artefacts and human users. The regulatory environment, though touched upon as a relevant topic, has been mostly framed as either the motivation for research initiatives or the external constraints for research and development. In developing our work at DADA, we take a bidirectional approach by unpicking not only how the technological paradigms for IoT technologies can shift to improve compliance with the existing regulatory framework, but also how the regulatory environment can evolve to support the human-centred approach we advance. By 'regulatory environment', our work mainly addresses two normative realms: law and standards.

The legal thread of our investigation deals with the data protection legal framework, mainly the GDPR. Considering the sheer volume and potential sensitivity of the data collected and analysed by IoT devices, including DADA as a future IoT cybersecurity solution, the starting point of our inquiry is whether and to what extent data protection law applies to edge computing in smart homes. In our paper 'Who is responsible for data processing in smart homes?' [19], two key legal concepts have been foregrounded to highlight the impact of data protection law on the development and adoption of security- and privacy-enhancing technologies: joint controllership and the household exemption. We note that these two notions are not simply static, immutable rules, but rather an ever-adapting pair that have been shaped up through regulatory guidelines and case law over the years. The expanding scope of joint controllership – meaning developers and end-users of smart technologies are more likely to be held responsible as joint data controllers – and the shrinking household exemption – meaning end-users are less likely to be exempted from data protection obligations – will collectively create a regulatory environment where the research and uptake of IoT privacy and security technologies may be deterred by the potential compliance burdens. These trends are well-intended with the objective to provide seamless protection to data subjects but have failed to recognise the nuances of control and power in digital domestic life. We, therefore, concluded that '[p]aradoxically this may then result in a lower degree of privacy, as well as security, for smart home inhabitants' [19].

This message is further elaborated in Chapter 2 of this book, where we further unpack the legal principle of 'accountability' in a smart home environment and also in a more user-centric approach. This is achieved through the construction of the notion of 'domestic data controllers' and the advancement of differentiated responsibilities in smart homes. These discussions are relevant to our approach with DADA because it underlines how the current data protection legal framework does not fully capture the contemporary reality of digital life that is characterised by the mundanity of ordinary people exercising control over personal data as well as the complex techno-socio-legal dynamics behind the decision-making on IoT privacy and security issues by stakeholders. To support domestic data controllers to demonstrate accountability, we argued it would be essential to make sense of the interpersonal relations in the digitalised domestic politics, the role of technologies in this domain and the differentiated nature of power exercised by domestic controllers and vendors. All these have profound implications for policymaking, including how the regulatory environment may be improved with clear and fair guidance.

A second thread of our work focuses on cybersecurity standards. We have written on how these standards are currently showing a similar lack of acknowledgement of the latest socio-technical developments in smart homes [20]. For one thing, major technical standards for IoT security are predominantly developed with the stereotypical cloud-based architecture in mind. The recurring recommendations of those standards on how smart devices should be designed (e.g. the resilience to outages requirement) would be often also relevant for edge-computing architectures and actually more efficiently implemented by the latter. While cloud-based standards are needed considering the number of IoT devices relying on this architectural model, standards can also set out directions for best practice and, therefore, should be more aspirational in attempting to change current industry practices, especially in the context of the rapid developments in edge-computing. For another thing, current standards focus mainly on technical and external threats, leaving a significant gap in addressing the internal human threats in smart homes. For example, domestic abusers may exploit IoT devices to monitor, harass, intimidate, control or manipulate other members of the household, but most, if not all, of the current cybersecurity standards have failed to provide guidance on how to anticipate and minimise such risks. Standards could potentially help in removing affordances related to in-home human threats, and further research in this field is required. In this regard, the routine activity theory (RAT) can be a helpful conceptual framework for uncovering the values of edge-computing and translating such strengths into actionable strategies to defend against security threats, whether technical or human in nature, and whether from within or outside the home [21]. Again, the shortcomings of the current standards will have policymaking implications, especially the urgent need to deepen our understanding of different types of security risks, and the roles and limitations of technical standards.

Through our research into the status quo of data protection law and cybersecurity standards, we aim to communicate a message to the academic community one that echoes the underlying idea of DADA: Human-centred IoT security is not just about technological design but also about normative development. A supportive regulatory environment, created with the right set of legal rules and technical standards, will promote security in smart homes. For academics and policymakers alike, this means further interdisciplinary work is needed to comprehend the human factors in compliance, design and regulation in the area of domestic IoT. The policymaking implications of DADA will be further discussed in Section 9.4.3.

9.4.2   *Extracting practical insights from industrial involvement*

In conjunction, we want to ensure that our work engages with practical challenges of designing for cybersecurity in IoT development. As such, we focus on two strands of our work here, where industrial insights have been key in charting the problem space.

First, we conducted a series of exploratory semi-structured interviews with different stakeholder groups from the IoT sector. Whilst industry practice around IoT security was a key focus, we also wanted to understand the wider IoT ecosystem and thus spoke to NGOs and government bodies. This provided us a wider appreciation of the emerging threat landscape, priorities for industry, strategies for anticipating and managing these risks, and what direction the industry is headed in securing IoT.

For example, in relation to motivations and solutions, the motivations for building secure IoT systems ranging from fear of harder regulation and reputational harm to emerging threats, such as how to manage vulnerabilities at scale (e.g. a washing machine bug in thousands of homes leading to a critical national infrastructure threat, not just an individual one). In terms of solutions, edge computing, greater need for life cycle security management, the value of MUD profiles and use of labelling of IoT risks all emerged as valuable. Such insights can guide academic research, providing interesting problems to be addressed.

Second, we are aware that developers have a growing role in addressing socio-technical harms of IoT systems, as seen in the Secure by Design work discussed below. Thus, we wanted to create a tool to help translate and make discussions around IoT cybersecurity more accessible. Acknowledging the value of reflective tools for thinking about law and ethics (e.g. ideation card decks) [22], we wanted to explore the value of play and developed a 'serious board game' for helping IoT developers consider human dimensions of securing smart homes. Conscious of moving past the framing of purely technical solutions, the goal was to create a game that engages with the complexities of managing home networks, guarding against a hacker who is compromising IoT devices. The game uses play to raise awareness about appropriate strategies to secure the home, the nature of risks and challenges domestic users face in using different skill sets to address these dangers. The game has been developed through a process of iterative development with different stakeholder groups from experts in cybersecurity and games, to those working on IoT, HCI and usable privacy and security. As such, our process has been shaped by their insights, where industry, as well as academic expertise, has played a key role in guiding gameplay, aesthetics and themes covered. Furthermore, with Covid-19, we needed to adapt our planned game development approach. Originally, it was to be a physical game but we still managed to use Tabletopia (an online board game platform), to iterate and test our prototype, to great success.

9.4.3 Shaping the prospect by informing policymaking

DADA started as a research project at a time when large-scale cybersecurity attacks have raised cross-departmental concerns in the UK government [17], followed by the publication of a code of practice for consumer IoT security [23] and later a set of regulatory proposals [24]. At the time of writing, the Department for Digital, Culture, Media & Sport (DCMS) has conducted a formal consultation on its initial positions (May–June 2019) [24], feeding into its revised proposal open for a second round of comments (July–September 2020) [25]. In a separate but related review, the DCMS also carried out a review on cybersecurity incentives and regulation, with a call for evidence (November–December 2019) [26]. This highlights the importance of regulating IoT cybersecurity as a governmental priority and also represents an opportunity for DADA to translate research findings into something that can potentially impact the regulatory environment surrounding smart technologies.

We have submitted our responses to all three inquiries [27–29] with a view to raising some of the legal issues we have identified in the journal articles and the practical considerations flagged up in our engagements with industrial stakeholders. Responding to public consultations, however, has the limitation that these consultations always take the form of a set of pre-determined, sometimes strictly structured questions, and occasionally, there is a preferred position, be it explicitly specified in the consultation document or inferred by the way the questions have been framed.

Exposing the 'blind spots' of these inquiries can therefore be somewhat challenging because going beyond the scope of the questions may result in the answers being disregarded. From the three IoT-related inquiries initiated by the government, there is a clear lack of emphasis on the human aspects of security in smart homes. The regulatory proposal for the May to June 2019 consultation, for example, views the regulatory challenge being 'vulnerable devices becom[ing] the weakest point in an individual's network' and '[c]ompromised devices at scale [posing] a risk for the wider economy through distributed denial of service (DDOS) attacks such as Mirai Botnet in October 2016' [30]. Accordingly, the first proposed regulatory option – which became the selected model in the July to September 2020 version [31] – focused entirely on the three technical safeguards: 'no default passwords', 'implement a vulnerability disclosure policy' and 'keep software updated'.[e] Our response highlighted the need to take into account the user-friendliness consideration of managing IoT security mapping these design requirements to the existing cybersecurity guidelines, such as the 'make installation and maintenance of devices easy' principle in the government's own code of practice. We submitted that 'most of the ten guidelines additional to the "top three" are already legally required under data protection law and cybersecurity law' and therefore mandating all 13 principles 'would not *per se* create a significant or disproportionate amount of compliance costs to retailers or manufacturers' [27].

As regards the organisational dimension of addressing cybersecurity threats, the July to September 2020 review has touched upon the lack of ability and motivation for businesses to put in place security measures. Many of the consultation questions, however, are based on the assumption that the level of incentives and barriers varies along the spectrum of the size of business (e.g. small, medium and large organisations). Yet, through our expert interviews, we found that organisation size is not the only decisive factor, other parameters such as the organisation's position in the supply chain, the market structure of a particular sector and the business model can also significantly affect how motivated a business can be to manage cybersecurity

---

[e]These are known as the 'top three' principles in the Code of Practice for Consumer IoT Security. See Department for Digital, Culture, Media & Sport. *Code of Practice for Consumer IoT Security* [online]. 2020. Available from https://www.gov.uk/government/consultations/consultation-on-regulatory-proposals-on-consumer-iot-security [Accessed 26 Sep 2020].

properly. As such, we submitted that '[a]n effective cybersecurity strategy will need to acknowledge the heterogeneity within and across sectors on those dimensions' [26].

There is clearly a delicate balance between foregrounding the under-discussed issues and remaining in scope when it comes to responding to governmental consultations. DADA as a research project has endeavoured to communicate the message of a human-centred approach in cybersecurity to policymakers by carefully aligning this with how the challenges and solutions have been framed. For future projects, other forms of engagement, such as a more proactive initiative to contribute to the scoping of the consultation in an earlier stage, may prove more effective if the timing of the project lifecycle allows.

9.4.4 Lessons of DADA on compliance by design

Our work on compliance by design in domestic IoT has enabled us not only to ensure DADA as a research project is privacy-aware, value-driven, ethically sustainable and legally compliant but also, more importantly, to explore approaches to understanding and interacting with the surrounding regulatory spaces that matter to future developments of security- and privacy-enhancing technologies for smart homes. Through different threads of research and outreach activities with the academic, industrial and policymaking communities, some of our experiences may be of value to future research projects.

First, for interdisciplinary projects, there can be a strong role for social scientists to play in co-shaping the technical approach, provided that messages are clearly translated across discipline-specific languages. The initiative to proactively engage with audiences coming from a more technical background is the key.

Second, with a multi-stakeholder approach, it is essential that the priorities of different groups are clearly identified so as to inform the adjustment of the engagement approaches. Industrial partners, for example, would have starkly different motivations behind improving IoT security from policymakers. Consequently, in order to generate greater impact, it would be helpful to explain how the human-centred approach is in line with their own overall agenda.

Third, managing interdependencies and continuity across different strands of work has proved significantly crucial. For example, the RAT theory employed in our academic work has ended up being the conceptual framework for the design of the serious game. Also, the findings in our interviews with experts from the industry have also laid the empirical groundwork for our policy engagement activities. Effective communications between, and timely reflections on, all fronts of the work have made this much more manageable.

Fourth, with a large part of our work taking place during the COVID-19 pandemic, adaptability and resilience have turned out especially important to our empirical research. While the plans to engage with industrial stakeholders through interviews and the game were affected by the restrictions, eventually it was possible to move these activities online. It also offered us the opportunity to reflect on how different groups of stakeholders have responded to our new approaches, and what the more effective ways to engage with them would be going forward.

9.5   Acknowledgement

This work was supported by the Engineering and Physical Sciences Research Council [grant numbers EP/L015463/1, EP/M001636/1, EP/N028260/1, EP/M02315X/1, EP/R03351X/1].

This chapter is based on the following original works:

- Piasecki, S., Urquhart, L., and McAuley. D. (2021) Defence Against the Dark Artefacts: Smart Home Cybercrimes and Cybersecurity Standards. *Computer Law & Security Review: The International Journal of Technology Law and Practice*. (In Press).
- Chen, J., Edwards, L., Urquhart, L., McAuley, D. McAuley, D. (2020) Who Is Responsible for Data Processing in Smart Homes? Reconsidering Joint Controllership and the Household Exemption. *International Data Privacy Law*. 2020; 10(4) pp. 279–93.

Many thanks to our project intern Adam Jenkins, PhD researcher in usable security at School of Informatics, University of Edinburgh. He has been key in the game design and iterative testing process.

References

[1]   Symantec. *Endpoint protection [online]*. 2016. Available from https://www.symantec.com/connect/blogs/iot-devices-being-increasingly-used-ddos-attacks.

[2]   Amar Y., Haddadi H., Mortier R. 'Privacy-aware infrastructure for managing personal data'. *Proceedings of the 2016 ACM SIGCOMM Conference*. 2016:571–2.

[3]   Richard M., Haddadi H., Henderson T., McAuley D., Crowcroft J. Human-data interaction: the human face of the data-driven society (October 1, 2014). Available from https://ssrn.com/abstract=2508051.

[4]   Crabtree A., Rodden T., Tolmie P., *et al*. 'House rules: the collaborative nature of policy in domestic networks'. *Personal and Ubiquitous Computing*. 2015;**19**(1):203–15.

[5]   Sonar K., Upadhyay H. 'A survey: DDOS attack on IoT'. *International Journal of Engineering Research and Development*. 2014;**10**:58–63.

[6]   Kushner D. 'The real story of stuxnet'. *IEEE Spectrum*. 2013;**50**(3):48–53.

[7]   Scarfone K., Mell P. 'Guide to intrusion detection & prevention systems'. *NIST Special Publication*. 2007;**800**:94.

[8]   Apthorpe N., Reisman D., Sundaresan S., Narayanan A. 'Spying on the smart home: privacy attacks and defenses on encrypted IoT traffic'. *ArXiv*. 2017:arXiv:1708.05044.

[9] Crabtree A., Mortier R., Rodden T., Tolmie P. 'Unremarkable networking: the home network as a part of everyday life'. *Proceedings of the Designing Interactive Systems Conference*; 2012. pp. 554–63.

[10] Edwards W.K., Poole E.S., Stoll J. 'Security automation considered harmful?'. *Proceedings of the 2007 Workshop on New Security Paradigms*; 2008. pp. 33–42.

[11] Bauer L., Cranor L.F., Reiter M.K., Vaniea K. 'Lessons learned from the deployment of a smartphone-based access-control system'. *Proceedings of the 3rd Symposium on Usable Privacy and Security*; 2007. pp. 64–75.

[12] Yang J., Edwards K., Haslem D. 'Eden'. *Proceedings of UIST*. 2010:109–18.

[13] Mortier R., Rodden T., Lodge T. 'Control and understanding: owning your home network'. *2012 Fourth International Conference on Communication Systems and Networks*; 2012. pp. 1–10.

[14] Yang J., Edwards W.K. 'Icebox: toward easy-to-use home networking'. *IFIP Conference on Human-Computer Interaction*. Berlin, Heidelberg: Springer; 2007. pp. 197–210.

[15] Balfanz D., Durfee G., Grinter R.E., Smetters D.K., Stewart P. 'Network-in-a-box: how to set up a secure wireless network in under a minute'. *USENIX Security Symposium*; 2004. p. 222.

[16] Ullmer B., Ishii H., Jacob R.J.K. 'Token+constraint systems for tangible interaction with digital information'. *ACM Transactions on Computer-Human Interaction*. 2005;**12**(1):81–118.

[17] Department for Digital, Culture, Media & Sport. *Secure by design report [online]*. 2018. Available from https://www.gov.uk/government/publications/secure-by-design-report [Accessed 1 Jul 2021].

[18] Rossi A., Haapio H. 'Proactive legal design: embedding values in the design of legal artefacts' in Schweighofer E., Kummer F., Saarenpää A. (eds.). *Internet of Things. Proceedings of the 22nd International Legal Informatics Symposium IRIS 2019*. Bern: Editions Weblaw; 2019. pp. 537–44.

[19] Chen J., Edwards L., Urquhart L., McAuley D. 'Who is responsible for data processing in smart homes? reconsidering joint controllership and the household exemption'. *International Data Privacy Law*. 2021;**10**(4):279–93.

[20] Piasecki S., Urquhart L., McAuley D. 'Defence against dark artefacts: an analysis of the assumptions underpinning smart home cybersecurity standards'. *SSRN Electronic Journal*. 2019.

[21] Cohen L.E., Felson M. 'Social change and crime rate trends: a routine activity approach'. *American Sociological Review*. 1979;**44**(4):588–588.

[22] Urquhart L.D., Craigon P.J. 'The moral-IT deck: a tool for ethics by design'. *Journal of Responsible Innovation*. 2021;**30**(4):1–33.

[23] Department for Digital, Culture, Media & Sport. *Code of practice for consumer IoT security [online]*. 2018. Available from https://www.gov.uk/government/publications/code-of-practice-for-consumer-iot-security [Accessed 1 Jul 2021].

[24] Department for Digital, Culture, Media & Sport. *Code of practice for consumer IoT security [online]*. 2020. Available from https://www.gov.uk/government/

consultations/consultation-on-regulatory-proposals-on-consumer-iot-security [Accessed 1 Jul 2021].

[25] Department for Digital, Culture, Media & Sport. *Proposals for regulating consumer smart product cyber security - call for views [online]*. 2020. Available from https://www.gov.uk/government/publications/proposals-for-regulating-consumer-smart-product-cyber-security-call-for-views [Accessed 1 Jul 2021].

[26] Department for Digital, Culture, Media & Sport. *Cyber security incentives & regulation review: call for evidence [online]*. 2019. Available from https://www.gov.uk/government/publications/cyber-security-incentives-regulation-review-call-for-evidence [Accessed 1 Jul 2021].

[27] McAuley D., Koene A., Chen J. *Response to consultation on the government's regulatory proposals regarding consumer Internet of Things (IoT) security [online]*. 2019. Available from https://doi.org/10.17639/4esm-9705 [Accessed 1 Jul 2021].

[28] McAuley D., Haddadi H., Urquhart L., Chen J. *Response to the government's call for views: proposals for regulating consumer smart product cyber security [online]*. 2020. Available from https://nottingham-repository.worktribe.com/output/4880636 [Accessed 1 Jul 2021].

[29] McAuley D., Chen J. *Response to DCMS call for evidence: cyber security incentives and regulation [online]*. 2020. Available from https://doi.org/10.17639/SWKM-5T76 [Accessed 1 Jul 2021].

[30] Department for Digital, Culture, Media & Sport. *Consultation on the Government's regulatory proposals regarding consumer Internet of Things (IoT) security [online]*. 2020. Available from https://www.gov.uk/government/consultations/consultation-on-regulatory-proposals-on-consumer-iot-security/consultation-on-the-governments-regulatory-proposals-regarding-consumer-internet-of-things-iot-security [Accessed 1 Jul 2021].

[31] Department for Digital, Culture, Media & Sport. *Proposals for regulating consumer smart product cyber security - call for views [online]*. 2020. Available from https://www.gov.uk/government/publications/proposals-for-regulating-consumer-smart-product-cyber-security-call-for-views/proposals-for-regulating-consumer-smart-product-cyber-security-call-for-views [Accessed 1 Jul 2021].

Chapter 10

Anticipating the adoption of IoT in everyday life

Paul Coulton[1], Adrian Ioan Gradinar[1], and
Joseph Galen Lindley[1]

Realising the potential economic and societal benefits of emerging and future technologies such as the Internet of Things (IoT) is dependent on a critical mass of potential users adopting them, this is often driven by whether users consider them to be acceptable. However, the processes that drive adoption and acceptability are rarely taken into consideration when researching emerging and future technologies. More often than not, either adoption is regarded as something that will naturally occur once the technology is made available to the market or the process of adoption is considered to be someone else's future work. The result is that the discovery of challenges and barriers to adoption and acceptability occur only after potentially problematic design patterns have become established and concretised at the core of devices and services. This, in turn, can result in even the most mundane designs having unintended consequences or compromised impact.

In this chapter, we focus on IoT-connected products that are often referred to as 'smart' in our IoT-enabled 'smart homes'. The espoused promise of the smart home is that it will make our lives easier by giving us more free time, improving our energy consumption and saving money. However, one factor that is frequently absent from these discussions is the tsunami of data that is generated and collected as we add millions of IoT products and services to our home networks. While the nuance of the emergent human–data relationships may not be of immediate concern to the majority of their users, when this significant activity is unexpectedly brought to the fore it can challenge our expectations and perceptions of personal privacy in our homes. Such disruptions to notions of privacy then unbalance our perception of IoT devices' acceptability causing users to either resist the adoption of new devices or potentially reject devices that had previously been adopted.

Addressing this challenge requires new approaches to design for future IoT products and services. The underlying human–data relationships need to become legible. Moreover, new ways of allowing potential users to experience such futures before problematic aspects are introduced are equally important. This brings future

[1]Imagination, School of Design, Lancaster University, UK

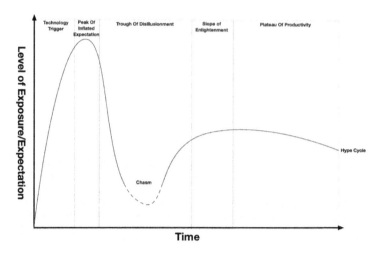

Figure 10.1   Adoption hype cycle

adoption and acceptability concerns to the centre of current design challenges. To this end, in this chapter, we present several examples of projects that utilised the Design Research method of Design Fiction to explore these challenges. This research is based on work conducted within the PETRAS Cybersecurity of the Internet of Things Research Hub to explore critical issues in privacy, ethics, trust, reliability, acceptability, and security and the Objects of Immersion research project, The Living Room of the Future.

10.1 Adoption

A popular lens on adoption is Gartner's much-referenced *hype cycle* (Figure 10.1). Whilst the hype cycle has a scant empirical foundation in any specific domain or context [1], its familiarity to researchers and commercial innovators alike, coupled with the compelling rhetoric such diagrams provide relating to technology research and development, makes it a highly useful figurative aid for conceptualizing adoption of technology [1]. The hype cycle places technologies on a graph of time (*x*-axis) against expectations and/or exposure (*y*-axis).

Starting from a particular technology, the exposure and expectations grow quickly to a peak of inflated expectation – the fever pitch when early adopters and the media are very excited about the potential of a new innovation. This initial hype quickly falls away leading into a trough of disillusionment – the sad reality that most new technologies do not work immediately, and the adoption process can be drawn out. Exposure and expectations then grow again, this time more slowly, up the so-called slope of enlightenment – this is the actual, wide-scale adoption. Finally, the technology stabilizes at the plateau of productivity – at this point, technology is no longer new: it is normal or 'domesticated'. The so-called 'chasm', which sits at the bottom of the trough of disillusionment, was added to the diagram at a later stage to account for technologies that never make it up the slope of enlightenment – for example, the Sinclair C5 personal transportation system. It's also the case that, sometimes, technologies – even if they make it across the chasm – actually jump back to re-enter the peak of inflated expectation such as virtual reality (VR) or artificial intelligence (AI).

Bell and Dourish highlighted that 'we' (technology researchers) have a penchant for suggesting that the actual adoption of the technologies we research is 'just out of reach' or 'around the corner', and that considering how this is achieved, or possible unexpected consequences, is left as someone else's problem [2]. This is problematic because if we wait to see what potential societal impacts emerge before we consider how to address them, the challenge is much harder and is often intractable as the issues are 'locked in' to the underlying technology and how it is used [3]. Of course, researchers are not able to *fully* envisage the gamut of potential futures for emerging technologies, but this doesn't mean we shouldn't try. This leaves us with the question of how do we effectively explore future adoption?

10.2   Technology futures

Considering the future is generally seen as an integral part of any design activity.

> Visions of the future are particularly important for designers, because designers have to imagine both the future conditions that will exist when their designs actually come into use and how those conditions will be changed by the creation of their new design [4].

The general approach to envisioning futures has been to present futures through scenarios based on qualifiers, the most common qualifiers being probable, plausible, possible, represented in Figure 10.2. In some cases, we might also add the preferable

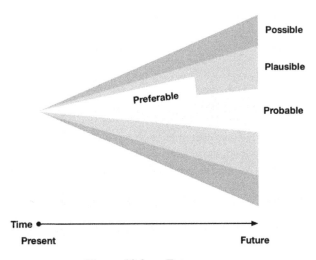

Figure 10.2   Futures cone

[5] as a moveable concept within any of the other qualifiers. The qualifiers are subjective but can be considered as: possible – *might happen*; plausible – *could happen*; and probable – *likely to happen*. Note the outer area of the cone could be considered the 'impossible' relating to concepts outside current scientific knowledge and if used would likely be considered fantasy.

We have not fully addressed the area of the figure indicating preferable. A preferable future could be described as what we believe should happen and thus could be applied within any of the three previously described qualifiers of probable, plausible, possible. This characterisation of preferable is potentially problematic because it effectively privileges the creator of the future scenario potentially promoting elitist views of a 'better world'. It should always be accompanied by a critical reflection on the question *preferable to who, and why*?

Another problematic feature of the futures cone is how we acknowledge the influences of the past. Marshall McLuhan said in his book, *The Medium Is the Massage*, 'We look at the present through a rear-view mirror. We march backwards into the future' [6]. Although McLuhan meant this primarily as a criticism, it serves as a reminder of the significant influences of the past on our perception of both the present and the future. This is not to say we should completely ignore the past, as we may have lost potential futures through the decisions we made, but rather we should be aware of its influence. Further, we should acknowledge that there is no universally accepted view of the past, the present or indeed the future (as Figure 10.2 suggests) – but rather these are individually constructed based on both reality and fiction [7] to create an ultimately particular reality [8]. This plurality of perspectives is vital as it also acknowledges the dominance of western visions in technology futures.

> The notion of oww [One-World World] signals the predominant idea in the West that we all live within a single world, made up of one underlying reality (one nature) and many cultures. This imperialistic notion supposes the West's ability to arrogate for itself the right to be 'the world,' and to subject all other worlds to its rules, to diminish them to secondary status or to nonexistence, often figuratively and materially. It is a very seductive notion […]. [9]

Rejecting *oww*, and if we accept there are multiple simultaneous points of view then arguably what might be deemed plausible or probable can more meaningfully be collapsed into a single plausible qualifier. This prevents contention over the perceived difference and reduces the chance that would overshadow otherwise productive discussions. With these points in mind, we proposed an amended futures cone (Figure 10.3) that provides a more nuanced lens through which to consider futures [10].

Moving on from this discussion of the characterising futures, we need a method through which we might practically consider future adoption of emerging technologies with various stakeholders. Whilst there are numerous methods proposed scenarios, sci-fi prototyping, etc., in this chapter we are focusing on design fiction that is an approach that aims to concretize futures by considering what a world might be

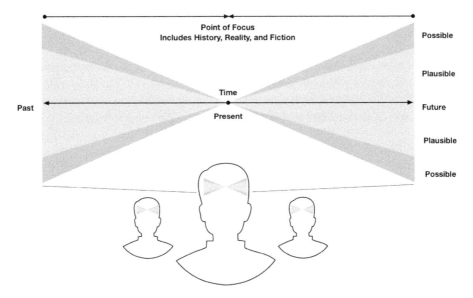

Figure 10.3   Plurality futures diagram

like in which emerging technologies have become domesticated into our everyday lives effectively rendering them as mundane as shown in Figure 10.4.

Unlike critical design that often presents such visions as dystopias using arte- facts that are often designed to sit in exhibitions, galleries or museums [11], design fiction appropriates formats more common in the real world. For example, product videos, device documentation, manuals, patents, media coverage, marketing materi- als, etc. In this way it evokes the traditions of vapourware and vapourworlds [12, 13] deployed by technology companies as representations of the future.

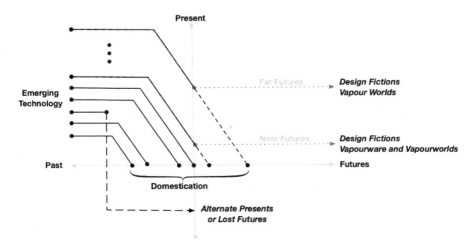

Figure 10.4   Emerging technology futures.

Vapourware is a term commonly used to describe software and hardware that is announced, sometimes marketed, but is never actually produced [14]. There are a variety of explanations as to why vapourware is produced such as unrealistic expectations of technology or overestimations of technical competence, but it has also been used nefariously by companies to inflate share prices, to create extra publicity for their brand or even to deter competitors entering a market [12]. Vapourworlds is a term we use to describe material produced by commercial organisations that do not seek to promote a particular product but rather a future in which that company and its products are an integral component [12, 13].

Design fiction draws upon these approaches and can help us to shift our gaze from the foreground of the present to the horizon of the future and then back again. Having glimpsed possible futures, design fiction helps us to consider both the broader range of societal implications of adoption and the wider political, regulatory, and social requirements that may be required for achieving adoption [1].

10.3   Design fiction as worldbuilding

Design fiction is still a relatively new concept within design research and still exhibits some traits of 'teenage angst'. In particular, design fiction has had an identity crisis whereby there are currently a number of explanations of what it is, how it is produced, and what it is for. This means that there are currently competing understandings and framings of the practice resulting in ambiguity within any discussions produced about design fiction. To make our position clear within the context of these examples, we consider design fiction as a world-building activity [15]. This means that the individual bits and pieces that make up a design fiction (the objects and artefacts produced by practice) are diverse and varied but the end result of design fiction is always the creation of a fictional world [13].

> Design Fictions are collections of artefacts that, when viewed together, build a fictional world. The artificially built world is a prototyping platform for the very designs that define it, meanwhile those designs reciprocate in kind and prototype the world. [15]

In practice, within a single design fiction, the specific selection of forms and media used manifest themselves as a number of standalone artefacts, which together build the world. Two metaphors are suggested for describing how the individual artefacts relate to the world. First, let us imagine a design fiction world as a distinct entity, one that we can see the overall shape of, but whose complex internal structure is hidden from view. What we can see, however, is a series of entry points into that world. Each artefact that contributes to making up the design fiction plays its role as a metaphorical entry point to the fictional world as shown in Figure 10.5.

The second metaphor, which works in unison with the first, is inspired by Charles and Ray Eames' iconic film about the relative size of things in the Universe, Powers of 10 (https://youtu.be/0fKBhvDjuy0). The film shows our world from a number of frames of reference (literally drawn as squares in the film) starting with a

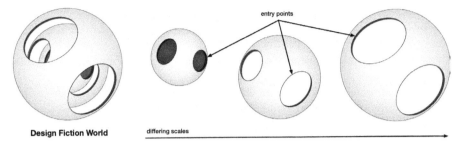

Figure 10.5   Design fiction worlds (scales and entry points)

1 meter squared section of an image that includes a couple sitting having a picnic but then zooming out and increasing the visible area by one power of 10 every 10 s (e.g. 1, 10, 100, 1 000 m). This changing scale is a device that encourages the viewer to constantly reconsider the scene being viewed. It is important to note that by adopting this metaphorical framing we are not suggesting adherence to the configuration 1 power of 10 per 10 s, but rather that the basic concept of shifting scale can be applied to the consideration of design fiction worlds and the artefacts that create them. We can think of each individual artefact that constructs the world as a representation of that world but at a different scale. The fictional world becomes a unique kind of prototyping platform testing and interrogating the very space artefacts which define it; meanwhile, those artefacts return the favour and test and interrogate the world. It is through this back-and-forth prototyping relationship design fiction derives its value. In the following sections, we will illustrate how design fiction can be utilised through specific projects to address the challenges of acceptability and adoption in the context of IoT technologies.

10.4   Case studies

10.4.1   Game of drones

Whilst the general focus for this chapter is predominantly how design fiction might address various challenges for IoT in the home, i.e, privacy ethics, security, trust, etc., we start with a project that serves as an exemplar of creating design fictions. When we submitted Game of Drones as a 'work in progress' (WiP) paper [16] to the 'CHI Play' Conference in 2015, we wondered whether we would be derided or praised because Game of Drones is a fictional account of a research project that never happened, presented in a real research paper submitted to a real conference. Whilst it may be surprising to some that such a paper passed review and was even accepted, it is important to understand the intent behind this paper was not subversive but rather to consider new ways to produce new knowledge [17]. The purpose of this project was dual: we wanted to explore a potential future use of drones for civic enforcement activities and also to progress a programme of research that aimed to develop design fiction as a research method. In this case study, We want to illustrate the value of this approach by exploring how drones helped us develop a design fiction, and how design fiction helped us to highlight the wider issues relating to the design of such a drone-based system.

The term 'drone' covers a broad range of unmanned aerial vehicles, but it is the proliferation of small quadcopters for personal use that has raised them to prominence in the public consciousness. Multi-rotor copters come with sophisticated flight controllers and on-board sensors that make them ever-easier to control. Their ease-of-use and relatively low cost have facilitated a huge range of controversial, sometimes amusing and often innovative applications. For example, delivering drugs to prison inmates, a platform for espionage, flying cats and Halloween ghosts, a plethora of photographic applications, aerial light painting and competitive first-person view drone racing. Amazon's Prime Air, Facebook's internet drone and a huge range of wildlife conservation drones are further examples of innovative commercial, corporate and research uses of the same technologies. What these activities demonstrate is that while there is a high degree of 'interpretive flexibility' around drone technologies, their full significance for society is still being established' as they start to be 'domesticated' and adopted into our everyday practices.

In Game of Drones, we were interested in exploring the potential use of drone-based civic enforcement systems. We wanted to understand what the technological and legal challenges of such a system would be, and to ask whether such a system would be an acceptable proposition and to initiate a discourse that could unpack the ethical and societal questions relating to such a system's adoption.

The design fiction world we built for Game of Drones was constructed using a variety of artefacts and then the whole 'world' was packaged into the submitted research paper. The WiP paper format provided the opportunity to focus on individual elements of the imaginary system and write about how they fitted together, as opposed to needing to create believable research results that would likely be expected of a full paper. The structure of the paper also allowed us to evaluate whether our world was plausible to the communities that may become involved in developing such technologies. By adhering to a normal paper structure we rendered a 'future mundane', in which drones had become an everyday part of the urban landscape. The paper describes a user trial of the drone enforcement system (DES) in which drones are used to provide enforcement services to local authorities. Specifically, it presents a 'gamified' system, which allows retired members of the police and armed services to act as remote drone pilots helping to enforce by-laws relating to parking offences and dog fouling in a small UK city. The whole interaction takes place through a game-like interface, and points are awarded to pilots for recording activity, and ultimately catching other citizens infringing upon the rules. Alongside the paper, we submitted a supporting video (https://youtu.be/6b_30d7yW2s) that consisted of real footage recorded from a drone but was composited with a game-like interface and claimed – fictionally – to show the system 'in the wild'. In the following paragraphs, we will discuss important elements that shaped the design of the system presented in the paper and video.

10.4.1.1   Addressing the legality of drones

When the design fiction was created in 2015 the UK legislation the adoption of commercial services, such as the one described in Game of Drones, would be unfeasible because of Civil Aviation Authority Protocol 658 (Article 167) that governs small unmanned surveillance aircraft of less than 7 kg in weight. In particular, the article stipulates that, currently, drones must not be flown within 50 m of any person, structure or vehicle, and when flown via a first-person view (FPV) camera on the drone, they are required to adopt a 'Buddy Box' system whereby another person maintains a line of site view and can take over control of the drone if required. Within the realms of our fictional world, we therefore had to consider a future in which this article no longer applied and thus superseded Article 167 with our own law that allows remote FPV flight for users in possession of a 'Drone Pilot Proficiency Certificate' within certain height and distance limitations. Although only part of our more comprehensive design fiction world, this change in legislation is a design fiction prototype in its own right and was arguably a portend of the US Federal Aviation Administration's subsequent implementation of compulsory drone registration and mandatory certification for commercial pilots and the recent additional restrictions imposed in the UK in relation to airports. This serves to highlight how design fiction can be used to address policy or regulatory issues surrounding a particular technology and highlight potential barriers to adoption.

10.4.1.2   Considering the required Infrastructure

A number of technical details about hardware are included in Game of Drones, most notably a contemporarily available consumer model of a drone and camera (cited as being used in the trial), as well as a sketch of the docking station design (Figure 10.6a), photographs of signage and a diagram of the control device. While the drone hardware primarily played a supporting role in the design fiction, it

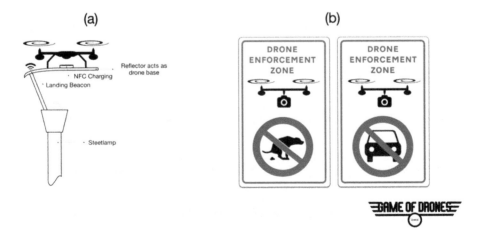

Figure 10.6   Drone landing station and signage

allowed us to consider how their current capabilities would impact upon the proposed system design. With this in mind, the drone docking station was designed based on a real type of lamppost and would have been a necessary part of the infrastructure for this system due to the limited flight time of these battery powered vehicles. To further bolster the plausibility of the fiction, we incorporated wireless charging technology (citing real research) into the docking stations, and because it would be necessary to make landing on the docking stations far simpler, we incorporated automatic landing beacons. We note that subsequent to creating our design fiction and publishing the paper, Amazon was awarded patent US009387928 in July 2016 that describes a remarkably similar lamppost-based docking station for drones to the one we proposed. Patents can not only be a useful way of representing possible futures but also provide a useful source of information relating to potential futures as they effectively represent the desired futures of the companies that produce them.

10.4.1.3   The devil is in the detail

A number of extra details were added about the trial, all of which were intended to be highly reminiscent of reality but with subtle twists for the Game of Drones world applied to them. These all not only add further to the design fiction's plausibility, but also draw upon cultural triggers to spark meaningful discussion. Most of us are familiar with parking or dog fouling notices, as these are oft-cited issues discussed by the public relating to their local urban environment; hence, we made real 'Drone Enforcement Zone' signs (Figure 10.6b) that utilize the official UK designs for road signage. In addition, real GIS data was used to construct a map of the trial city, complete with enforcement zones (based upon existing city council maps of parking zones) and landing stations placed to facilitate coverage based on our flight distance restrictions and practical recharging as shown in Figure 10.7. Programmatically enforced no-fly zones are mentioned for special areas such as the railway line to acknowledge current discourses about the potential hazards caused by drones.

Finally, the paper claims that the trial participants were ex-service (police and military) personnel, as they would likely have a diligent approach to enforcement. A note about financial rewards suggests that for this iteration of the system, users are not financially rewarded for recording more infringements, hinting at the possible ethical dilemmas of gamifying enforcement. It might seem that we went to a lot of trouble for such small details but we believe they add important texture to the fictional world, making it appear more plausible, and in doing so aim to stimulate more meaningful discourse.

For instance, 'the drone pilots are also encouraged to record any activity they consider "unusual" to ascertain the use of drones has potential for crime prevention beyond enforcement activities' [16] could suggest to some visions of a 'big brother' style dystopia, while for others it may be reminiscent of neighbourhood watch schemes. This ambiguity is deliberate and done with the aim of encouraging discussion about the desirability of such systems and their effect on society.

Legend
— Parking Control Zones
— Dog Walking Routes
☐ Parks

Figure 10.7   Map of drone landing stations and enforcement zones

10.4.1.4   Reflections

Game of Drones built a fictional world in which drones were used as part of a gami-fied civic enforcement system. It did so convincingly enough that two out of three of the reviewers seemed to believe it was real despite our admission in the paper's conclusion that it was part of a Design Fiction and therefore a 'fictional account' [17]. This level of acceptance, despite the evidence, is fascinating not because of the misinterpretation, but because it demonstrates how powerful technological visions of the future even to those shaping such futures (e.g., technology researchers). In this particular case, not only is the proposed drone-based enforcement system *plausible,* it also seems to be *feasible* to the reviewers. Whilst at the time this form of civic-based enforcement system seemed quite an extreme vision, the recent Covid-19 has seen a rapid rise drone use from spraying disinfectant on streets to enforcing lock-down in rural areas. Indeed, the images from China of a drone telling people to wear a mask and the footage from Derbyshire police shaming people walking their dogs in the UK Peak District national park are almost identical to scenes in the Game of Drones video. The aim of the design fiction was not to predict this future but rather highlight the potential future the emerging technology was leading towards in terms of wider adoption that we will explore for IoT in the following examples.

10.4.2   Allspark

This project explored a popular use case for IoT systems, intelligent energy infra-structures or 'smart grids'. The speculation was focused on a fictional energy company called Allspark. The Allspark project began not through a consideration of smart meters per se, which often appears in discussions of energy and IoT, but rather the somewhat neglected topic of batteries. Note this particular fiction does not address the important topic regarding the sustainability of IoT products themselves [18] or indeed batteries that present significant environmental challenges.

As our global electricity generation slowly moves towards sustainable sources, temporal energy storage is becoming an important element in ensuring our ability to cope with varying energy demands [19]. Although it is now quite common to generate electricity from wind and solar energy, the supplies are intermittent because the wind doesn't always blow and the sun doesn't always shine. Companies have started selling large batteries to install in your home that can store power generated when it is windy or sunny and use it later at a time when it is needed. The same technology is beginning to be used on an industrial scale, which means that at peak times energy companies use huge arrays of batteries, which are charged by spare solar and wind energy. This avoids temporarily spinning up so-called 'Peaker' power plants, which run on polluting fossil fuels. We wanted to use design fiction to explore the role the IoT might play in relation to how such battery technology and smart energy grids may manifest in next-generation product design. We set out to explore the question: what if energy consumption could be optimised using batteries and the IoT, what would that world be like?

The initial research centred around electricity delivery systems and battery storage and highlighted a huge amount of wastage, particularly when electricity is converted from alternating current (AC) to direct current (DC), which has actually significantly increased over recent years. For example, when power is generated by solar panels on the roof of a house is then normally converted to AC immediately before either being used in the house or sent back to the grid. That conversion causes a loss of energy of approximately 30%. It is also the case that the majority of our modern electronic devices use DC power, even though the power is delivered to the house using AC, which requires conversion also resulting in a loss of energy. What if we could avoid some of the conversions? One way to do this would be to redesign household electronic devices so that they would get their power from small rechargeable batteries rather than from wall sockets. So, the first entry point into our design fiction was a universal, portable, rechargeable battery that would be used on an array of household products.

In a house equipped with the Allspark energy system, users would own multiple batteries and each one could be used to power a range of different devices. The smaller batteries would be charged directly from a much larger household battery (most households would have only one of these). The large batteries would usually be charged directly from solar panels on the roof of the house (and in some circumstances when there is spare capacity in the electricity grid). Because the solar panels, big batteries and small batteries, all operate using DC, there is a significant power saving when the system is configured like this. We began to imagine how these products would fit together and be marketed, naming the smaller 'utility' batteries Runner (Figure 10.8a) and the larger fixed batteries Director (Figure 10.8b) – drawing on terminology from the film industry.

Figure 10.8   Allspark battery modules

In order to help visualise how the system would work in a typical home and how it would integrate with the existing power distribution network a further entry point (Figure 10.9) that shows a wiring schematic. Using the Allspark system, the main electricity grid remains the same – making this design fiction more plausible as it does not necessitate an entirely new infrastructure. However, *within* houses themselves, many appliances would have to be replaced to either run off a newly installed high voltage DC circuit (e.g. the washing machine, cooker and electric car) or from one of the Runner batteries (e.g. the laptop, tablet or lamp). Further developing the 'zoomed out', or large scale, entry points for this design fiction, we produced fictional marketing materials as a way of thinking through what products could be powered from batteries (Figure 10.10).

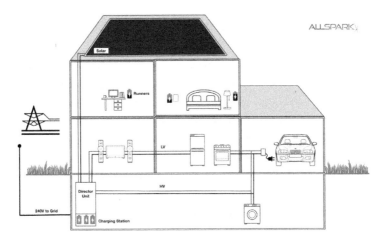

Figure 10.9   Alternative home wiring

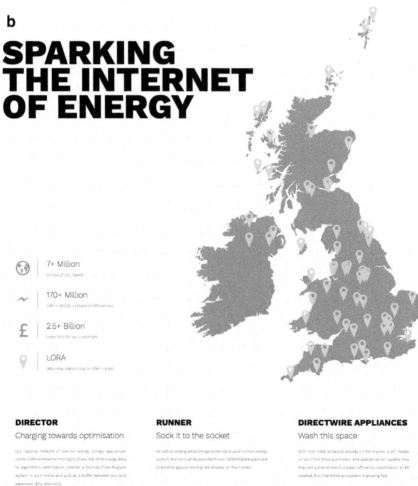

Figure 10.10   Allspark promotional material

The entry points so far – Runner, Director, household wiring diagram and advertising for battery-powered appliances – are effectively all zoomed out over-views. The more detailed entry points arose through the consideration of the role the IoT could play in the Allspark system. Although a 'dumb' version of this system could bring efficiency to power consumption, to really optimise the system all of the elements need to be integrated. The energy grid operators would need to know how much energy is currently stored across every household's Directors and Runners, and they need to know, as precisely as possible, how much energy will be used in the coming hours. By making every single Runner and Director battery an IoT device, it would be possible to gather the information necessary to drastically optimise elec-tricity consumption and take significant steps towards a renewable-first grid.

In the design fiction world we created, the Allspark system would oversee Internet-connected batteries across hundreds of thousands, or millions, of homes (Figure 10.10).

Using the data provided by these smart batteries, Allspark would be able to very accurately predict, and potentially manage, the demand. Ultimately, Allspark could minimise the need for on-demand generation from fossil fuels. In a system like this, it would be very likely that the operator, such as Allspark, would want to incentivise their customers to use devices at particular times. One way this could be achieved is with variable pricing, depending on supply and demand. The entry point below is more zoomed in than the others and shows a screen in the Allspark app. Householders would utilise this app in order to plan their electricity usage around the price of electricity from the grid: how sunny it is, how many daylight hours there are and how much charge there is in their battery system.

Through a 24-h period, we can see how the market price of electricity (if it is bought or sold from the grid) changes dramatically depending on various factors. During the night time (between sun down at 5.40 p.m. and sun up at 7.36 a.m.), market price is at a high if winds are light. The app predicts that during this period the house should use battery power. Towards the end of the night, as the price of grid electricity goes down, the battery begins to charge from the grid. The app entry point (Figure 10.11) helps us to understand not just how the price, charge and solar factors interact but shows how the Allspark system might try to influence customer behaviour. It includes an option to select 'Nudge Aggression', which would impact upon how many notifications users get asking them to change their behaviour (an example is shown in the top-left of figure 10.11, asking the user to turn off their air conditioner for 10 min in order to get a cost benefit of £0.50).

The entry point shown in Figure 10.11 – an Allspark-approved washing machine – shows how individual appliances would become integral parts of the whole system. Employing a basic nudge technique to try and influence behaviour towards more efficiency, appliances like washing machines would automatically schedule so that they run at a time that maximises available energy. Rather than indicating to the user how long is left before the wash is finished, it would display the latest possible time for when the wash would complete. We use the term 'energy temporality' to describe the way that a smart grid will likely have a knock-on effect on how we use and interact with our electrical appliances and may ultimately require

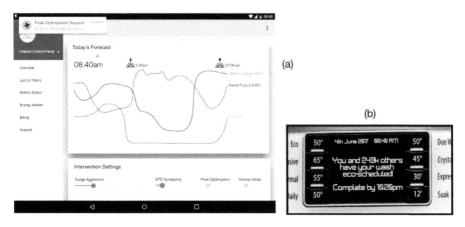

Figure 10.11   Allspark feedback

a change in design criteria. For example, if appliances are to be used at night making them quiet might be an increased priority.

10.4.2.1   Reflections

This particular manifestation of design fiction could be used by product designers to develop their understanding of how future energy distribution will impact upon their designs; alternatively, it could be a useful tool for energy companies that need to refresh our energy infrastructure. Lastly, it may be used as a communication and policy tool to demonstrate how to increase potential customers adoption by making IoT more meaningful. Using design fiction in this way leverages the power of showing precisely what *specific* strategies for meeting medium-term emission targets look like, and in doing so aims to contribute towards negotiating acceptable IoT devices with an increased chance of adoption.

10.4.3   Living Room of the Future

In this case study, we highlight the flexibility of the design fiction approach through the Living Room of the Future (LRofTF), which we characterise as an experiential design fiction [20]. The LRofTF mixes both real and fictional elements to allow us to situate the audience in a near-future world in which the negotiability of data access is brought to the fore. The LRofTF explores this by looking at how media broadcasters may utilise the potential of a technology called object-based media (OBM) to deliver more immersive experiences to audiences in home environments. OBM allows the customisation of media, like radio and television, based on audience-specific data. For example, it may customise a soundtrack based on your music preferences. OBM delivers personalised viewing experiences by considering the programme as a collection of smaller elements created during production (these are referred to as media objects) and describing how they need to semantically relate to each other in order for the programme's flow or narrative to make sense. This system

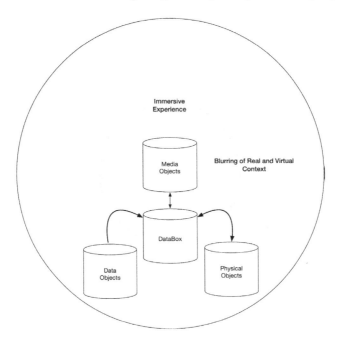

Figure 10.12   Relationship of object types for living room of the future

allows the media objects, in theory, to be dynamically reassembled into many possible personalised versions of the same programme. In addition to using OBM, the LRofTF uses IoT devices and external data sources to personalise the media even further, for example, by using the current weather to alter how the screen media is displayed or using personal data to create customised sound tracks for programmes as shown in Figure 10.12. Finally, the IoT objects provide a physical means to contribute to an immersive media experience; for instance, the smart lights may adjust their colour and brightness automatically to match the overall look and feel of the content being shown on the screen.

We chose to build this prototype around a living room, since this is a well-understood space within our own homes that many people in the UK (who were our primary audience) are familiar with. Whilst the initial version of the LRofTF was designed as part of a public exhibition for a specific installation in the FACT gallery in Liverpool (UK) [21], it has been redesigned with new interactions and a new narrative for events at the Victoria and Albert Museum and the Tate Modern in London before going on permanent display in a 'Future Home' at the Building Research Establishment in Watford as shown in Figure 10.13.. In the next sections, we describe the physical, media and data objects that sit at the foundation of delivering this experiential future. We have chosen to make this separation in writing to provide a greater level of understanding; however, it is important to note they were not conceptualised in this manner, but rather holistically to provide a unified experience.

Figure 10.13   Living Room of the Future installation

10.4.3.1   Physical objects

The LRofTF was designed to represent a potential near future, and we identified a selection of off-the-shelf IoT products to form part of the experience, which included programmable lights, a heating/cooling fan, programmable window blinds and smart plugs. In addition to these commercially available products, we created a set of bespoke artefacts: a clock-radio whose speaker provides ambient sounds as part of the media; a series of sensors to detect audience interactions with objects in the room (including a drink coaster and a remote-control device); a coffee table with in-built hand sensor, visual display and thermal printer; and a voice-activated LED 'eye' that provides a personality for the living room and acts as the sensor for its face-scanning technology. Whilst the commercial products and the printer may be considered as 'outputs' of the LRofTF, the sensors should be seen as 'inputs' that generate data which the system then uses to personalise the experience.

10.4.3.2   Media objects

The version of the LRofTF described in this case study uses a short drama called The Break Up, specially commissioned by the BBC's Research and Development department to highlight the potential of dynamic programming for television. The Break Up is a special type of programme that utilises an innovation known as 'Perceptive Media' that had previously been demonstrated for radio [22]. Perceptive Media, in contrast to interactive storytelling (e.g., the Netflix Black mirror episode Bandersnatch) which relies on audiences to influence a storyline through direct action, utilises contextual information relevant to audiences passively, and data gathered using a range of sensors, to subtly alter the media. Although the overall story arc remains the same for each viewing, ambient aspects of the narrative tweak the ways media are presented in order to create a more engaging, context-specific, experience for the audience.

The Break Up was written and filmed in such a way that the entire narrative can be shifted to accommodate the viewer. For example, there are two contrasting endings (one positive and one negative) and two paths through the story (one emphasising the male character and one highlighting the female). There is even an alternate version of the story, using the same script, where the gender roles of the characters are swapped and rather than existing in the present day it takes place in a science fiction alternate universe – allowing for so-called 'genre spiking'. Further, it allows for dynamic changes of the soundtrack to better reflect each viewer's individual experience and tastes.

10.4.3.3   Data objects

The media objects in the film can be reconfigured based on data objects that means that the system will construct a new version of the programme based on the contextual information about the viewer gathered through the available data points. This version makes use of real data points such as the current weather, location and time in addition to fictionally suggesting it uses data points such as music preferences, political leanings, social media postings, house heating habits and metadata gathered from pictures. Taking the data points in conjunction with information gathered from the IoT sensors in the room (e.g., whether the audience is smiling, if they are moving around in their seats or whether looking away from the screen) and processed by the OBM system allows the delivery of a completely personalised version of the film. While the physical and media objects are the only tangible aspects, it is the data objects – despite being invisible – which directly affect how the audience experience LRoTF.

10.4.3.4   What about privacy?

Given that each IoT device uses different protocols and shares data differently, we had to create a bespoke system for translating these data into a format that the LRofTF could understand. In order to address the privacy challenges of the experience (which acted as if it accessed various kinds of highly personal data), all data moving through the system is managed through an instantiation of Databox [23] providing a unique ecology for exploiting personal data in privacy-preserving ways. For example, Databox can enable a media provider to utilise algorithms that process data referring to an individual's viewing habits in order to offer bespoke content. However, uniquely, it can do so without disclosing personal data directly to the provider. Instead of distributing personal data to remote cloud servers for processing, processing takes place on-the-box, preserving privacy by ensuring no personal data need to leave the home or be accessed remotely.

10.4.3.5   The experiential future

The Living Room of the Future experience is split into three parts: the introduction, the personalised media experience and the 'reveal'. These parts are described in the following subsections providing an overview of design considerations:

Introduction

To begin, the participants seat themselves on the sofa in front of the television screen. The experience is then introduced by the voice of the living room that seeks to gain consent from users to collect, process and store their data (the LRofTF prints out a permission slip using the thermal printer embedded in the coffee table, which the audience must sign in order for the system to proceed). Based on the data collected, the LRofTF then produces a unique version of the Break Up for that particular audience.

Personalised media experience

In the second part of the experience, the film is played based on a profile generated by the system. During this film, various IoT objects in the room begin to contribute to the experience. For example, at the start of the film, the blinds come down and the room's lighting adapts to each scene (the system 'knows' the outside weather and picks up a relevant colour gradient). When the lead character in the film is outdoors, the fan switches on, matching the wind blowing her hair. The music within the film is chosen dependent on the profile generated by the system, as is the chosen ending (which depicts the character either leaving or staying with her abusive partner). By the middle of the story, if the audience appears bored (based on sensory inputs such as face scanning), an IoT smart plug is triggered by OBM to turn on an ultraviolet (UV) light during which a short section of the science fiction film is shown to 'enliven' the audience, before returning to the main drama. The impact of particular data interactions that affect the drama do not immediately affect the media objects, which means that while each experience was uniquely tailored to the audience, they would not necessarily be able to see why or how. Therefore, the tablet in the coffee table highlights when data is being collected and subsequently used.

Reveal

Finally, as the audience has only experienced one of the many possible adaptations of the drama, an explainer video shows the variations that could have occurred, and why, as shown in Figure 10.14.. At the end, the voice of the living room asks the audience to comment on their experience. In order to illustrate the audience reaction, we filmed a number of consenting participants to create a GoggleBox style video (https://youtu.be/cjxbXbF_TPE) which provides a novel way of representing data related to the experience.

10.4.3.6   Reflections

The experience was designed to highlight the lack of control when dealing with providing consent and the generally unperceived transactional nature of data collection. Consent, even after the introduction of the General Data Protection Regulations (GDPR), often ultimately comes down to a binary choice of using the IoT service or not [24]. This is foregrounded through the living room's voice that will always keep cajoling the audience for a positive acknowledgement to any consent questions even when the audience continually says 'no', the system says that this is a shame as

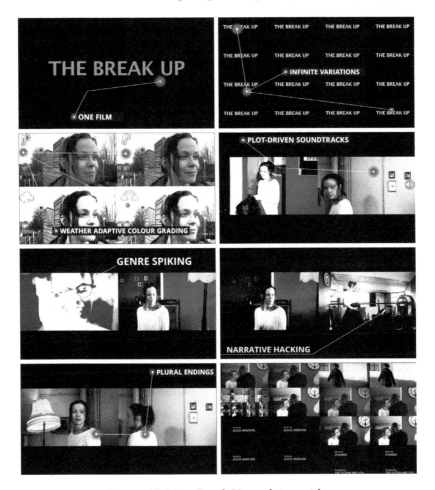

Figure 10.14   Break Up explainer video

they will miss out on the video, but they are welcome to exit through the gift shop. It is interesting that during the hundreds of times the experience was run, only one person declined the fictional face recognition software scanning their face and when presented with the potential termination of the experience, the participant quickly changed their mind. This perhaps indicates how engaging voice can be as an interaction and a problem for future IoT systems using voice in that, if their security is compromised, they may present nefarious actants a highly effective means of phishing.

Alongside consent, LRoTF served to highlight the transactional nature of data and expose how often those transactions are generated simply by living in our homes. This was illustrated on the display and the thermal printer embedded in the coffee table. The display endeavoured to make data collection and how it were used legible by presenting this in real-time as the experience unfolded. This output onto a printed receipt for participants to take at the end of their experience to highlight that the data was also theirs if they wish to take greater control. The underlying questions being around the theme, how might transactional data practices impact acceptability and adoption?

10.5 Conclusions

As we stated at the start of this chapter, within research focused around emerging technologies adoption, IoT innovations are typically viewed as someone else's problem. This conundrum is thus forwarded into some other proximate future, despite an economic argument for adoption often being the driver of the very research agendas that fund innovation. This is potentially problematic as there may be significant societal and technological challenges that ultimately decrease the likelihood of adoption. Hence, the suggestion is that in some cases it is beneficial to incorporate a consideration of the wider societal and technical implications that could arise from particular instantiations of IoT technologies. In this work, we have presented design fiction as Worldbuilding as a viable means to respond to these challenges. Though, notably, *not* as a way to predict future adoption as there will always be a plurality of potential futures, but rather to unpack what wider societal and technical challenges require consideration if future adoption is to be driven by acceptability.

10.6 Acknowledgements

The work featured in the chapter was - funded by the EPSRC [grants EP/N023234/1, EP/N023013/1 and EP/N02317X/1, EP/S02767X/1] and the AHRC funded project *Objects of Immersion* [AH/R008728/1].

References

[1]   Lindley J., Coulton P., Sturdee M. 'Implications for adoption'. Proceedings of the 2017 CHI Conference on Human Factors in Computing Systems, May; 2017. pp. 265–77.

[2]   Bell G., Dourish P. 'Yesterday's tomorrows: notes on ubiquitous computing's dominant vision'. *Personal and Ubiquitous Computing*. 2007;**11**(2):133–43.

[3]   Lanier J. *You Are Not a Gadget: a Manifesto*. Vintage; 2010.

[4]   Berry D.J. (eds.) 'Man-Made futures: readings in society' in Cross N., Elliott D., Roy R. (eds.). *Technology and design*. London: The Open University Press; 1974.

[5]   Voros J. 'A generic foresight process framework'. *Foresight*. 2003;**5**(3):10–21.

[6]   Fiore Q., McLuhan M. *The Medium Is the Massage*. New York: Random House; 1967.

[7]   Gonzatto R.F., van Amstel F.M.C., Merkle L.E., Hartmann T. 'The ideology of the future in design fictions'. *Digital Creativity*. 2013;**24**(1):36–45.

[8]   Law J., Urry J. 'Enacting the social'. *Economy and Society*. 2004;**33**(3):390–410.

[9]   Escobar A. *Designs for the Pluriverse: Radical Interdependence, Autonomy, and the Making of Worlds.* Duke University Press; 2018.

[10] Coulton P., Burnett D., Gradinar A.I., Bohemia E. (eds.) 'Games as speculative design: allowing players to consider alternate presents and plausible futures' in Lloyd P., Bohemia E. (eds.). *Proceedings of Design Research Society Conference 2016. Design Research Society.* Brighton, UK.2016. pp. 1609–26.

[11] Auger J. 'Speculative design: crafting the speculation'. *Digital Creativity.* 2013;**24**(1):11–35.

[12] Coulton P., Lindley J. 'Vapourworlds and design fiction: the role of Intentionality'. *The Design Journal.* 2017;**20**(sup1):S4632–42.

[13] Coulton P., Lindley J.G. 'Game vaporware as design fictions'. *Proceedings of Mindtrek 2016. ACM, New York.* Mindtrek 2016, Tampere, Finland, 17/10/16; 2016. pp. 341–9.

[14] Atkinson P. 'Delete: a design history of computer vapourware'. London: Bloomsbury Academic; 2013.

[15] Coulton P., Lindley J., Sturdee M., Stead M. 'Design fiction as world building'. Proceedings of the 3rd Biennial Research Through Design Conference; Edinburgh, UK; 2017. pp. 163–79.

[16] Lindley J., Coulton P. 'Game of drones'. Proceedings of the 2015 annual symposium on computer-human interaction in play (CHIPlay), Oct; 2015. pp. 613–18.

[17] Lindley J., Coulton P. 'Pushing the limits of design fiction: the case for fictional research papers'. Proceedings of the 2016 CHI Conference on Human Factors in Computing Systems; San Jose, USA; 2016. pp. 4032–43.

[18] Stead M., Coulton P., Lindley J. 'Spimes not things: creating a design manifesto for a sustainable internet of things'. *The Design Journal.* 2019;**22**(sup1):2133–52.

[19] Lindley J.G., Coulton P., Cooper R. 'Not on demand: Internet of things enabled energy temporality'. *DIS '17 Companion Proceedings of the 2016 ACM Conference Companion Publication on Designing Interactive Systems.* Edinburgh, UK: ACM; 2017. pp. 23–7.

[20] Coulton P., Lindley J.G., Gradinar A.I., *et al.* 'Experiencing the future mundane'. Proceedings of RTD 2019. Research through Design 2019; Delft, Netherlands; 2019.

[21] Sailaja N., Crabtree A., Colley J., *et al.* 'The living room of the future'. Proceedings of the 2019 ACM International Conference on Interactive Experiences for TV and Online Video, Jun 4; 2019. pp. 95–107.

[22] Gradinar A., Burnett D., Coulton P., *et al.* 'Perceptive media: adaptive storytelling for digital broadcast'. Proceedings INTERACT 2015 The 15th IFIP International Conference on Human-Computer Interaction; Bamberg, Germany, 14–18 September; 2015.

[23] Mortier R., Zhao J., Crowcroft J., *et al.* 'Personal data management with the databox: what's inside the box?'. Proceedings of the 2016 ACM Workshop on Cloud-Assisted Networking; Irvine California USA; 2016. pp. 49–54.

[24] Lindley J.G., Coulton P., Cooper R. (eds.) 'The iot and unpacking the hef-falump's trunk' in Arai K., Bhatia R., Kapoor S. (eds.). *Proceedings of the Future Technologies Conference (FTC) 2018: Advances in Intelligent Systems and Computing.* **Vol. 880**. Vancouver, Canada: Springer; 2018.

Index